SAILING AND SEAMANSHIP

U.S. COAST GUARD AUXILIARY

Contents approved by the
National Association of
State Boating Law Administrators
and recognized by the
United States Coast Guard

FOREWORD

Sailing is a historic means of travel and transportation and at one time was man's main means of adventure and exploration. Early sailors went to sea at a young age and spent a lifetime learning how to sail and survive with ships, navigational instruments, and techniques which are crude by today's standards. Skippers of yesteryear's sailing ships were called masters, yet many of their ships were wrecked and lives lost through a combination of human error and weather.

Although modern technology has made sailing an affordable form of recreation, human error and hazards from the elements are still just as prevalent as they were in the historic past. This course of instruction has been prepared for the United States Coast Guard Auxiliary by knowledgeable and experienced member sailors. They wrote this unique text for the purpose of helping you become a competent and safe sailor. Information is available here for all, from the beginner to the experienced "salt."

As Commandant of the United States Coast Guard, I salute the members of the Auxiliary for their concern for safe boating and for their development of this course. I also commend you for having the foresight and prudence to thoroughly prepare yourself for boating's challenges, as well as its pleasures.

Smooth sailing!

J. S. GRACEY
Admiral, U. S. Coast Guard

Preface

SAILING AND SEAMANSHIP has been produced by the United States Coast Guard Auxiliary to provide you a unique and excellent combination of sailing theory, seamanship techniques, legal responsibilities, the latest Federal regulations, and other subjects which will assist you to become a more informed and proficient sailor.

The Coast Guard Auxiliary is a volunteer, civilian organization dedicated to assisting the United States Coast Guard in its mission of Boating Safety. As sailing is increasing in popularity, the course and this text form an integral and important contribution to the saving of lives and property.

The instructors who present SAILING AND SEAMANSHIP are well experienced in sailing and specially qualified for teaching. They are convinced that a graduate of this course will enjoy sailing more and will be less likely to have accidents or problems on the water.

This text and course material are a contribution by members of the Coast Guard Auxiliary National staff in cooperation with the Coast Guard's Office of Boating Safety, Consumer and Public Affairs. We hope that you will enjoy and benefit from out efforts and find that SAILING AND SEAMANSHIP is a text of the highest standards.

Sincerely,

Martin S. Herz
National Commodore
United States Coast Guard Auxiliary

Contents

Chapter 1

What Makes A Sailboat?

Although there are literally hundreds of types of sailboats afloat today, all sailboats are basically similar. In this book, we will concentrate on more common kinds of boats, but the principles that apply to them will generally hold true for the exotic, unusual craft as well.

In order to understand how sailing works, a beginner must first pick up a basic sailing vocabulary. As one of man's most ancient activities, sailing has developed over the centuries a language of its own. Although many of the words may seem strange at first, there's a reason for nearly all of them. Sailors' jargon exists because the terms have no equivalent in ordinary speech. Once you become accustomed to using sailors' terminology, it will come naturally. And it's a lot easier in the long run to have at your command a word like **halyard,** for instance, than to grope for the approximate equal in everyday English — **rope or wire that raises and lowers a sail.**

Hulls and Hull Types

There are two basic parts of any sailboat — the **hull** (or hulls) and the **rig.** Because hulls are common to all watercraft, let's consider them first. A sailboat hull is simply the load-carrying part of the vessel. Besides supporting the crew, their equipment, the engine (if any) and the mast and sails, the hull also has the functional requirement of moving efficiently through the

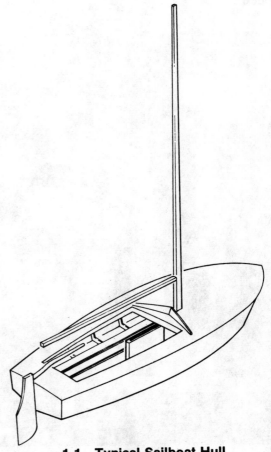

1-1   Typical Sailboat Hull

water in the direction the boat is steered, and at the same time resisting forces that attempt to push it in other directions. A third requirement is that the hull stay reasonably upright, opposing the pressure of wind on the sails.

As sailboat designers are painfully aware, the three design objectives are sometimes in mutual opposition, and it can be a very tricky job to reconcile them. All boats, sail or power, are compromises, but sailing craft embody more trade-offs in their design than do other types. Most modern sailboats give nearly equal attention to stability, load-carrying ability and a speedy hull, with perhaps a slight tilt toward one factor or another, depending on the designer's special aims. As one gets into the nearly "pure" racing sailboats, more and more is subordinated to emphasize speed-producing elements. At the other end of the spectrum, on some craft where sailing is a secondary aim, the hull is designed first and foremost for comfort instead of speed.

1-3 Motor Sailer

1-2 International Class Type Hull

Hull Chine

A few years ago, when nearly all boats were built of wood, the most obvious basic distinction between hull types was that of shape: **hard chine** or **round bottom.** Round or at least curved bottoms have been the traditional hull shape for centuries. They are easy to move through the water, but are also easy to tip or **heel.** Their construction in wood planking requires both time and skill, and as the cost of workmanship has become a larger and larger factor in boatbuilding expense, round-bottom boats have become increasingly costly.

By contrast, flat-bottom boats are easy to build, even for amateurs. With the advent of sheet plywood, flat-bottom craft became outstandingly inexpensive, but their tendency to

1-4   Hard Chine Hull

1-5   Round Bottom Hull

1-6   Hull - Carvel Wood Construction

1-7   Hull - Plywood Construction

1-8   Tipping Tendency

pound in even a slightly choppy sea caused designers to draw in a mildly V-shaped bottom. The **chine** — or intersection between side and bottom — remained **hard,** or abrupt, giving the hull type its name. Hard-chine craft sail well as long as they remain upright, and they have considerable **initial stability:** They resist tipping easily. To illustrate for yourself the relative tipping tendencies of hard-chine and round-bottom hulls, lay a round bottle and a rectangular cardboard milk container in water. The bottle will spin easily around its axis, while the carton — with its hard chines — will not.

Fiberglass

With the advent of fiberglass-molded hulls, it was as easy to produce a curved hull as a flat one. More important, fiberglass engineering makes use of some curvature in strengthening the hull. Because of this fact, and the great predominance of fiberglass hulls today, most boats' shapes are more or less curved and the hard chine has been considerably modified.

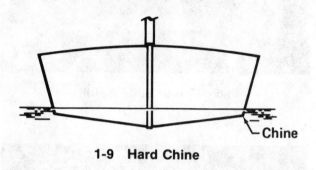

1-9 Hard Chine

Displacement vs Planing Hulls

Sailboats can be divided into classes related to performance: There are **displacement hulls** on the one side and **planing hulls** on the other. The difference between them has to do with the way they function in the water. Any floating object at rest displaces an amount of water equal to its own weight. If you could freeze the water around and below a floating vessel, then remove the boat without cracking the ice, the hole left behind could contain an amount of water equal to the boat's weight.

Hull Speed

As a boat begins to move, it still displaces its own weight of water: It must push aside the water ahead, while the water behind rushes in to fill the space vacated by the hull. This sounds like a process that requires a lot of effort, and it is. What's more, a boat which can only move by displacing its own weight in water is restricted to a relatively low top speed. Without going into the technicalities involved, it is true that displacement boats generally cannot go faster than a certain speed which is closely related to the boat's length. You can figure your boat's maximum displacement speed — called its **hull speed** — quite easily: take the boat's length at the waterline, often known as its **LWL**, in feet, and derive the square root of that figure. Multiply

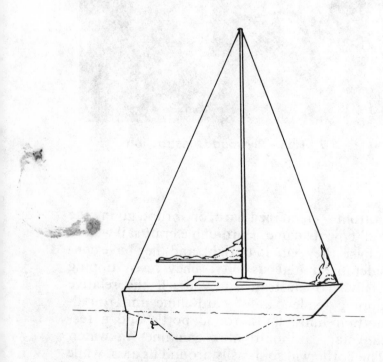

1-10 Displacement Hull at Rest

1-11 Displacement Hull Underway

this number by 1.34, and this is the boat's approximate maximum speed in nautical miles per hour. (A nautical mile is approximately 6,080 feet, as opposed to 5,280 for a land mile. One nautical mile per hour is called one **knot**.)

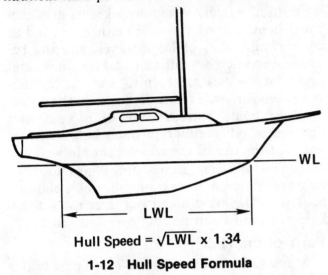

$$Hull\ Speed = \sqrt{LWL} \times 1.34$$

1-12   Hull Speed Formula

It doesn't matter if the boat in question is propelled by oars, sails or engine, nor does it matter how much power is applied; unless the boat can escape from displacement-type movement through the water, it cannot increase its speed much above 1.34 x the square root of the water-

line length. What this means in practice is that a displacement boat which is 16 feet long at the waterline cannot go much faster than 5.36 knots. A considerably larger boat, 25 feet on the waterline, will only go about 6.7 knots.

The normal displacement-type sailboat won't even go this fast most of the time. A boat that can average a speed in knots equal to the square root of its waterline length in feet — 4 knots for a 16-foot boat — is doing very well. What's holding the boat back is both friction from the water and the wave formation caused by the boat's motion through the water. The speed-reducing waves are not the familiar, V-shaped swells that form the boat's wake. In addition to these waves, the displacement hull forms two transverse — at right angles to the hull — waves, one near the bow and another at a variable distance back toward the stern. As the boat gathers speed, the stern wave drops further aft, until at hull speed the boat is virtually suspended between the two. The only way to escape is for the boat to receive enough additional propulsive force to ride up and over the bow wave, and then move, over instead of through, the water, rather like a ski moving on snow. This kind of motion, very familiar to powerboat people, is

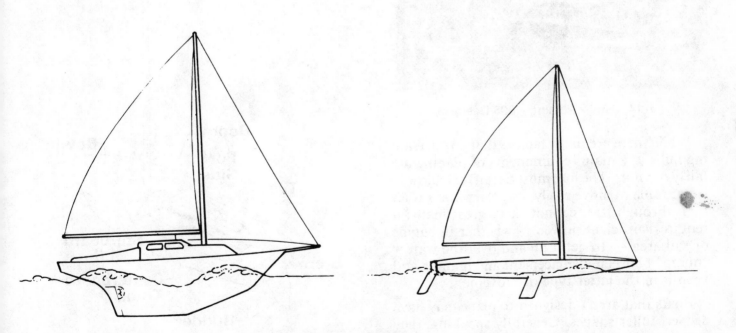

1-13   Wave Formation - Displacement vs Planing Hull

called **planing.** While there are practical limits to planing speed in a boat, there is no theoretical maximum speed — iceboats, which have virtually no surface friction to contend with, have been clocked at well over 100 miles per hour.

1-14 Hull - Planing - 505 Design

While there are many factors that go into sailing hulls, the main requirements of planing are fairly obvious. The hull must be fairly shallow in shape, able to move easily over the water rather than through it; it cannot carry great loads; it requires sufficient power — whether in engine or sail area — to get it up and over the watery "hump" between displacement and planing and keep it in the latter type of movement.

Boats that aren't designed to plane may have deeper, fuller shapes. Generally speaking, they can carry greater loads relative to the size of the

boat, and the power available is less — because more power will not move them faster than design hull speed. To counterbalance the weight of masts and sails, displacement hulls frequently have a weighted appendage called a **keel,** which we'll discuss later. When deep keeled displacement boats are overpowered either by wind or by surfing ahead of large waves, steering becomes erratic or difficult, larger bow and secondary waves are formed and the hull actually tends to ride relatively lower in the water. Planing boats seldom have deep keels and achieve stability either through hull shape or through the use of the crew as counterweights: Anyone who's seen sailing photos has undoubtedly encountered at least one shot of a planing boat with the crew **hiked out** over the side to keep the craft from heeling over too much.

Parts of the Hull

Many sailboat terms are so much part of the language that you'll find you know them already. Words like **starboard** and **port,** for instance. Some other terms are less well known. Let's run through the ones that pertain to the hull.

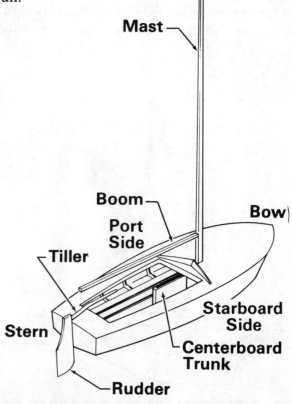

1-15 Basic Sailboat Nomenclature

As in all boats, the front or **forward** end of a sailboat is the **bow**, pronounced as in the exclamation, "ow!" The other, or **after,** end is the stern. Facing forward, **port** is to your left and **starboard** to your right. If you measured the length of the boat along the deck from bow to stern, the dimension would be labeled as **length over all**. When the dimensions of sailboats appear in magazines or sales literature, this term is frequently abbreviated **LOA.** As you already know, length at the waterline is called **LWL** for short. The width of the hull at the widest point is her **beam,** and the depth of water required to float her is known as the boat's **draft.** Many sailboats have retractable appendages called **centerboards** or **daggerboards,** so in this case two figures may appear for draft — **board up** and **board down.**

The **waterline** is the line of intersection of the surface of the water and the boat's hull. A line painted along and above the waterline when the boat is floating upright is called the **boot top** or **boot stripe.** It serves as a useful reference point to determine if the boat has been properly loaded. When the waterline shows clear around the hull and parallel to the surface of the water, the boat is said to be correctly **trimmed.** If the hull is down by the bow or stern, or tipped to one side or the other, or too high or low in the water, she's **out of trim.**

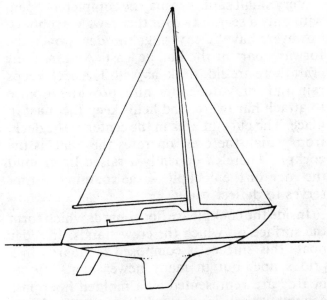

Boat is out of trim by having weight too far aft - she is down by the stern. Note that waterline of boat is visible at bow while stern is squatted down. The center of effort would be well aft of the center of lateral resistance providing this boat with a likelihood of excessive weather helm.

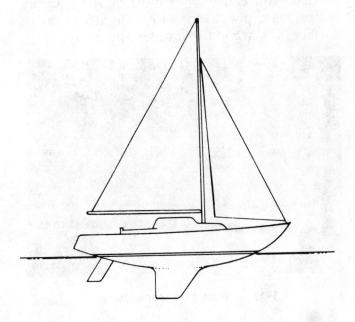

Boat shown above is properly trimmed, fore and aft. She is well balanced as evidenced by waterline's attitude relative to surface of water.

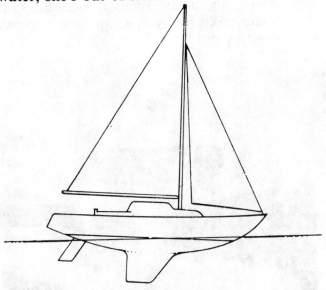

Boat is out of trim by having weight too far forward - she is down by the bow. Note that waterline of boat is visible at the stern, as opposed to vessel in illustration above.

1-16   Hull Trim-Correct vs Out-of-Trim

Very small sailboats may be completely open, with only a seat or two for the crew. Most boats, however, have a covering, the **deck,** over the forward part of the hull at least. And in many craft there are side decks as well. The deck keeps rain and spray out of the hull, provides a place to attach hardware, and helps keep the mast in place. The cut-out area in the center of the deck, from which the crew operates the boat, is the **cockpit.** There's frequently a raised lip around the edge of the cockpit — the **coaming** — that serves to deflect water.

Inside the cockpit are **floorboards** which form the surface on which the crew stands. In older boats this surface is composed of boards in a grid shape, but in many newer boats, floorboards are represented by a molded fiberglass cockpit **sole,** or deck. Like other walk-on surfaces aboard, it should be **non-skid:** The effect may come from paint with sand in it, or (more commonly) from a molded-in pattern. If your boat doesn't have non-skid where it's needed, you can buy, at most boating supply stores, waterproof tape with a slightly abrasive surface. It's a good investment in safety.

1-17   **Non-skid Deck Surface**

Most hardware on a sailboat is connected with handling the sails, but some pertains to the hull itself. Even the smallest boat should have a **cleat or eye bolt** at bow and stern for the attachment of mooring or towing lines. Cleats may be wood, metal or plastic, but they should be bolted through the deck and preferably through a backing plate under the deck as well. More

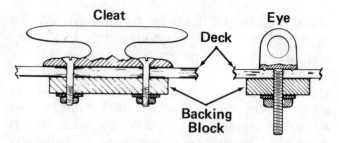

1-18   **Typical Thru-Bolted Cleat**

and more fiberglass sailboats have built-in **flotation** between the outer skin of the hull and the inner skin, called the **liner.** This flotation is usually in the form of rigid plastic foam, inserted in quantity sufficient to keep the water-filled boat plus her crew afloat.

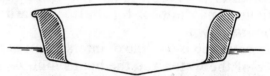

1-19   **Cross Section of Hull Flotation**

Some boats have **self-bailers** built into the bottom. These are valves which operate to draw bilge water from the hull — but they only work when the boat is moving at a good clip. Don't count on them to empty the boat when she's at rest: For that you'll need a pump or bailer. Some self-bailers actually take in water if the boat isn't moving, and must be shut off once the boat slows down. If you have such a device built into your boat, make sure you know how it works before setting out.

1-20   **Typical Self-Bailer in Hull**

Keel and Centerboard

As noted above, sailboat hulls are designed to pursue a straight-ahead course with as little disturbance of the water as possible. At the same time the boat is moving forward, wind pressure on the sails is frequently attempting to push it to the side. This lateral or sideways movement caused by the wind is called **leeway** and is partially counteracted by the hull shape. When the boat is moving in the direction the wind blows it is moving to **leeward** (pronounced "loo'ard").

The portion of the hull shape that minimizes leeway is called either a **keel** or **centerboard** depending upon which is used in the design of the boat. This fin-shaped feature in the bottom of the hull allows forward movement, but increases the side profile of the hull thereby increasing lateral resistance. The obvious difference, of course, is that the keel is normally fixed in place — bolted or molded to the hull — while the centerboard is raised and lowered through a slot in the bottom. Within the hull, the board is housed in a structure called the **trunk.**

Fixed Keel

A keel has the additional advantage — in normal construction — of no moving parts, hence nothing to break or jam. A lead keel bolted to the bottom of a boat's hull is also soft enough to absorb the sudden jolt of a grounding on rock or coral without damaging the hull. But keels have their disadvantages, too: Lead is an expensive metal, and the depth of a keel may add so much to a boat's draft that she is excluded from many shallow-water sailing areas. In addition, a boat with a fixed keel is difficult to launch from a highway trailer and it will probably never have the potential for planing.

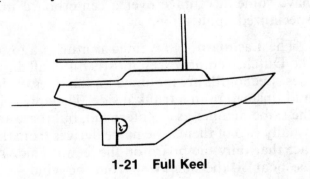

1-21   Full Keel

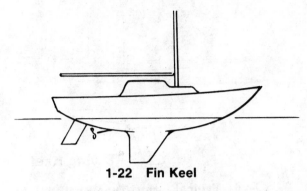

1-22   Fin Keel

Less obvious but really more important is the fact that the keel is usually weighted and the centerboard normally is not. While many boards are metal and quite heavy, their weight relative to the boat's displacement is small. A keel, however, may contain an amount of weight — usually in the form of lead **ballast** — equal to half the boat's total displacement. This much weight is there for a reason. While the shape of the keel performs the function of preventing or minimizing leeway, its weight helps add to the boat's stability by counter-balancing the heeling or overturning forces of wind on the sails and the weight of the mast, rigging and sails.

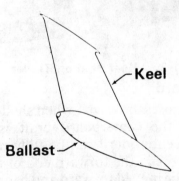

1-23   Externally Ballasted Keel - Bulb Type

Swing Keel

Some designers have produced **swing-keel** boats: In these, the weighted keel can be partially retracted into the hull or locked in the fully-lowered position. For many people, swing-keel vessels are a good compromise, for while their sailing with the keel raised is sometimes limited, they can be launched from a standard trailer and they can be motored to and from deep water.

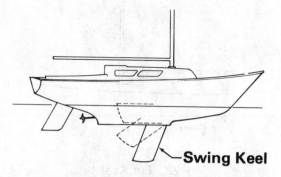

1-24   Typical Swing Type Keel

1-25   Keel Boat on Trailer

Centerboard

In most cases, however, when shallow draft is important the centerboard craft is the first choice. A centerboard can be fully raised, and since it pivots at the forward end of the board, the fin can be moved forward and backward as it rises and falls. As we shall see, this has an important effect on the boat's sailing ability under certain conditions. To counterbalance its advantages, a centerboard has several drawbacks:

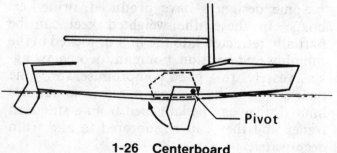

1-26   Centerboard

To begin with, it is easily damaged if the boat should hit an underwater obstruction. Although the centerboard will sometimes pivot up into its trunk when it hits something, it's more likely to splinter or crack (if wood), bend and jam in the trunk (if metal) or exert a sudden strain on the trunk and the hull, often leading to a serious leak.

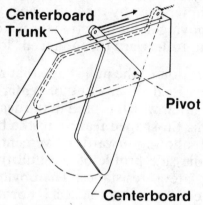

1-27   Centerboard and Trunk

Centerboard trunk leaks are not as common in fiberglass boats as they were in wood craft, but they still happen, and they are still among the most stubborn defects to repair.

Finally, a centerboard has the disadvantage of taking up space in the boat. Although some trunks don't protrude very much above the floorboards, they are still visible, and it's difficult to use that area of the cockpit or cabin for anything else. Some high trunks require bracing to the sides of the hull, and it's sometimes possible to make these braces into seats, but for the most part a centerboard trunk is merely a problem in an already crowded area.

Besides a centerboard, there are three other types of fin used in boats. Each is designed to have some advantage over a centerboard in a specialized application.

The **Leeboard** — invented centuries ago by the Dutch, and now seen mostly on small dinghies. Leeboards are mounted on the sides of the hull, instead of in a trunk inside. They pivot in the same manner as a centerboard, but there are usually two of them. The name derives from the fact that only the board on the leeward side of the boat — the side **away** from the wind — is lowered at any one time. Leeboards are not as efficient as centerboards, but they don't take up space in the boat, and they are a lot cheaper — even in pairs. They are, however, also prone to damage when coming alongside piers or other boats.

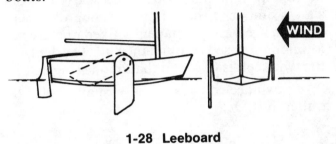

1-28 Leeboard

The **Bilgeboard** — Sometimes seen on flat-bottomed sail racers, bilgeboards are paired like leeboards, but are placed on either side of the cockpit. They are said to aid in sailing efficiency, but they also make for more complicated construction.

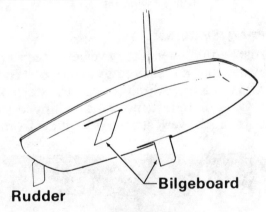

Rudder   **Bilgeboard**

1-29 Bilgeboard

The **Daggerboard** — By far the most popular alternative to the centerboard, the dagger slides up and down in its trunk, instead of pivoting. It has the advantage of simplicity over the centerboard, requiring no **pennant,** or line, to raise and lower it. In small boats, the daggerboard usually has a handle fixed to the top to make lifting easier. The problem with a daggerboard is that, since it's not pivoted, it must when raised extend above the top of its trunk. This has two implications: First, the trunk cannot be capped at the top, which leads to a considerable amount of water splashing into the cockpit. Second, when fully raised the dagger greatly interferes

with operations in the cockpit and may even get in the way of maneuvering. Its cheapness and simplicity have, however, made it a standard installation on smaller boats. Although a centerboard **may** pivot upward out of harm's way if a submerged object is struck, a daggerboard almost certainly cannot slide upward, and it is thus considerably more vulnerable.

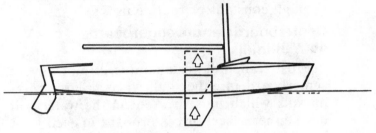

1-30 Daggerboard

Using the Centerboard or Daggerboard

One advantage of both the centerboard and the daggerboard over the fixed keel is that they can be raised or lowered in varying heights to counter the effects of leeway and minimize underwater hull resistance. The racing skipper knows that when running downwind with the board raised the boat will move faster than another boat which has its board down. This same skipper will have to drop the board when reaching or beating if leeway is to be minimized.

In Chapter 9 you will understand that the underwater shape and hull profile can be varied by adjusting the board height (either centerboard or daggerboard) and that the ultimate trim and steering of the boat are affected by the height of the board. The amount that a skipper varies the board will depend upon experience and confidence as well as individual preference. Many successful skippers drop the centerboard or daggerboard completely and never raise it except when sailing into shallow water or onto a beach.

Care of the Centerboard or Daggerboard

As either the centerboard or daggerboard is adjustable, care should be taken to make sure that it can be raised or lowered with ease. Occasionally a tight fitting board or the trunk itself will swell or expand when the boat is left in the water for a period of time resulting in damage to the trunk itself as well as extreme difficulty in raising or lowering the board when required.

Centerboard boats which must be left in the water require attention to prevent the centerboard itself from being jammed in the trunk in the "up" position by marine growth. In addition to regular haulouts and bottom painting, proper prevention could be underwater hull cleaning or brushing and movement of the centerboard through constant or routine use.

Centerboards and Daggerboards on Multihulls

Most trailerable catamarans do not have a centerboard in either hull whereas large catamarans which must be kept in the water will have either a keel or centerboard in each hull. The design and depth of the hulls will often provide enough area that a centerboard or keel is not required. Ballast for either centerboards or keels is not usually required because the design of the two hulls, side by side, provides great initial stability, resistance to overturning forces.

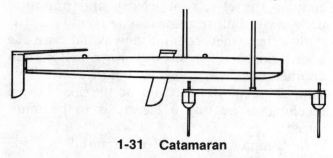

1-31 Catamaran

Trimarans will have either a centerboard or a keel in the center hull which might be either ballasted or unballasted, depending upon the size of the hull and the speeds for which the craft is designed. Trailerable trimarans will usually have an unballasted centerboard.

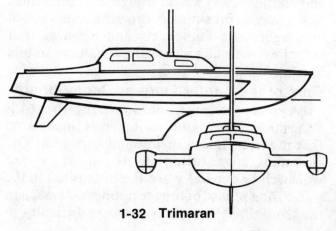

1-32 Trimaran

Twinkeels

The twinkeel or bilge keel is a popular keel design in some shallow water areas or areas subject to extreme ranges in tide. Twinkeels provide an opportunity for a boat so designed to rest on its bottom upright at low tide if necessary. This design is similar to that of the bilgeboards except that the keels are permanently fixed and are not lowered or raised through the hull. The depth of the twinkeels is less than that of one single keel.

A twinkeeled vessel is usually of the trailerable size.

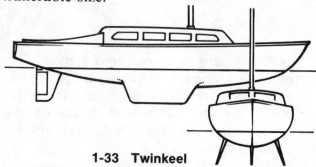

1-33 Twinkeel

Steering Systems

Most people, even if they've never seen a boat, are aware that it is steered by means of a **rudder**. A rudder is a fin located toward the stern of the boat. On small craft, it's usually hinged to the transom, at the very stern. As it pivots from side

1-34 Rudder

to side, the rudder has one face or the other to the pressure of water streaming past the moving boat. The pressure of water on the rudder blade pushes the stern to one side or the other.

On most smaller sailboats, the rudder is worked by a simple lever called a **tiller,** which makes it possible to turn even a fairly large rudder on a fast-moving boat without too much effort. On larger craft steering wheels are quite common and provide even more mechanical advantage than do tillers. A steering wheel on a boat works in the same manner as the one on your car: Turn the wheel to the right, the boat turns to starboard, and vice versa.

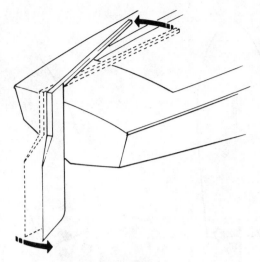

1-36 Rudder Action

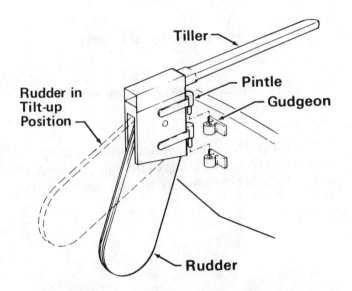

1-35 Typical Transom Mounted Rudder

A tiller, on the other hand, operates in reverse: Push the tiller to starboard, and the boat swings to port. What happens is that the boat's stern is thrust sideways by water pressure against the rudder blade. As the stern swings to starboard (let us say), the boat pivots around its keel or centerboard, and the bow must swing away to the other side — to port, in this case. It takes beginning sailors a little while to get used to this fact of tiller steering, but once one has become accustomed to pushing the tiller in one direction to have the boat turn in the other, it's quite natural.

In steering a boat with a tiller, a few things are important to remember: First, don't forget that

the boat pivots like a weathervane around a point somewhere near **amidships** — the center of the boat. In this, a boat is quite unlike a car, which follows its front wheels through a turn. A boat turning is more like a car skidding — the bow describes a small circle, while the stern swings in a wider circle outside it. This means that careless skippers frequently hit docks and other boats with their own boats' sterns when turning sharply.

Second, bear in mind that a rudder cannot function unless water is moving past it. For this reason a boat must gain speed before it can be steered — unless, of course, it's anchored in a place where water is running swiftly past the hull while the boat is standing still, as in a river.

Third, consider that a rudder pushed too hard to one side or the other acts more like a brake than a turning force: With the face of the rudder at right angles (or nearly) to the moving water, the boat's tendency is simply to slow down and even become unmanageable. One of the first things to learn about any boat is how far the tiller must be put over to one side in order to make the boat turn. Chances are it's less than you think.

This, then, is the basic boat: a hull to carry crew and equipment, a keel or centerboard to keep the boat from sliding sideways, and a rudder (with tiller or wheel) for steering. So far, our boat could be any type, because we have not yet come to grips with driving power.

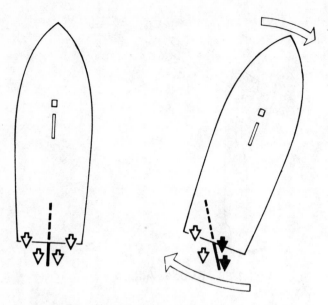

1-37   Rudder Turning Boat

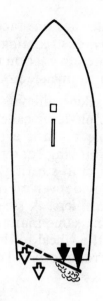

1-38   Braking Action of Rudder

The Rig

The rig is the collective term for the various elements that form a sailboat's power system. There are basically three interacting parts — the spars, the rigging, and the sails.

Spars

Spar is the general term for the rigid members that support and extend sails and other parts of the rigging. The primary spar is the **mast,** a vertical member that holds the sails up. Most boats also have at least one **boom,** which holds out the foot of the sail at right angles to the mast. The mast and boom are joined by a kind of universal joint called a **gooseneck,** which allows the boom to pivot up, down or sideways. There are other types of spars — gaffs, yards, spinnaker poles, to name the most common — but they are restricted to specialized boat types or advanced forms of sailing, and will be dealt with later.

As noted above, spars may be made of several kinds of materials. Because of its strength, relative light weight, and good durability, aluminum is now far and away the most popular spar material, and seems likely to remain so. On some smaller boats where bending spars are useful, fiberglass spars, rather like oversize fishing poles, are occasionally seen. Older boats and

ones of traditional appearance may retain wood spars, either hollow sections glued together or solid pieces of timber.

Whatever the construction material, spars have much the same kinds of fittings attached to them. As we shall see in a later section, it's

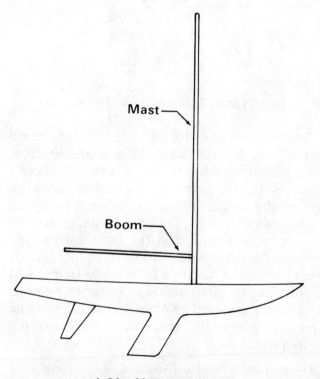

1-39   Mast and Boom

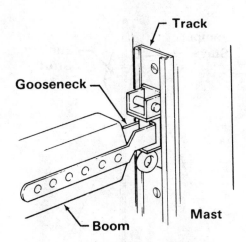

1-40 Gooseneck Installation

important to be able not only to extend a sail, but also to vary the amount of tension along any one of the sail's edges. The sail control fittings on the spars perform this function. Once we've had a chance to consider how the sails are shaped and made fast to the spars, we can consider the various types of fittings and how they work.

For the moment, consider first the basic (in several senses) fitting called the **step.** This is a socket in the bottom of the boat, often set directly into the keel, the vessel's backbone, of the vessel. The mast fits into or onto the step, which is so shaped that the spar's **heel,** or base, cannot slide off. In most boats, the mast is held in place by being passed through a tight-fitting hole in

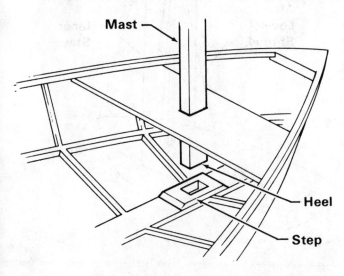

1-41 Typical Small Boat Mast Step

the deck or a forward seat. Often, in larger boats, the mast passes through the cabin roof, where a reinforcing **collar** is placed to help take the strain of the spar. On some small boats, this arrangement is enough support for the mast, but on most a certain amount of rigging, varying with the size of boat, is necessary to keep the mast up and straight.

Standing and Running Rigging

There are two basic types of rigging — **standing** and **running.** The function of each is fairly well expressed by its name. Standing rigging stays put; it supports the mast under tension. Running rigging, by contrast, moves: it runs through **blocks** (the nautical term for pulleys) to raise and lower or extend and pull back the sails.

Standing Rigging

The standing rigging of the average small sailboat is not complicated. It's especially easy to comprehend if you remember that its purpose is to keep the mast upright and straight. (There are exceptions, but this statement remains true for most boats, large and small.) Remember also that any pull on the mast from one direction must be matched from the opposite side, if the spar is to remain in position and untwisted.

Standing rigging which keeps the mast from falling forward over the bow or backward over the stern consists of one or more **forestays** and **backstays.** As you might easily guess, a forestay is in the forward part of the boat. It runs from a metal plate on deck — the **tack fitting** — to a position at or near the top of the mast, and it keeps that spar from toppling backward. In opposition to it is the backstay, which runs from the stern up to the masthead. In some cases where the rudder and tiller are in the way, two backstays are fitted, running to corners — the **quarters** — of the stern. And sometimes a backstay is shaped like an inverted Y, for the same reason.

When, for reasons of design, the forestay doesn't end near the masthead, tension to balance the backstay is provided by short, horizontal spars called **jumper struts,** over which

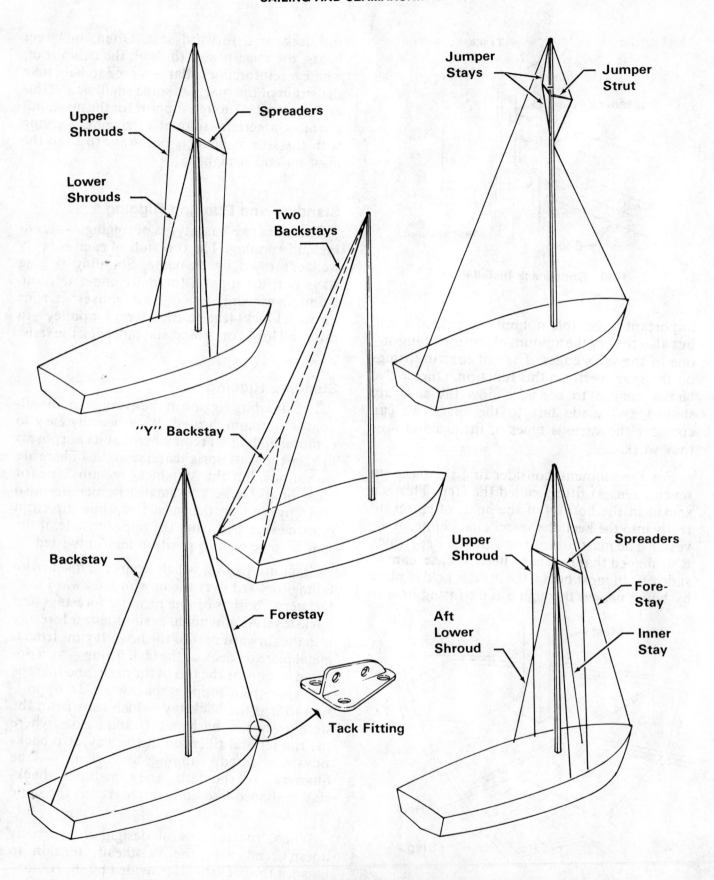

1-37   Rigging Nomenclature

run **jumper stays.** On small boats, where the mast is thick and strong enough to take such strains, jumper struts and stays aren't necessary.

A mast is kept from falling to the side by standing rigging, called **shrouds.** On small boats there is usually only one set, running from the side of the hull up to the masthead. Sometimes, to make a more mechanically effective lead of the shrouds to the masthead, a pair of horizontal spars called **spreaders** are fitted about two-thirds the way up the mast. The spreader, as its name suggests, simply widens the angle at which the wire reaches the masthead, giving a more effective sideways angle of pull.

The shrouds which run over spreaders to the masthead are called **upper shrouds,** or just **uppers.** Other shrouds run from the sides of the hull to the mast just beneath the intersection of the spreaders; these are **lower shrouds** or **lowers.** There may be one or two pairs of them. On some boats, an **inner forestay** does the same job as the pair of forward lowers.

Both shrouds and stays are normally made of stiff wire rope, generally stainless steel. Since it's necessary to balance off the stresses of the various pieces of standing rigging against their opposite numbers, adjuster fittings are provided at the bottom of each stay and shroud. The stand-

ard type of adjuster is called a **turnbuckle,** usually cast in bronze or stainless steel. It allows for a limited amount of adjustment of wire tension, a process called **tuning,** dealt with in more detail in Chapter 9.

The turnbuckles are in turn fitted to **toggles,** small castings that allow the turnbuckle to lie in the same straight line as the stay or shroud to which it is fitted. And the toggles, in turn, are secured to **chainplates** — heavy metal straps bolted and/or fiberglassed to the hull or its principal **bulkheads.**

Running Rigging

While standing rigging is almost invariably wire, running rigging may be wire or rope or both. The two most common types of running rigging are **halyards,** which raise and lower the sails, and **sheets,** which control the shape of a sail. There are other kinds of running rigging, but they are specialized in nature, to be discussed later.

1-44 Wire-Rope Halyard

Each sail has at least one halyard, which normally takes its name from the sail it raises. Because rope stretches, halyards are frequently half rope and half wire, so that when the sail is

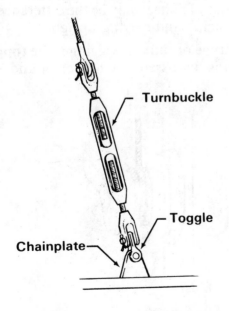

1-43 Shroud or Stay Fittings

Turnbuckle

Toggle

Chainplate

fully raised, all the tension is taken by non-stretching wire. Sheets, which are also named by the sail they control, are normally Dacron line: Dacron rather than the popular nylon because nylon stretches a great deal, and Dacron doesn't. In a sheet, one can tolerate a slight amount of stretch, but too much stretch is not good — whereas it is helpful in shock-absorbing lines connected to anchors. The type of wire used for halyards is quite flexible, and different in construction, if not in material, from the wire used for stays and shrouds.

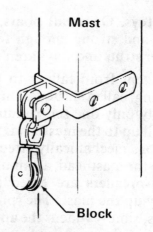

1-46 Halyard Block

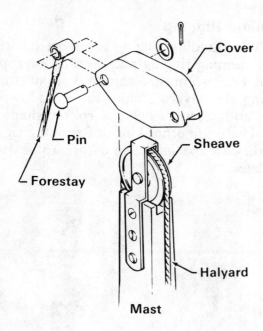

1-45 Masthead Fittings

Each sail has a halyard, but in some cases the same halyard is used by more than one sail, as we shall see. Halyards run either through rollers — called **sheaves** — set into the top of the mast, or through blocks attached to the mast, depending on how high the sail is to be raised. Most halyards terminate at cleats on the mast itself, and in many cases (especially aboard larger craft) the halyard is led around a winch to increase the tension on it and, by extension, on the sail it is raising.

Once raised, a sail must be adjusted so it sets at a particular angle to the wind. The lines controlling this adjustment are the **sheets.** They normally run from the after corner of the sail,

known as the **clew,** or from the mainsail boom down to the cockpit. Mechanical advantage of the sheets may be increased by the use of winches or block-and-tackle systems as required. The end of a sheet is made fast to a cleat. While the traditional, anvil-shaped cleats are often seen, more and more skippers are turning to one or another style of quick-release **cam** or **jam** cleats. In these devices, the rope is simply led through a gripping pair of jaws which hold it fast until it's forcibly released by a crew member. The attachment is as secure as cleating the line, and a great deal quicker both to make fast and to let free — and in smaller boats, quick release of a sheet may be the difference between capsizing and staying upright.

A third type of running rigging is the **topping lift,** which is discussed in Chapters 4 and 9.

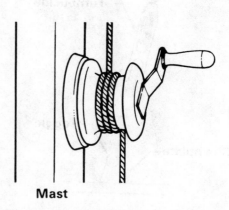

1-42 Halyard Winch

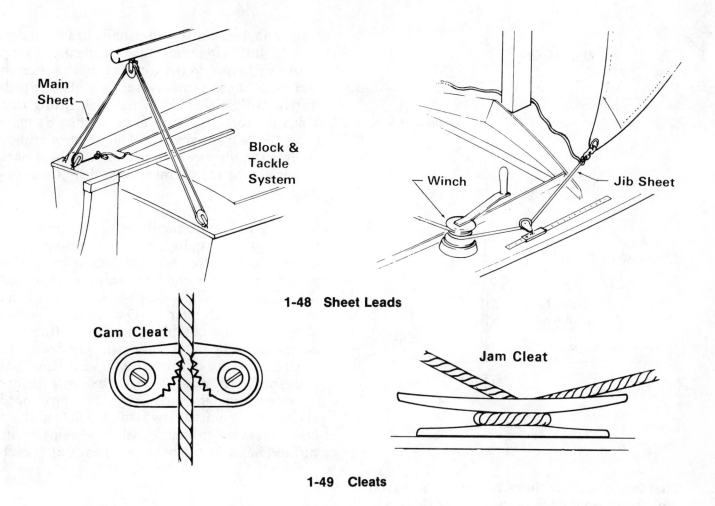

1-48 Sheet Leads

1-49 Cleats

Sails

All this structure — spars, standing and running rigging — exists to make the sails function efficiently. Today's sails are, for the most part triangular, and are known as **jib-headed, Marconi** or **Bermudan:** All three terms are synonymous. Back in the days when sailboats functioned as fishing craft or ferries, the sails employed in everyday business were known, quite appropriately, as the **working sails.** Boats have changed, and working sail isn't quite as useful a term as it once was, but for convenience' sake we shall use it here, for lack of a better.

The most common American sailboat type is called the **sloop** — a vessel with a single mast and two sails, one set ahead of the mast and one behind. The latter sail is called the **mainsail,** usually shortened to **main,** and the former is the jib. The sails have a number of terms associated with them, and it will help to learn them.

The triangular mainsail has the same names for its three corners as does the jib — the **head,** at the top; the **tack,** at the forward lower corner; and the **clew,** at the after lower corner. Either sail's leading edge is the **luff,** sometimes referred to by old-timers as the **hoist;** its lower edge is its **foot,** and its after edge is the **leech.** Each sail is formed from a number of cloths sewn together in one of several patterns. Because a sail, unlike a flag, is really a three-dimensional shape (think of an airplane's wing), the cloths are joined to create this form, either flat or full. The sail's edges are reinforced with rope or extra thicknesses of cloth, or with wire sewed to the luff of the sail.

A mainsail is attached to the mast along its luff and to the boom along its foot. The normal

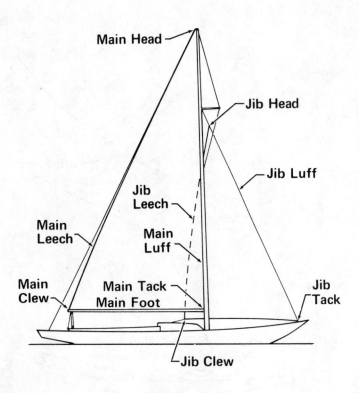

1-45   Sail Parts

three cringles. But the jib usually has no boom, only its luff being made fast, by means of snap hooks or **hanks,** to the forestay; both the leech and the foot are normally free sides. The jib tack fastens with a shackle to the tack fitting that holds the forestay, and of course the jib's head takes the halyard shackle. The jib clew cringle accepts the jib sheets — usually a pair of lines that lead aft to cleats on either side of the cockpit.

Today's sails are nearly all made from synthetic fabric, usually Dacron but sometimes nylon. Dacron stretches less than nylon, and is used for mainsails and jibs, while nylon is used for sails where slight shape deformation is no problem (see Chapter 9). Dacron sails require little or no care compared to their cotton predecessors: It helps, if sailing on salt water, to wash the salt out of them from time to time, and one should if possible dry the sails before stowing them in their bags for prolonged periods to avoid mildew, which will not affect Dacron except to make unsightly stains on its surface. Sails should be stowed neatly after each

hardware used are **slides,** which ride along a surface track on the top of the spar, or **slugs,** which fit a groove recessed into the mast or boom. Sometimes a roped edge of the sail fits inside the track groove. The sail's leech is the free side, and it is normally reinforced and to a great extent supported by wood or plastic **battens,** strips set into pockets at right angles to the leech. The reason for these supports is that the mainsail's leech, unlike its luff or foot, is cut into a convex curve called the **roach,** for greater sail area.

At each corner of the sail is a **cringle,** a circular metal reinforcement for attaching hardware: The halyard is made fast to the head cringle; the gooseneck is fitted to the tack cringle; and the **outhaul,** a carriage riding on the boom to extend the foot of the sail, is fitted to the clew cringle.

The jib is a somewhat simpler sail to describe: It has, as noted, the same names as the main for its three sides, three corners and for its

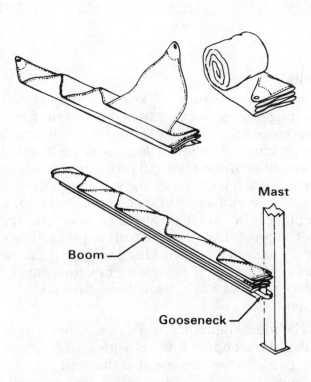

1-46   Folding Sail for Storage

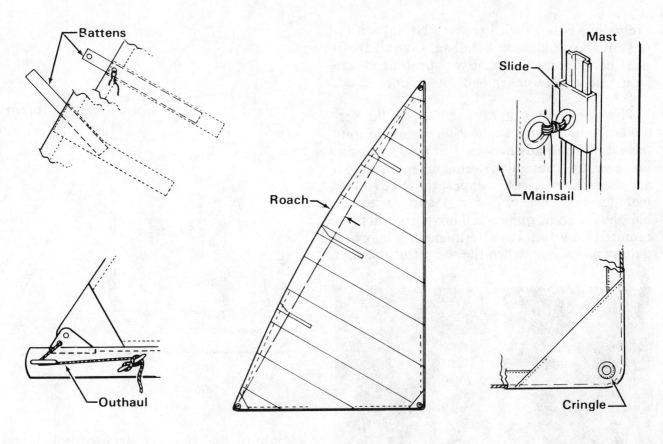

1-52   Sail Construction

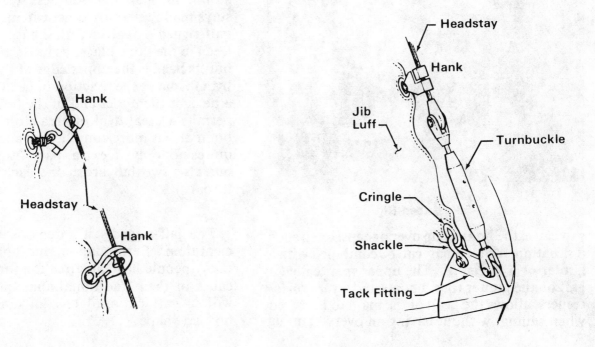

1-53   Typical Jib to Forestay Attachment

1-54   Tack Fitting

excursion, either furled (on the boom) with a sail cover or folded, in a sailbag. Like all artificial fibers, Dacron is sensitive to prolonged sunlight, and it will weaken badly if left uncovered.

There are other shapes of sail besides the Bermudan, and in some applications these variants have important advantages. For the most part, however, the triangular Bermudan main and jib are the most efficient, cheapest to make (if one includes the cost of the rig) and easiest to handle. On some quite small boats, the tall mast required for an effective Bermudan rig may be a danger at anchor, when the weight of the spar

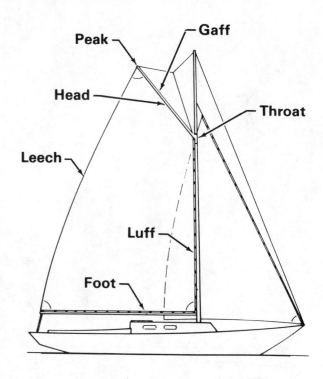

1-56   Parts of Gaff Rig

1-53   Lateen Rig

can cause the boat to tip over or **capsize**. In such a situation, a short mast can be combined with a **gunter** or a **lateen** rig. The upper spar, called a **gaff** on the gunter rigged boats and a **yard** on lateeners, allows the head of the main to be raised when sailing, without having an overwhelming

weight of spar to make the boat unbalanced at anchor.

In the early years of the 20th centry, before aluminum spars and stainless steel shrouds and stays made tall spars practical, most boats were **gaff-rigged.** A gaff mainsail has a luff, foot and leech in the same places as its Bermudan cousin, but its **head** is the upper edge of the sail, limited by a **throat** at the junction of head and luff, and a **peak** at the upper end of the head. A gaff sail permits a great deal of area close to the water, but it also is more complicated and generally requires not only an extra spar — the gaff itself — but also two halyards, one each at peak and throat.

The gaff-rigged sail is demonstrably less efficient than a Bermudan sail most of the time, but many people have an affection for gaff sails because of their traditional appearance. A sloop with a gaff mainsail has, of course, a jib of normal shape.

Chapter 2

How A Boat Sails

A sailboat's rig is its engine, and the fuel, of course, is the wind. As you become a better sailor, you'll want to know more about how the wind works (some additional reading is suggested in the Bibliography), but at this stage a few simple facts are all you need.

The Nature of Wind

By definition, wind is air in motion. When you stand on a pier and feel the breeze on your face, what you're sensing is the **true,** or geographic wind — moving air as perceived from your position. With a little experience, you'll learn to tell how strongly the wind is blowing and what direction it's coming from. (Wind directions, by the way, are always given in relation to where the wind is blowing **from:** Thus, a north wind is blowing from north to south.)

A moving vehicle, on land or sea, creates a "wind" of its own as it moves through the air. Suppose, for example, that you're in a powerboat on a day when no true wind is blowing at all. You're chugging in a northerly direction at 10 knots. If you raise your head above the windshield, you'll feel a "north wind" of that same strength — 10 nautical miles per hour — blowing straight at you. This is the boat's **wind of motion.**

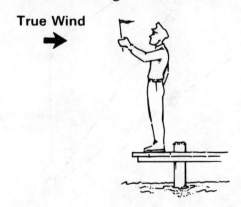

True Wind

2-1 True Wind

Wind of Motion

2-2 Wind of Motion

Now take the example one step farther: You're again in a powerboat, again moving north at 10 knots. But this time, there is a wind blowing **from** the north at five knots. What do you feel, riding in the boat? **A 15-knot wind** — your boat's wind of motion, added to the true wind. This result is called **apparent wind:** The wind perceived from a moving vehicle. On a windless day, the apparent wind is of course the same as the wind of motion, but otherwise it's the combined force and direction of true wind and wind of motion.

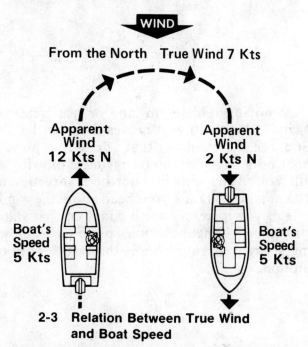

2-3 Relation Between True Wind and Boat Speed

Sometimes the apparent wind is less than either of its two components: Imagine that we're still in our powerboat, moving at 5 knots to the north into a north wind that's blowing at seven knots. We turn the boat in the opposite direction, while maintaining its speed: Now we're going south at 5 knots, with a seven knot wind blowing from directly astern of us. In this case, our apparent wind is 7 knots **minus** 5 knots, or a mere 2 knots.

Apparent wind is easy to calculate when the wind is directly ahead or astern. It's a bit more complicated when the wind is blowing from somewhere on either side of the boat. In a situation like this, if we know the true wind's speed and direction (which we can observe before we set out) and the boat's speed and direction, we

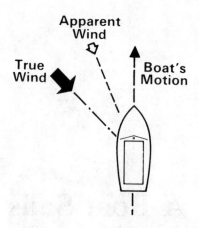

2-4 Apparent Wind

can figure out the apparent wind by use of a diagram called a **wind vector.**

On small boats, no one bothers with this kind of technical detail, except perhaps for very intense racing skippers. All you as a sailor have to know is the general idea of apparent wind and what makes it up, because it's apparent wind that conditions not only the directions in which your boat can sail but also how much or little sail you should raise: Many sailors who don't consider apparent wind get an unpleasant surprise when, after sailing with the wind for some time, they suddenly head their boat into the

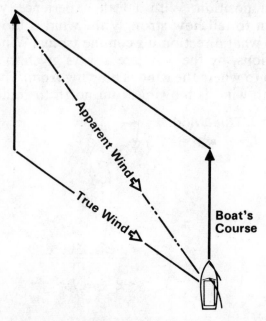

2-5 Wind Vector Diagram

breeze — only to find that what appeared a gentle zephyr when heading downwind is quite blustery when going the other way.

To be aware of wind direction, most skippers use a form of wind vane or **telltale.** It may be a rigid, pivoting vane at the masthead, a cloth pennant, or a strip of fabric tied to one of the shrouds: The idea is the same in each case — to locate the vane in a place where it can easily be seen and where the wind hitting it will not have been deflected by the sails or rigging. On most small boats, the only practical location for a vane is at the masthead, but because the wind at the top of a larger boat's mast may be blowing in a slightly different direction than the breeze at deck level, big sailboats usually have extra telltales tied or taped to the upper shrouds about four or five feet from the deck, and another, for measuring the wind astern, made fast to the backstay.

On cruising sailboats, where the mast may be 30, 40 or even 50 feet high, an electronic device

2-7 Telltales on Shrouds

at the masthead may measure both wind direction and speed, for readout on a pair of instrument dials in the cockpit. While this sort of instrumentation is available for quite small craft, it's really not necessary.

2-6 Mast Head Wind Devices

2-8 Cockpit Instruments

Points of Sailing — Running

It's easy to visualize a sailboat moving with the wind behind it — being pushed downwind. When the wind is more or less directly astern of a boat, she is said to be **running**. For most efficient sailing, the main and jib should, if possible, be at right angles to the apparent wind (which is, in this case, from the same direction as the true wind).

Because the mainsail is likely to **blanket** the jib if both sails are extended to the same side of the boat, when running the sails are set **wing-and-wing** — fully out on either side of the vessel. A boat sailing directly before the wind can be somewhat difficult to steer, responding sluggishly to her rudder. In addition, the wind direction is constantly changing in small degrees, and it's possible for the wind to get behind the fully extended mainsail and blow it — boom and all — across the boat to fully extended on the other side. This maneuver is called a **jibe** and is perfectly acceptable when done properly and on purpose (see Chapter Three); an **accidental jibe,** however, can put serious strains on the rigging and should be avoided.

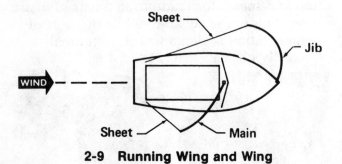

2-9 Running Wing and Wing

Sailing Wing and Wing

The best way to keep the boom in its place, especially on very windy days, is to sail with the wind coming from either **quarter** — over the corners of the transom. On this heading, the mainsail will be reasonably efficient and you should be able to set the jib on the opposite side. You may require a portable spar called a **whisker pole** to keep the jib standing and filled. A whisker pole is a light aluminum tube with a snap hook at one end and a narrow prong at the

other. The snap hook fits to an eye on the forward side of the mast, while the prong goes through the jib clew cringle. When the jib sheet is pulled back, the pole acts like a boom.

It takes a good deal of practice to be able to sail a boat wing-and-wing, and for a long time it will seem that it's more trouble than it's worth. If your boat has a very small jib, it may indeed be too much effort to bother winging it out — concentrate at least for the time being on sailing with the main alone.

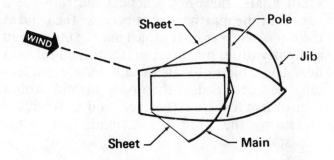

2-10 Wind Over the Quarter - Using Whisker Pole

Try to keep the sail at right angles to the apparent wind, watching either the telltale on the backstay or the masthead vane. To adjust the angle at which the wind strikes the sail, you can either turn the whole boat, or play the mainsheet in and out. Many experienced sailors never cleat the mainsheet at all, and certainly the sheet should always be ready to let run, to spill the wind from the sail in a hurry. At the same time, it's tiring and dull to have to hold a piece of line all day. Perhaps the best compromise is the use of one of the quick-release cleats mentioned earlier.

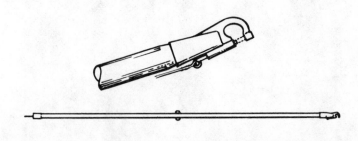

2-11 Whisker Pole and Fittings

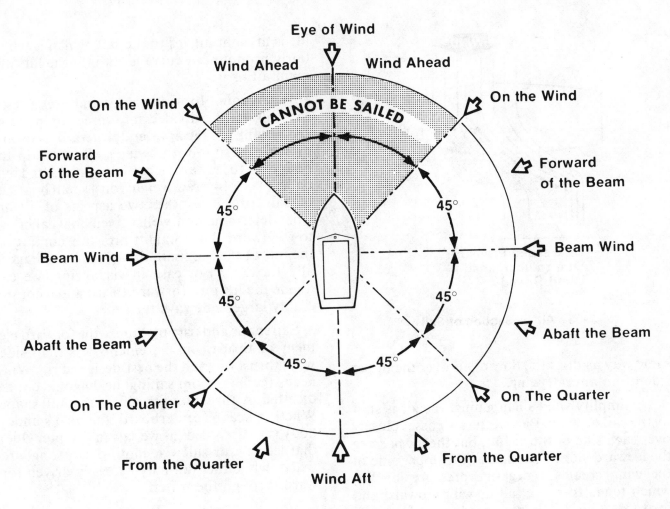

2-12   Eye of the Wind

Points of Sailing — Close Hauled

We can easily understand how a boat can sail before the wind, but it's harder to understand how a boat moved by the wind can sail into the direction from which the wind is blowing — yet modern, well-designed sailboats can sail to within 40° of the **true** wind. And even ordinary, nonperformance craft can usually sail to within 50° of the direction from which the wind is blowing. For purposes of discussion, we normally say that the average boat can sail to within approximately 45° of the **wind's eye** — the direction from which the true wind is coming.

That means, of course, that a sailboat skipper in a reasonably good boat has a choice of headings covering 270 degrees of the conventional 360° circle. This is a major improvement over the old square-rigged sailing vessels of the age of sail. They could only sail about 200 of the 360°.

A sailboat heading at approximately 45° to the true wind is said to be sailing **close hauled**. She may also be referred to as **beating to windward,** being **on the wind** or simply **beating**. All these terms mean the same thing — the boat referred to is sailing as close to the direction from which the wind is blowing as she efficiently can.

How is it done? Essentially, a sail on a boat going to windward is performing like an airplane wing. The technical term for it is **airfoil**. You remember that in Chapter One we mentioned a sail as having a three-dimensional shape built into it. That shape — a curve — is such that the flow of wind over the **leeward** side of the sail (the side away from the wind) acts the

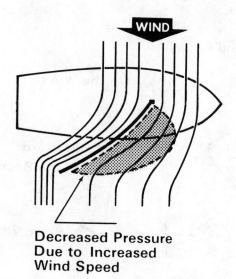

Decreased Pressure
Due to Increased
Wind Speed

2-13 Airfoil Section of Sail

same way as does the flow of air over the upper side of an aircraft wing.

To simplify what's happening, the air is split by the sail or wing. Part of the air passes closely over each side of the airfoil, but the air passing the leeward side of the sail or the upper side of the wing creates a negative pressure, or **lift,** which tends to move sail or wing upward and forward. This lift is generated in the forward quarter of the sail, along the luff and a relatively small distance back; the direction of the

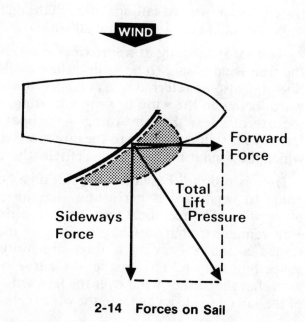

2-14 Forces on Sail

lift is at right angles to the sail, which is why a fairly pronounced curve is cut into the luff of a mainsail or jib.

When going to windward, wind pressure on the sails can be divided into three components — **heeling, sideways, and forward.** Heeling pressure is simply the wind's effort to tip the boat over to leeward; it can be counteracted by a ballast keel, by crew weight (on a small boat), or by sail trim. The other two aspects of lift are what determine how well a given boat can move to windward: The total lift pressure, coming off the luff of the mainsail, drives the boat diagonally forward. For ease in visualizing, we can divide the lift into forward thrust and a considerably larger sideways thrust.

Sail shape and trim maximize the forward element of thrust, but it remains less than sideways thrust on even the best-designed rig. What keeps the boat from sailing the diagonal course dictated by thrust on the sails is the hull shape. Whether keel or centerboard, the boat's underbody is so designed (as we saw in Chapter One), that leeway, or sidewise motion, is strongly resisted, while the hull may be easily driven forward through the water.

Function of Jib Close Hauled

Thanks to great refinements in hull and sail design, today's sailboats move to windward very efficiently, all things considered. Both sails function in this process, but the jib — if it is a large one, as many are today — contributes more lift than does the main, by virtue of the fact that lift over the mainsail surface is at least partially canceled out by the effects of turbulence caused by the mast, while air striking the jib luff is only mildly disturbed by the forestay, jib snaps and sail luff.

Not only does the jib provide its own lift to windward, it also helps funnel wind across the leeward surface of the mainsail. Many authorities believe that this creates a "slot effect" which accelerates the wind over the main and thus makes its lift more effective.

If lift is to be created, the wind flow must pass smoothly over the surfaces of the sail, with as little turbulence as possible. In order for smooth

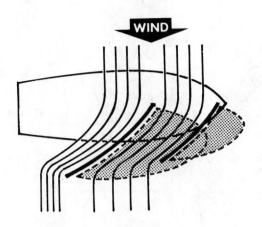

2-15 Sail Slot Effect

flow to occur, the sail must be at the proper angle to the wind. If the angle between sail and wind is much too small, the sail will **luff,** or shiver, along its windward edge; a luffing sail is an obvious warning that one is far too close to the wind. It is possible, however, to sail with enough wind in the sails to fill them, yet at an in-

correct angle, so that lift isn't nearly as great as it should be. Until fairly recently, it was hard to sail to windward efficiently, and most people took many hours of practice to develop a "feel" for when the boat was moving most efficiently to windward.

Now such a feel, while useful in getting the last ounce of drive from a boat, isn't really necessary. Thanks to a recent development, a person at the helm can now "see" how the wind is moving over the sails of his or her boat. Simply thread two or three pieces of knitting yarn, in a color that contrasts with the sail, through the jib luff at evenly spaced intervals. These tell-tales, usually called **woolies,** should be four to six inches back from the jib luff and eight inches to a foot in from the mainsail luff. They should be long enough — six inches or so on either side of the sail — to hang freely, yet not so long that they catch in seams or get snagged when the sail is bagged or set.

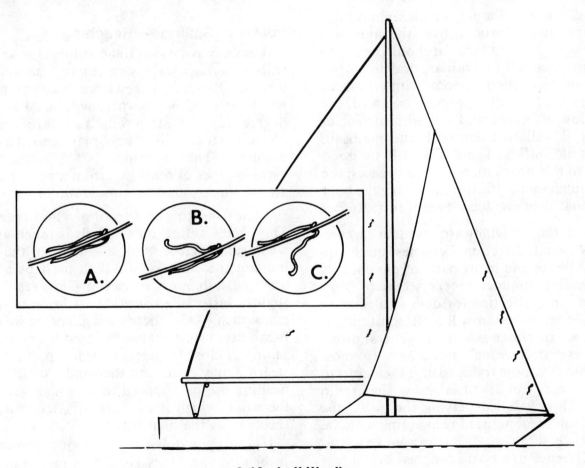

2-16 Luff Woolies

When sailing to windward, pull the jib sheet as tightly as possible and hold it, while edging the boat up into the wind. As the jib approaches its optimum angle with the wind, both windward and leeward woolies will stream straight back across the sail. If the boat is too close to the wind, windward streamers, on the concave side of the sail, will begin to lift and twirl, graphically indicating the air turbulence around them. When the boat heads too far off the wind for the set of the jib, the leeward streamer will begin to twirl.

For most vessels, there is an area of two to five degrees of heading where the sail trim is good enough so the woolies will stream evenly. As a general rule, the leeward wooly can be seen through the sail fabric, at least in sunlight, but many people have their sailmaker put a small, clear plastic window in the sail where the key jib wooly — about one-third the length of the luff up from the deck — is located.

Having trimmed the jib for maximum efficiency, one can then proceed to do the same with the mainsail. On most boats, it should be possible to trim each sail till both are drawing properly, but on some modern boats with very large jibs, when the foresail is properly trimmed, the air will flow off its leeward side with such velocity that it will interfere with the mainsail, causing mild luffing. There is usually no good solution to this problem, but in many cases, the jib is so much more effective in moving the boat upwind that it really doesn't seem to matter.

When sailing to windward, the fact of ever-changing wind direction becomes quite apparent. Although in many parts of our country the prevailing summer breeze seems to blow from the same direction for days at a time, in fact its actual direction will shift constantly a few degrees to either side of its general direction. These shifts aren't noticeable to most people, but to sailors trying to urge their craft to windward, they can be crucial, as we shall see in Chapter Three. Called **playing the puffs,** the helmsperson's technique of responding with the tiller to each slight wind shift can make a dramatic difference to a boat's progress over a reasonable distance.

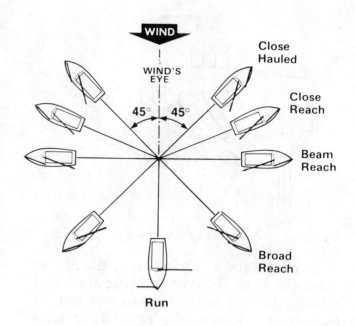

2-17   Points of Sailing

Points of Sailing — Reaching

A boat may be said to be sailing close-hauled within perhaps five degrees of its optimum windward course. Likewise, a boat is running when the wind is anywhere within a 10- or 15-degree arc dead astern. That's a total of perhaps 25° in the total 270° a boat may head at a given moment. The remaining 245° consists of various types of **reaching,** from almost-beating all the way around to almost-running.

Almost-beating is known as **close reaching.** The wind's action on the sails is much as it is when sailing close-hauled — most of the force moving the boat is lift, with perhaps a little more push than when beating. Close reaching is slightly faster than beating — because of the extra push — and there's a slight degree of extra flexibility, too. Because the boat is not already sailing as close to the wind as it can, the person steering may head into the wind a trifle (called **heading up,** as opposed to turning away from the wind, which is **heading off**), trimming the sheets in as the boat turns.

Use of the woolies is just about the same as in beating, and they should be just as helpful. As the boat's bow is turned farther away from the wind, she approaches a **beam reach,** which occurs when the apparent wind is blowing over the boat at more or less right angles. A beam reach combines excellent lift over the leeward side of the sail with good thrust on the windward side. For this reason, beam reaching is usually a boat's fastest point of sailing. As we shall see in Chapter Three, it also offers maximum maneuverability and is probably the safest point of sailing for the beginner.

Beam reaching, the woolies should still be reasonably effective, at least the ones on the leeward side of the sail. If in doubt, try the old trick of letting the sails out till they begin to luff just a little, then trimming them back in till the luffing stops, then trimming them a hair more. This rule-of-thumb system should leave you with the woolies reacting effectively.

As the wind moves aft from a beam reach, one is said to be on a **broad reach.** Probably the woolies will cease to be effective, as the force moving the boat is mostly thrust from astern, with just a little lift remaining over the leeward side of the sail. Broad reaching is safe, reasonably fast in any kind of wind, and quite exhilarating. The only common mistake new sailors make is to fail to let the sails out far enough. Trimmed in, the sails seem to be catching more wind; the boat heels and appears to be roaring along. In fact, however, easing (letting out) the

sheets a bit may bring the boat back up on her feet, and while she may not appear to be going as fast, she will really be moving more swiftly. The proper way to trim sails for broad reaching is the luff-and-let-out system described above. A speedometer will help you determine if your boat is moving at her best, but instruments like this are expensive and fragile, and their use is largely restricted to bigger boats.

The differences between beating, close reaching, broad reaching and running or the three types of reach are not instantly apparent, nor do they matter a great deal in practice. The important thing to learn is proper sail trim for each heading, and for this the concepts of beating, reaching and running are useful.

Perhaps the best way to test sail trim is to get another boat identical to yours and sail the same courses, with each skipper varying sail trim, one at a time. The most effective trim for every major heading will soon become apparent, and it will soon become second nature. Another good way to learn sail trim is to sail with someone who knows your kind of boat. Don't be afraid to ask him or her questions about what's the best practice. Most sailors are only too eager to impart what they know, and your only problem may be absorbing more information than you really need.

Basic Sailboat Maneuvering

So far, we've considered the three major points of sailing — close hauled, reaching and running — and the subdivisions of reaching, but without any thought as to which side of the sails the wind may be striking. In a modern fore-and-aft rigged boat, in which the sails at rest lie along the boat's centerline, the wind can, of course, blow on either side of most sails. When the breeze is coming over a boat's starboard side, so that the main boom is extended out to port, we say the boat is sailing on **starboard tack.** When the opposite is true, and the wind is coming over the boat's port side, she is said to be on **port tack.**

Identification of Tack

A boat is always on one tack or the other, even when running directly before the wind: In that case, we use the position of the main boom to determine tack; if the boom is extended to **port,** the boat is on **starboard** tack and vice versa. We assume for identification purposes that the wind is striking the boat on the side opposite to that on which the boom is extended.

Thus any description of how a boat is sailing at the moment includes both point of sailing and tack: "We were close hauled on starboard tack," for instance, or "reaching on port tack." It's important to know which tack your boat or any other in sight may be on. The legal question of which of two sailboats has right of way in a pos-

sible collision situation is largely determined by who is on what tack (See Rules of the Road, Chapter 6).

Aside from the legal question, however, the concept of port and starboard tack is a useful one to understand. In Chapter Two, we showed how most sailboats could at any moment sail a heading on any of 270° of a 360° circle. Only the two 45° segments on either side of the wind's eye are not sailable by the average boat. A little thought will reveal that a boat can then sail

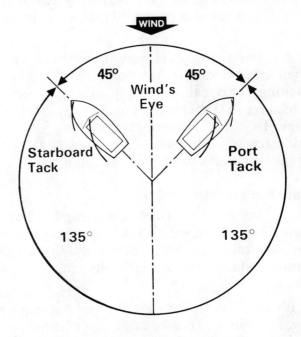

3-1 Starboard vs Port Tack

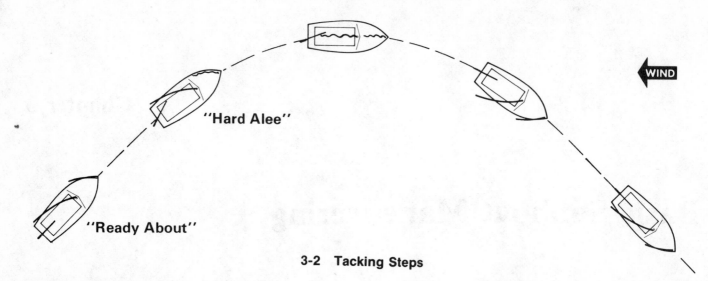

"Hard Alee"

"Ready About"

3-2 Tacking Steps

headings equal to only 135° without taking the wind on the opposite side of the boat.

If, for instance, a boat is running on starboard tack, with the main boom fully extended to port, and she changes course only slightly to bring the wind to the port quarter, the main boom will swing across the boat to the starboard side, and the vessel is now on port tack.

By the same token, if a boat is sailing fast and well while close hauled on port tack, and the skipper steers her through the wind's eye, she will soon be heading at about 90° to her previous course, and the sails will fill from the other side. She will be on starboard tack, close hauled again.

The two paragraphs above describe in a nutshell the two basic sailing maneuvers, **jibing** and **tacking** (also called **coming about),** both of which result from the need to change tacks from time to time. Because **tacking** is generally admitted to be the more important of the two maneuvers, let's examine it in detail first.

Tacking (Coming About)

Tacking can be defined as **moving the boat's bow through the wind's eye from close hauled on one tack to close hauled on the other. Coming about** means exactly the same thing as tacking.

It's obvious that during the tacking maneuver, the sails will not be drawing or helping the boat to move. They will in fact be causing drag

as the boat continues to move forward while turning. It's important, therefore, to make the tacking maneuver as quick as possible, to retain the boat's momentum. At the same time, if the

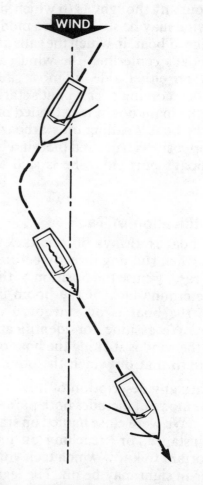

3-3 Jibing

rudder is too far over, it acts as a brake, which also cuts down on the boat's forward speed. Thus, a well-executed tack is a proper compromise between a turn that's too slow, causing air drag, and one that's too abrupt, causing water drag.

Let's run through a tack to see how it works in practice. We'll assume that we have a small boat with a mainsail and a jib, handled by a crew of two. One of the two is the skipper, and for convenience's sake we normally assume that the skipper is whoever's steering at the moment. The important thing, in any case, is to make sure that there's only one skipper. You can discuss a sailboat maneuver before you do it or afterward, but never during the action itself. To do so is just asking for trouble.

The skipper decides when to tack. The reason may be a wind shift (that is, a change in direction), another boat in your way, or simply the desire to turn. Having decided to come about, the skipper says, "Ready about." This is short for "Get ready to come about." Each crewmember has a job to do in getting ready. The skipper must be sure the boat is moving at a good, steady speed; he or she must also be ready to release the main sheet if necessary (it shouldn't be, but the skipper should be prepared); the crew normally handles the jib sheet. He or she must uncleat **but not release** the cleated end of the sheet so it's ready to let go.

When the skipper sees everything's in hand, he or she calls out, "Hard alee." At the same time, the tiller is put over to **leeward — away** from the direction the wind is coming from, called **windward.** In steering by wheel the direction in which to turn it may differ, according as the wheel is "right" or "left-handed". The desired effect is that of pushing the boat's stern to leeward, and, consequently, the bow swings into the wind.

The maneuver should be swift enough so the boat is still moving easily ahead as she turns. As the bow comes up more and more into the wind, the sails will begin to flutter, or **luff** — first the jib, then the main. As soon as the jib luffs, **but not before,** the crew should release the sheet he or she is holding and grasp the other one, taking

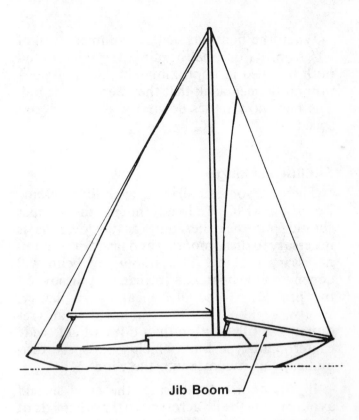

Jib Boom

3-4 Jib Boom

in the slack, but not forcing the sail to set on the other side of the boat.

Normally, the mainsheet may remain cleated as the boat comes about. The sheet made fast to the boom only allows the spar to swing across the cockpit, so the mainsail doesn't need to be tended. The jib sheet, on the other hand, is usually double, with the ends running to cleats at each side of the cockpit. To make the jib set on the opposite side of the boat, the other half of the jib sheet has to be taken in and cleated. (Some jibs, by the way, have a boom — the **club** or **jib-boom** — and sheet like the mainsail; these jibs are known as **self-tending** sails because they sheet themselves properly on the opposite tack.)

As the bow swings into the eye of the wind, the sails will luff straight down the boat's centerline. Then, as the bow continues its turn, the sails will begin to fill out on the other side. As the jib luffs over the deck, the crew takes in the sheet on that side, until the sail begins to stop luffing and draw. It's not necessary to work the mainsheet — the mainsail will usually fill and adjust itself.

When the boat has made a complete turn of 90° from its original heading, the sails should both be filled in approximately the same position on the new tack that they were on the old. The boat now settles down and begins to gain speed.

Skillful Tacking

There are some small tricks to skillful tacking. To begin with, as already noted, the skipper should put the tiller only as far over as is necessary to turn smoothly and fast, without unnecessary braking. This amount of helm will depend on the boat, and you can only discover it by practice. Generally speaking, a heavy, narrow keel boat has more momentum and requires less tiller action than does a light, wide centerboard-type hull, which loses speed dramatically as it comes into the wind.

In the course of tacking, the crew should avoid pulling the jib across onto the other side of the boat prematurely. Doing so only causes the sail to **backwind** — to take the breeze on its forward side, braking the boat's forward motion and turning the bow back to the old tack. The

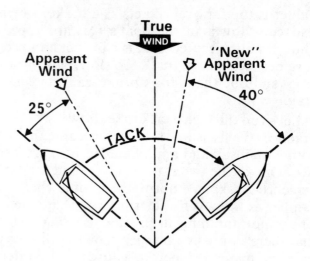

3-6 Tacking - Apparent Wind Effect

crew should, when possible, simply allow the jib to come across the boat, easing out the old part of the sheet and taking in the slack of the other part, so there's no great amount of loose line flapping on the foredeck, with the consequent likelihood of its getting tangled.

While most boats do tack through 85-95 degrees, remember the effect of apparent wind, noted in Chapter Two: Just before tacking, with the boat moving well close hauled, the apparent wind will probably be about 20° off the bow. When the tack is completed, and the boat has begun to move off on the new heading, the apparent wind will probably be more like 40° off the other side of the bow. As the boat gains speed, the apparent wind direction will move forward, and the sails must be trimmed, as described in Chapter Two, to match the apparent wind direction of the moment.

This means that the crew will normally not trim the jib in as far on the new tack as it was trimmed in on the old. Then as the boat regains its speed, the jib will have to come in a little, to account for the changing wind direction. Generally speaking, however, the mainsail is left alone during this part of the maneuver as the boom will probably swing over by itself; the crew will have been warned by the skipper's "hard alee" to avoid being struck by the swinging boom.

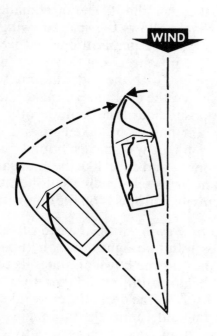

3-5 Premature Backwinding

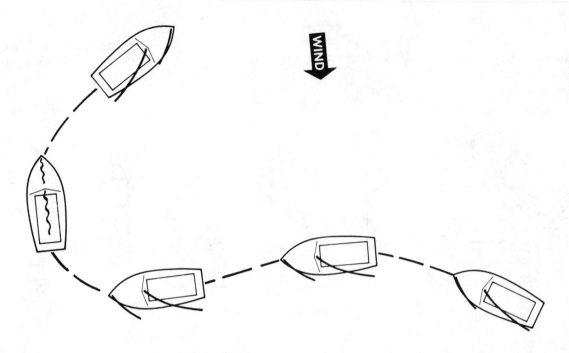

3-7 Avoiding Irons by Falling Off

Being in Irons

It sometimes happens, especially in small, light boats, that a vessel will get halfway through a tack and stall with the bow facing directly into the wind. This is called **being in irons,** and it happens to everyone from time to time. It usually happens because the boat wasn't moving fast enough when the tack was begun, or because the skipper tried to tack from a reaching point of sailing, without edging up to close hauled first. Sometimes you can get into irons on a very windy day if a wave slaps your bow as you're turning the boat, and stops you cold. Sometimes when there's very little wind, the boat will simply not tack at all.

To avoid getting into irons, make sure — especially while you're still not familiar with the boat — that you're moving fast and smoothly before trying to tack. Many skippers will **fall off** — deliberately head the bow **away** from the wind five degrees or so — and pick up a bit of extra speed before coming about.

On very windy days, when there are steep, short waves, put the helm over more abruptly than usual, and a bit farther. The idea is to get the bow through the **wind's eye,** wind blowing directly against bow, even at a sacrifice of forward speed, before the boat's forward momentum is stopped by wind or wave.

Conversely, on very calm days, put the helm over gently, not quite so much as usual, and let the boat ease through the turn. In this case, you're trying to maintain all the momentum you can, at some cost in turning speed.

Most boats will come about from a close reach, but many cannot do it from a beam reach, even if the sails are trimmed in during the turn. Better to trim the sails in slowly, while heading up to a proper close hauled heading, then make your tack from there.

Every boat tacks slightly differently from every other boat, and learning how to handle a new craft is just a matter of time and practice. A top skipper will spend an hour or two tacking and tacking again in a new boat, till he or she has the maneuver down pat and knows just what to expect.

But even top skippers can make a mistake. Sooner or later you'll be in the embarrassing position of finding yourself stalled — dead in the water, with the sails luffing helplessly down the boat's centerline. In irons.

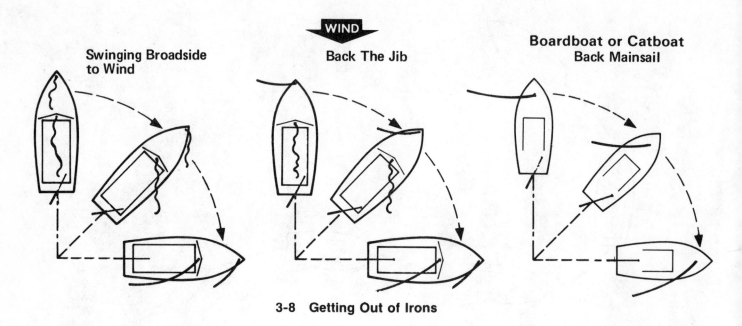

Swinging Broadside to Wind

WIND

Back The Jib

Boardboat or Catboat
Back Mainsail

3-8 Getting Out of Irons

Getting Out of Irons

Getting out of irons isn't particularly difficult. How you do it depends on what kind of boat you have. Here are several methods you can try to see which works best for you.

First, if yours is a light boat, just release the sheets, pull up the centerboard (if there is one), and wait. In a short time, the boat should swing around broadside to the wind, with the sails luffing out to leeward. Sheet in the sails and sail off.

Next, you can **back the jib.** Have the crew hold the jib clew out to one side of the boat, while you (the skipper) put the tiller over to the opposite side. Your boat will slip backward, and her stern will swing in the same direction the jib is extended, while the bow turns the other way. Once you're beam to the wind, you can straighten the tiller, sheet in both sails normally, and sail off.

On a boat with no jib, such as a boardboat or small dinghy, you can back the mainsail in the same manner. This may cause the boat to move straight backward, until you put the tiller over. Small catamarans will often begin to sail in reverse almost immediately after getting into irons. Just wait for the boat to pick up a knot or so of speed, then put the tiller over, while letting the sheet run.

There are only a couple of things to keep in mind when getting out of irons. First, before taking action, consider which direction you'll want to be heading after you get out of irons. If you back the jib, the bow will wind up headed in the opposite direction, but the stern will slide toward the side the jib is backed. Plan ahead.

In heavy winds, be cautious, as the boat comes beam-on to the breeze, about sheeting in. If you take the sheet in too quickly, the sudden wind pressure may spill the boat before it can get going. Better to sheet in just enough to let the

3-9 Getting Out of Irons by Backwinding the Jib

boat gain headway, then complete the sheeting operation when you're moving well.

Generally speaking, the heavier the boat, the more positive action will be required to get out of irons. As keel boats are normally heavier than centerboard boats of the same length, they'll need the jib backed and rudder hard over to get out of irons, while a centerboard boat may respond to rudder action alone. This is another of the things you'll have to learn about how your boat reacts.

Jibing

Recall our definition of tacking: moving the boat's **bow** through the eye of the wind. **Jibing,** pronounced Jybe-ing, occurs when you move the stern through the eye of the wind, in order to bring the breeze onto the other side of the sail. (Some purists may call this maneuver **wearing,** but it doesn't matter.)

The jibe is the downwind equivalent of tacking. Sometimes a wind change may be such that continuing along the tack you're on will mean you'll have to steer a course that's less direct than you'd like. Many smaller boats sail much faster on a broad reach than on a run, so they "tack downwind," using a series of jibes, first to one side, then to the other, and actually arrive where they're going faster than if they had sailed the straight-line course.

The essential difference between tacking and jibing is the wind direction relative to the sail. When you **tack,** the wind blows across the luff, the controlled edge of the sail; when you **jibe,** the wind hits the leech, the free side of the sail. Thus, when you're tacking, the sail flutters across the boat with no wind filling it until you sheet in. When you jibe, on the other hand, the sail always has wind filling it, except for the split-second when it's halfway across.

This means that jibing is potentially a less controlled, more violent maneuver than tacking. This does **not** mean you should be afraid to jibe your boat — a good sailor uses tack or jibe with equal confidence, according to what the maneuvering situation calls for. Until you can do the same, you're not handling your boat well.

Jibing may require a bit more maneuvering room than tacking, especially when jibing a small boat in a stiff breeze. This, too, is a question of control, and while a tack is a very predictable evolution, a fast jibe may result in a sudden burst of speed or a moment's out-of-control stagger. Allow enough room to cope.

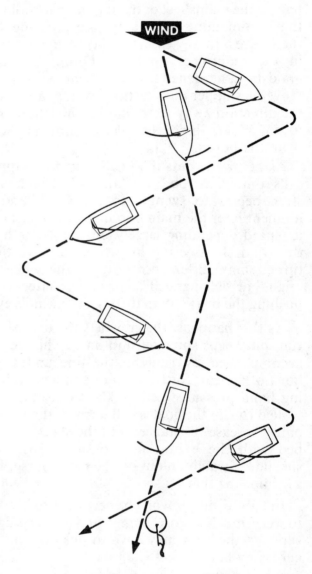

3-10 Jibing — Short vs Long Tack

The actual operation is very simple; let's assume the same kind of small sloop we had when discussing tacking, with a crew of two. To jibe, of course, you'll need first to put the boat on a run. If you're running **wing-and-wing,** jib set on opposite side to main, with a whisker pole extending the jib, remove the pole and stow it out of the way. The jib may or may not fill. Forget it. The sail which gets your principal consideration is the main.

The boat is now running, main boom fully extended. The skipper calls out, "Stand by to jibe," or words to that effect. The crew may handle the mainsheet or the skipper may hold it; that's something each crew must decide for themselves. In any case, the sheet handler takes in the mainsheet until the boom is nearly amidships, hardened in about as far as it will go. Now the skipper puts the tiller over, as always in the direction **away from** that in which he wants to go. When jibing, the tiller is put over away from the boom.

As he or she puts the tiller over, the skipper calls out, "Jibe-oh," or "Jibing." The boat's stern begins to swing into the wind, and a moment later the main boom will move across, its speed depending largely on the strength of the wind. In steering by wheel the direction turned may differ according as the wheel is "right" or "left-handed". The desired effect is of pushing the boat's stern through the wind's eye.

As this happens, the crew lets the mainsheet run, but keeps some tension on it. This can be accomplished by running the line under the horn of a cleat, for friction, or simply employing hand pressure. Let the sheet out in a controlled run, as the boat is still turning, then gradually increase resistance until the sheet is stopped with the boom short of hitting the lee shrouds. Straighten out on the new course. It's as simple as that.

In light winds, it won't be necessary to harden in very much before jibing, and in very light zephyrs, the crew may have to push the boom across by hand.

Uncontrolled Jibe

The important aspect of jibing is **control:** never allow the boom to swing across without controlling the sheet. In a brisk wind, aboard a small boat, the jar of boom's hitting shrouds can snap a wire, bend the boom or capsize the boat. If your boat has a single backstay, the boom can swing up as it moves across out of control and

snag on the backstay, with obvious possibilities, none good.

If your hands are tender, by all means wear gloves when handling sheets. Some sailors prefer fingerless mitts (it's the palms that need protection) made of chamois or some similar material. Others buy cheap cotton painters' gloves in the hardware store.

Remember that we mentioned one of the dangers of running as being the problem of knowing true wind strength? When heading downwind, your boat's speed is subtracted from the true wind strength, and the apparent wind you feel may be very much less than the true wind, which may slam the boom across with quite a crash, if you're not ready for it.

And watch your heads! The boom doesn't shout a warning as it comes across the cockpit, and more than one sailor has incurred a painful or even serious whack on the head from an unannounced jibe.

3-11 Uncontrolled Jibe

Sailing a Course

Any boat moving from point to point over the water can be said to be **sailing a course.** Much of the time nothing more is involved than heading directly toward the desired objective, but frequently, and especially in sailboats, things are somewhat more complicated.

If, for instance, the objective is directly upwind of a sailboat, it obviously is impossible to sail directly to it. The way to work a sailboat to windward involves a series of tacks, so that the boat zigzags its way to its ultimate destination. When it's necessary to sail a set of tacks to a windward mark, it's usually a good idea to choose a mark that is within sight. If the destination itself is out of range, then intermediate marks may be chosen, preferably ones that appear on nautical charts of the area (see Chapter 12).

about this question. Time spent tacking is, to be sure, time lost, and on the face of it, the same distance covered in many short tacks should take longer than a few long tacks. At the same time, however, it is easier to keep track of one's direction and position when short-tacking than when long tacks may take the boat well away from the base course. Finally, really skillful windward sailing involves being responsive — thus tacking — whenever a wind shift makes this advantageous, and that in itself implies frequent tacks.

If, for example, one is tacking toward a mark directly upwind, and the boat is on starboard tack, suppose the wind shifts 10° to port. This means that, to hold the same course relative to the wind while remaining on starboard tack, the boat will have to head 10° off the most direct zigzag. But if one tacks over to port, it will be

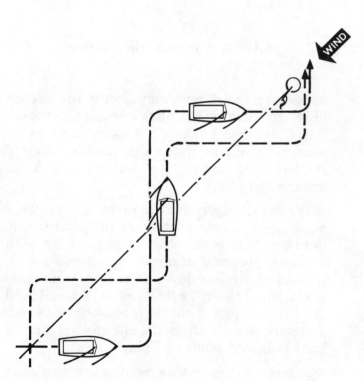

3-12   Sailing a Course Upwind

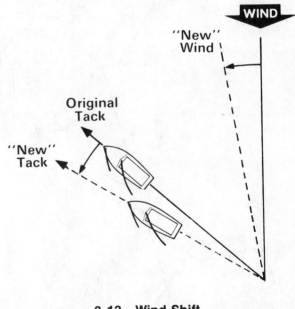

3-13   Wind Shift

Leaving aside the navigational aspect, the tactics of sailing an upwind course involve deciding whether to sail long or short tacks to either side of the base course — the straight-line course to the objective. Authorities are divided

possible to sail 10° closer than the former best zigzag. A wind change in one's favor is known as a **lift,** since it enables you to sail closer to the wind than anticipated. The opposite kind of wind shift is a **header,** since it heads you off from the course you'd planned.

Running downwind, as noted earlier in this chapter, it may frequently pay to head off the direct course to benefit from a considerable gain in speed reaching as opposed to running. The boat type and the wind strength will have a great deal to do with deciding whether this tactic is a good one in a given set of circumstances. Racing sailors frequently carry inexpensive plastic slide rules that read out the advantages and disadvantages of tacking downwind, revealing how much faster one must sail to make up the extra distance of an indirect course.

Normally, the way to change direction when running is to jibe, but sometimes, especially in rough weather, a controlled jibe may be rather

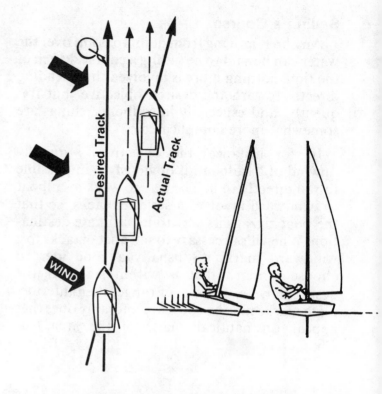

3-15   Daggerboard Up and Down

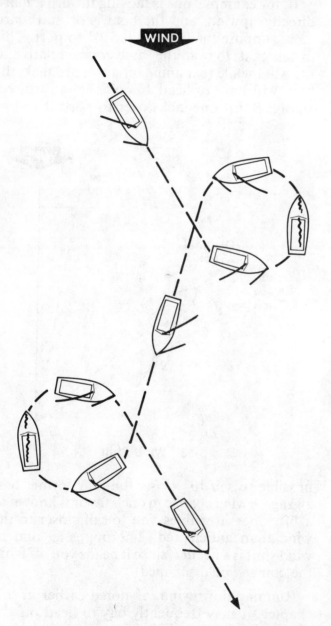

3-14   Running Down Wind In Heavy Weather

tricky, and the skipper may elect to sail a series of broad reaching headings, coming about each time the course is changed. This tactic keeps the wind relatively safely on the quarter, where a sudden wind shift is not likely to cause an unexpected jibe.

When tacking from a broad reach, it's usually necessary to come up toward the wind slowly until the boat is sailing a very close reach, with the sails properly trimmed, then come about. Instead of settling down on the opposite close reach, simply keep the boat coming around until the new downwind course is reached. It's a safe and only moderately inefficient way to handle a boat in heavy winds and seas.

A boat beating to windward or sailing a close reach makes a certain amount of leeway — the sideways slippage caused by wind pressure, which hull design cannot cancel out. The maximum amount of leeway under sail would be made by a centerboard boat close hauled, with the board fully raised. Try this with your own boat or a friend's. Put her on a close hauled heading with the board down, sailing right at

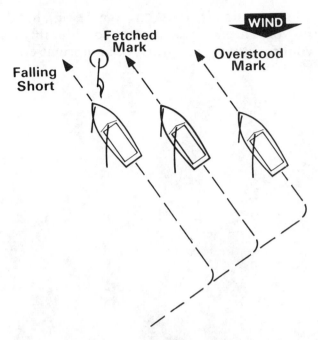

3-16 Fetching The Mark

make close hauled, close reaching and beam reaching, with the board all the way down, halfway down and fully raised. After a while, this kind of calculation becomes instinctive, but it takes practice.

When sailing toward a windward mark, the final tack is the crucial one. If you find yourself, following this tack, heading straight for your goal (allowing for leeway), then you have **fetched the mark.** If, after you've come about, you find you don't have to sail a close hauled course to make your target, you've **overstood** and should have tacked sooner. Far more common, however, is the problem of falling short, when one tacks too soon for the final leg, and then finds that another tack will be required.

some mark. Even better, try to line up a **range** — two marks in line. Sail toward it and see how your boat slides gently off to leeward. Now line up the marks again and try the same thing with the board all the way up. The difference will be dramatic.

Every skipper should have a pretty accurate idea of the amount of leeway his or her boat will

The temptation is to come about as soon as the mark is at 90° to your present heading. Theoretically, that should put you on a course directly toward it. In fact, however, once leeway enters the equation you'll find you will fall short. In addition, knowing exactly when the mark is at 90°, or directly **abeam,** is very tricky. More often than not, wishful thinking will cause you to tack too soon. Better to hold on another 30 seconds and overstand a bit.

3-17 Hiking Out

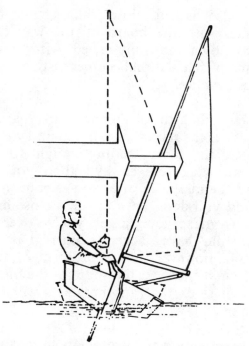

3-18   Sail Area Exposed During Heel

Stability and Angle of Heel

A sailboat normally heels in response to wind pressure, and we have seen (Chapter One) how the degree of heeling is partly controlled by hull shape and partly by ballast in the keel, if any. The third factor of importance, at least in smaller craft, is the disposition of crew weight. Even in a stiff wind, a small boat that's dramatically heeled can be brought level by the crew **hiking out** to windward. In older boats, hiking meant sprawling along the windward gunwale, but in most up-to-date craft, hiking straps are built in. The crew puts his or her feet under the straps; with one's seat on the gunwale, this allows the entire upper body to project out to windward as a living counterbalance. On some high-performance boats, the crew stands on the windward gunwale, seat supported by a trapeze hung from the masthead, and arches back to windward. This is the most effective use of human ballast possible, but it's not for beginners.

There are times when a boat should heel and times it shouldn't, and the degree of heel is also a variable. Within limits, heeling is a safety factor. When a sudden gust of wind strikes a boat's sails, and the boat heels, not only does the heeling action absorb some of the wind's force

(which would otherwise damage the rig), but the sails of a heeled boat present considerably less wind resistance than those of an upright craft.

3-19   Use of The Trapeze

On days of very light breeze, there may not be enough wind to make the sails assume a proper airfoil shape. The cloth just hangs there. But by heeling the boat five degrees or so, the sails may be induced to sag into the proper curve. In this case, heeling is induced by the crew sitting on the leeward, not the windward, side of the boat.

On some boats with long overhangs at bow and stern, heeling can effectively extend the length of the waterline. This means that the boat's potential speed, which is related to waterline length (Chapter One) is somewhat increased.

3-20 Crew's Weight Shifted to Lee Side in Faint Breeze (Induced Sag)

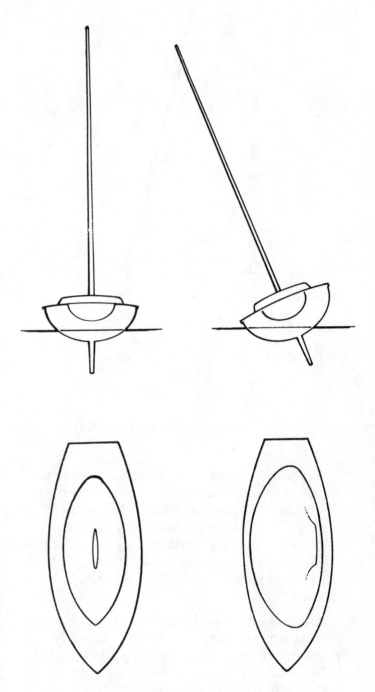

3-21 Waterline Changes by Heeling

Some sailboats can be slightly heeled to leeward in faint breezes to reduce the amount of hull surface in contact with the water, and thus lessen the friction impeding the boat's movement.

Some boats have a more effective underwater shape when slightly heeled, but this is generally true of older crafts. Today's high-performance daysailers are almost always at their best when sailed flat or very nearly so. In almost no case is a boat's performance going to improve beyond 20° of heel, and in most boats performance will deteriorate badly from 25° or so on.

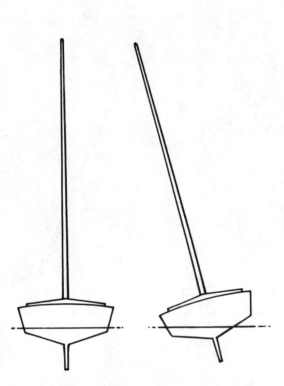

3-22   Surface Area of Hard Chine Hull

3-23   Catamaran

Stability in boats is a complicated matter of concern to naval architects. The amateur sailor needs only to know some basic characteristics of various kinds of hulls. Boats have two kinds of stability: **initial** and **ultimate.** Initial stability is a boat's tendency to resist heeling at all. Ultimate stability is the boat's ability to resist capsize.

Round bottom keel boats have relatively little initial stability. They heel easily — but only to a point. Once the counterbalancing effect of the ballast keel is felt, a round bottom boat will be very hard to heel any further. It has good ultimate stability.

Almost the opposite is true of hard chine centerboard boats. Their hull shape resists easy heeling, and they are very steady at first. But once there's enough heeling force to heel the boat more than a few degrees, the initial stability suddenly begins to lessen, until at some point it's easier for the hull to keep going over than to right itself. This is a matter of good initial stability and poor ultimate stability.

The most extreme case is that of the multihull — a catamaran with two hulls or a trimaran with three. Because of hull shape, these boats have tremendous initial stability, and a catamaran will seldom heel more than five degrees or a trimaran more than 10. But once the windward hull of a catamaran leaves the water, stability is on the point of evaporating and a "cat," once capsized, will tend to turn completely upside-down. A trimaran is more initially stable, but again, if sufficient force is applied to flip her, she will settle in a completely upside-down position. Both cats and tris are normally without ballast and have daggerboards, so there is no counterbalancing weight to bring them back up.

Each type of hull has its advantages and drawbacks. There is no "perfect" hull for all conditions, and in choosing a boat one must aim for that compromise between stability and other attributes (such as speed or maneuverability) that one's sailing area demands.

3-24   Trimaran

Chapter 4

Rigging and Boat Handling

As anchorages become more crowded and marinas more costly, sailors have turned in increasing numbers to trailering their sailboats (See Chapter 10). Even if you keep your boat at a pier or mooring, it may be helpful for you to know how to set up the rigging from scratch — a task well within the capabilities of most skippers of boats under about 25 feet in length.

Stepping the Mast

The difficulty of setting up the mast depends on two things: The size and weight of the spar itself, and the manner in which it's stepped in the boat. In our introductory chapter on parts of a boat we considered the simplest kind of step, in which the mast foot fits into or around a socket grounded on the boat's keel. Such a mast may first lead through a brace at gunwale level — either a hole in the deck or a seat.

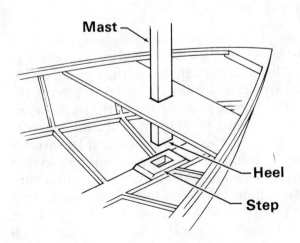

4-1 Stepping the Mast

4-2 Mast Step on a Hinge

On larger boats, such as small, trailerable cruisers, the mast may step on deck in a hinged fitting which allows it to be raised and lowered quite easily. In principle, stepping the mast in either case is much the same and should offer no problems if a few, orderly steps are followed.

First, select the location for mast stepping. If yours is a small boat without floorboards, or one in which the hull is thin enough so it flexes under your weight, then the boat has to be launched first. Make sure she is tied securely to float or pier, so she won't shift under you as you step aboard with the spar on your shoulder. If you step the mast while the boat is still on its trailer, as many do, first check to be sure that there are no overhead wires either near you or between you and the launch ramp. A small but significant number of sailors have been electrocuted in recent years when their metal spars or standing rigging came in contact with uninsulated wiring.

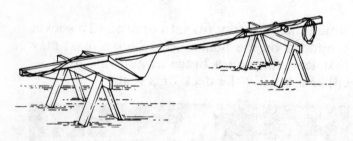

4-3 Mast on Horses

If you haven't done so already, tie off the stays, shrouds and halyards against the mast. The easiest way to do this is first to set the spar on two or three sawhorses for support. No tie should be higher up the mast than you can reach when the spar is stepped, for obvious reasons.

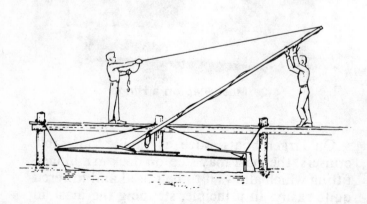

4-4 "Walking" the Mast Up

For masts that are deck-stepped in a hinged fitting, you may now place the mast foot in the hinge and secure it. If there's no way to secure the foot, or if the spar must first be guided through a deck hole, at least two people will be required to step even a rather small mast — one to locate the foot and the other to raise the spar.

Walk slowly and carefully forward, watching where you put your feet, and raise the mast to the vertical. At this point, one person will have to steady the mast (unless the deck-level support is enough to hold it upright) while another quickly makes fast the key pieces of standing rigging. These are the fore- and backstays and the upper shrouds, both port and starboard. Once these turnbuckles are attached to the proper chainplates and taken up enough to hold the mast reasonably steady, then it's no longer necessary for anyone to hold the spar erect.

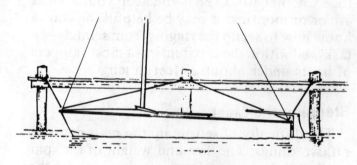

4-5 Mast Stepped

Make fast the remaining shrouds to their chainplates and be sure the halyards are free to run without being tangled in the rigging or the mast hardware. Although actual tuning of the standing rigging is a matter of trial and error, initial tensioning is no great problem. The wire running to the masthead, whether it be shrouds or stays, should be quite taut — enough so that it vibrates when plucked — while wire that runs partway up the mast should be tight enough so it doesn't flap to and fro, but should not have serious tension on it. Once you're sailing, you'll know soon enough if your turnbuckles need adjusting, so for the moment don't overdo.

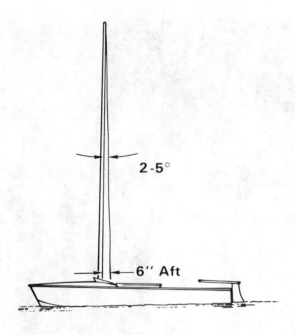

4-6   Mast Rake

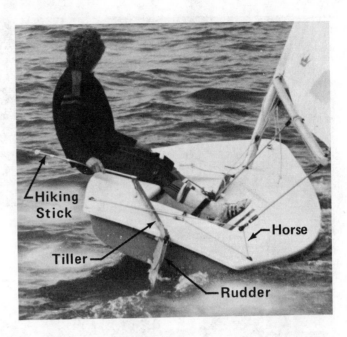

4-7   Rudder and Tiller - Note Hiking Stick

What's important is to have the mast standing straight in the boat. Sight over the bow to make sure the spar isn't tipped to one side or the other, and from the side to determine that the amount of fore-and-aft tilt, known as **rake,** is proper. On most boats, the mast is designed to rake aft slightly — two to five degrees at most. If yours is a class or production boat, other skippers or the manufacturer's literature will tell you the amount of rake that works best. Lacking this information, try a slight tilt aft — enough so that the halyard, allowed to swing free, will touch the deck about six inches aft of the mast step for a 20-foot spar.

With the mast in place, you can attach the boom to the gooseneck track or fixed fitting, whichever your boat is equipped with. Attach the mainsheet to boom and deck fittings, making sure the line is free to run through its blocks. If your boat has a **topping lift,** a light line or wire running from the masthead to the outer end of the boom, make it fast to hold the boom off the deck.

Now set up the rudder and tiller, if they're not already attached. On small boardboats having a rope or wire **horse,** a bridle under which the

tiller fits, be certain that the tiller is in fact under the horse. If the fittings on rudder and boat transom allow, the rudder should be locked in so it cannot float free. If you have a tilt-up rudder and the boat is not yet launched, be sure that the rudder is in the "up" position. Many boats with heavy centerboards are trailered with the board resting on a crossbeam of the trailer, so as to take the strain off the centerboard pennant. Before launching, check to make sure the board is fully retracted and the pennant tied off. Otherwise, the board will almost certainly jam in the trailer frame and make it impossible to launch the boat. Once afloat, however, the centerboard or daggerboard should be fully lowered.

4-8   Tilt-Up Rudders

4-9 Bending On Main - Feeding Foot into Boom Track

Making Sail

Before attaching the sails to the spars and forestay, head the boat more or less into the wind so that the sails, once hoisted, will luff freely. Ideally, a boat should be swinging free at a mooring when making sail, but in many cases you'll be at a pier or float where you line up only generally into the wind.

Work with the mainsail first. Usually, you'll have to take the sail out of the bag and find the clew — the lower aft corner, as you remember. Arrange the sail so the foot, from clew to tack, is untwisted and feed the sail onto (or into, depending on the attachments) the boom track, pulling the foot along the boom until the clew can be made fast to the outhaul. Next, make the tack cringle fast to the gooseneck fitting, and pull the outhaul toward the outer end of the boom until the sail's foot is taut.

Insert the battens in the batten pockets. Old-fashioned pockets had small grommets at the outer end, corresponding to a hole in the end of the batten. A light line secured the batten in its pocket. Nowadays, however, most sailmakers use the type of pocket illustrated, which holds the batten in place without tying. Battens should fit snugly into the pockets that hold them, but not so tightly that they stretch the fabric. Remember that the thinned-down end of a wood batten goes into the pocket **first.** It might seem that just the opposite would be true, but consider that a batten's job is to support the roach of the sail and to impart an even curve, hence the more easily bendable thin edge should be further forward in the sail, where the curvature is greater.

If your mainsail luff is fitted with **slides** (for an

4-10 Inserting Batten in Sail

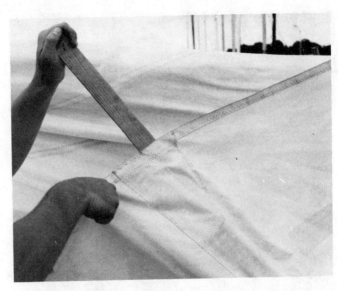

4-11 Detail of Batten and Sail Pocket

exterior track) or **slugs** (for a recessed track), you can slide these onto or into the track. There's nearly always a gate fitting at the bottom of the track so you can keep the slides or slugs in place, once attached. If, however, you have a mainsail with a roped luff, you won't be able to slide this into the mast groove until you are actually ready to make sail.

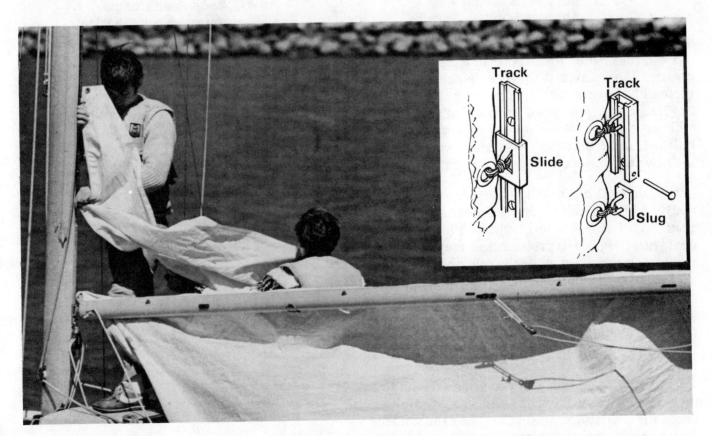

4-12 Bending on Main — Inserting Mainsail Slides — (Inset) Typical Slides and Slugs

4-13 Sail's Head Cringle - Attached with Bowline

4-14 Sail's Head Cringle - Attached with Shackle

Last, make the halyard fast to the sail's head cringle. Most halyards have a shackle or other piece of hardware for this purpose, but it's really not necessary. A type of knot called a **bowline** will serve just as well. Before making fast the halyard, sight up along it to make sure that it isn't twisted or snagged.

If your boat has only a mainsail, you're now ready to hoist it and go. But we're assuming that your boat has a sloop rig and you have yet to deal with the jib. (In practice, one crewmember will attach the main while the other handles the jib.) Bundle the mainsail loosely atop the boom (see how to do it below) and wrap it in place with a couple of **sail stops** — lengths of sail fabric or rubberized shock cord (the latter is recommended) that are carried for just this purpose.

Generally speaking, you can attach the jib to the forestay right from the sail bag, **if** you've taken the precaution to fold and bag the sail so that its tack cringle is right on top. Shackle or

4-15 Main Bundled Loosely on Boom

4-16　Making Jib - Attaching Tack to Stem

4-17　Bending On Jib - Hanking On

4-18　Jib Sheets - Spliced on to Jib Clew

snap the tack in place, then work up the luff of the jib snap by snap to the head. As you do so, it may help to run the luff through your hands to keep the edge from being twisted in the process of attachment. When you're done, check that all the jib snap jaws are facing the same way. Virtually all American sailmakers sew on jib snaps so their openings face to port.

When you get to the sail's head, make fast the jib halyard, using the same procedure as with the main.

The jib sheets are another story. Remember that they're nearly always double, with half the sheet running to one side of the cockpit and the other half to the other side. How you attach the sheets is an open question, and here are the methods among which you can choose.

Splicing — a splice is a permanent way of making an eye at the end of a line or attaching two lines together. It will never, when properly done, work free, no matter how briskly the sail luffs or flutters. A good splice is not heavy, so

two of them won't weigh down a corner of the sail. On the other hand, a splice can't be undone, so if you have more than one jib, you'll need more than one set of jib sheets, which is a nuisance as well as being expensive.

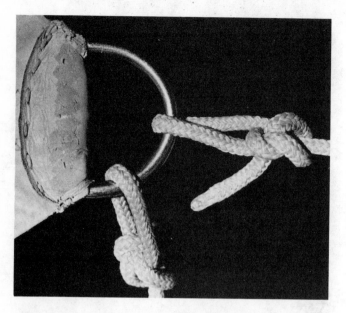

4-19 Jib Sheets - Bent on with Bowline

Tying — there's no reason you can't tie each part of the jib sheet to the jib clew cringle, using a bowline. This good knot is easy to tie, once you get the hang of it, and is also easy to untie. Normally, it will not shake itself loose except if badly tied and repeatedly shaken. A bowline is, however, a fairly large and clumsy knot, and two of them will weigh down the jib clew in light breezes, as well as offering potential snags when tacking.

4-20 Jib Sheets - Bent on with Fisherman's Bend

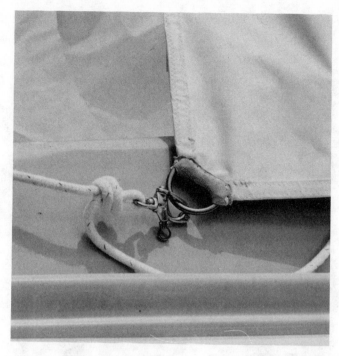

4-21 Jib Sheets - Attached with Snap Shackle

Snapshackles — for those who prefer or require a quick release, the snap shackle, into whose ring both parts of the jib sheet are spliced, is often the answer. Stainless steel or bronze snapshackles are relatively light and streamlined, but they are also expensive. And although they have been carefully engineered so as not to pop open, still they do so from time to time, and it can be very difficult to capture the wildly flapping clew of a big jib on a windy day. In addition. the hardware can be dangerous or damaging even if it doesn't snap open. More than a few sailors have received bloody noses from being whacked across the face by an untamed shackle.

When hoisting sail, a double-check of three things is recommended. First, be sure the boat is facing as nearly into the wind as possible. Second, check again before putting tension on a halyard to see that it's free and untangled. And third, be sure that main or jib sheets are ready to run free, so the sail won't hold any puff of breeze it may catch, and start your boat sailing before you're ready.

the halyard on a cleat. Now put tension on the downhaul until the sail's luff is approximately as taut as the foot and secure the downhaul line.

For rigs without a downhaul, you will have to raise the sail and put tension along the luff by pulling on the halyard. In most cases where this type of rig is fitted, there's a mainsail halyard winch fitted to the starboard side of the mast, and by taking four or five turns of the halyard wire around the winch drum, then turning the winch, you can increase tension on the mainsail luff. When the sail shows vertical creases along the luff, it's properly taut.

4-22   Main Halyard Coiled and Stowed on Cleat

4-23   Coiled Halyard Stowed Between Halyard and Mast

Raise the mainsail first, hoisting it quickly and smoothly. If your boat has a sliding gooseneck, release the downhaul line, allowing the sail to be raised all the way to the top of the track. On some smaller boats, there may be a halyard lock which will engage, holding the sail fully raised. On most boats, you'll have to tie off

The tail of the halyard — a length of line about equal to the height of the mast — now must be coiled and stowed where it cannot get free, but where it can be freed and released on a moment's notice. There are several ways of coiling and stowing a halyard.

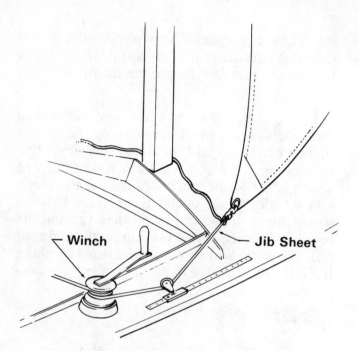

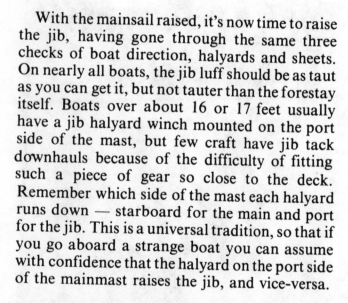

4-24   Jib Sheet Led Through Block

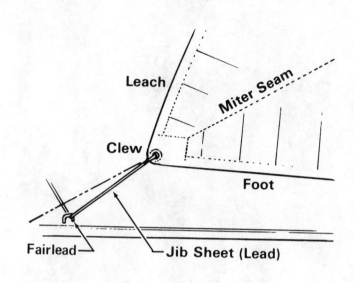

4-25   Jib Details at Clew

With the mainsail raised, it's now time to raise the jib, having gone through the same three checks of boat direction, halyards and sheets. On nearly all boats, the jib luff should be as taut as you can get it, but not tauter than the forestay itself. Boats over about 16 or 17 feet usually have a jib halyard winch mounted on the port side of the mast, but few craft have jib tack downhauls because of the difficulty of fitting such a piece of gear so close to the deck. Remember which side of the mast each halyard runs down — starboard for the main and port for the jib. This is a universal tradition, so that if you go aboard a strange boat you can assume with confidence that the halyard on the port side of the mainmast raises the jib, and vice-versa.

If a boat flies more than one jib at a time, both headsail halyards lead down to port; and if she is gaff-rigged, the two mainsail halyards — peak and throat — both lead to starboard.

With the jib fully raised, check the sheet leads. In order for the sail to set properly when filled with wind, the jib sheet should lead to the block or non-turning **fairlead** on deck. Many boats have a length of jib sheet track on either side of the deck, so the position of the jib sheet lead can

be varied. Most jibs are cut with a **miter seam** running from the clew to a point along the luff. The correct sheet lead is usually a little **below** an extension of the miter seam.

Once you're away from mooring or pier (see below), put the boat on a close-hauled heading on either tack. Now sight up the mast from the side and from forward, to make sure it's straight. If there's a bend or hook in it, use the turnbuckles on the appropriate shrouds or stays to straighten it out, but work slowly.

If the head of the mast is hooked to windward, try tightening the windward lowers; if it's hooked to leeward, tighten the windward upper shroud. When the masthead hooks forward, chances are you'll want to tighten the backstay.

Having got the mast straight on one tack, come about and repeat the process on the other. You may have to run several tacks before you have the rig properly adjusted, but once you've accomplished this, a dab of paint at the proper spot on the turnbuckle will show how far it should be turned next time.

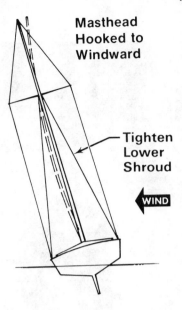

4-26 **Mast Bowed to Leeward**

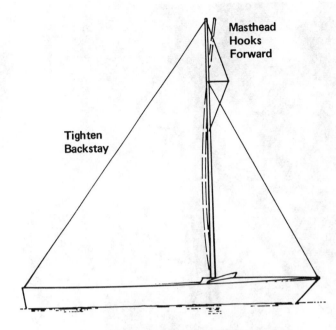

4-28 **Masthead Hooked Forward**

With the shrouds and stays at the correct adjustment, insert the cotter pins through the threaded stems and tape the turnbuckles with waterproof tape (available at any store handling sailing gear) so that the bent-over pins can't snag or tear the sails. Some skippers use inex-

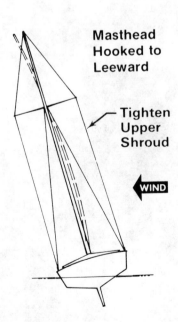

4-27 **Mast Bowed to Windward**

4-29 **Turnbuckle with Cotter Pins
Turned in to Prevent Sail Damage**

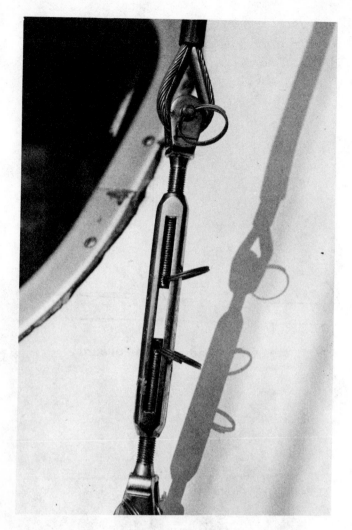

4-30 Turnbuckle with Ring Clips in Lieu of Cotter Pins

4-31 Chafing Gear — Plastic Tubing Over Turnbuckles

4-32 Stuffing Jib in Bag

pensive plastic tubing instead of tape. It can be employed over and over, but it's another thing to remember when hooking up the turnbuckles.

When returning from a sail, head into the wind before dropping sail, then do it in reverse order of raising the sails. Lower the jib first, then the main. To drop a sail, first capsize the halyard coil on deck — turn it upside-down so it's free to run when uncleated. One crewmember should tend the halyard to make sure the end doesn't snake up the mast out of reach, or to prevent a snag.

4-33   Folding the Jib

The jib may be simply stuffed into its bag with the tack fitting accessible at the top. If you're in a hurry, it won't do the sail much harm. It's better practice, however, to take the sail ashore and lay it out flat. Now flake it from foot to head as shown and then loosely roll the flaked sail before bagging for overnight or longer. This will prevent wrinkles in the sail fabric and, more importantly, will keep the artificial fibers from cracking as they may if the sail is jammed forcibly into its bag.

4-35   Dropping the Main

4-34   Rolling Jib for Bagging

The mainsail, too, should be folded and bagged (after the battens are removed, of course) in the same manner as the jib. On many larger boats, however, the main is furled on the boom and left there under a sail cover. This is quite acceptable and should do the sail no harm, provided that you first remove the battens, slack off the outhaul, and then furl the sail properly.

This is easy enough to do. As the sail is lowered, try to drop it slightly to one side of the boom. After detaching and securing the halyard, pull a large flake of sail out from the foot to form a semi-bag. Now flake out the rest

4-36   Furling — Dropping the Main and Rolling on Boom

4-37   Furling — Main Stowed on Boom

of the main within this fold. Roll it tightly on top of the boom in a smooth, sausage-shaped form. Secure it in place with shock cord sail ties —

three should be enough for the average length boom, and it's always a good idea to have one extra.

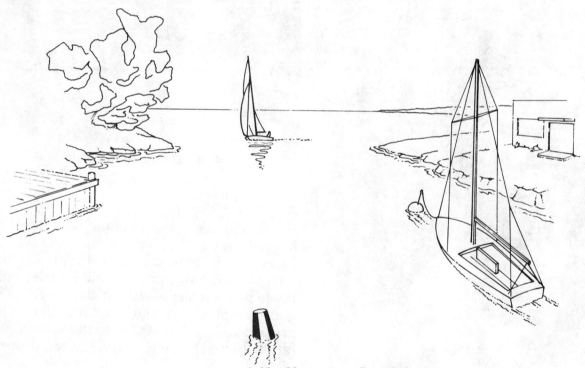

4-38   Moored on Buoy

Sailing Away

The most important part of getting a sailboat under way is planning ahead. And conversely, the easiest way to get into trouble is to leap before you look. Let's assume that our boat is swinging at a mooring buoy (See Chapter 7) in an anchorage. This is close to the ideal situation, as the boat can (at least in theory) sail off on any heading permitted by the wind direction. As a matter of practicality, of course, this is seldom true. One must take into account other boats, both anchored and moving, structures like piers and aids to navigation, water depth, and the shape of the harbor itself.

The wise skipper will also consider that what he or she is planning may not come off. If counting on sailing off in one direction and then tacking quickly to a new heading, bear in mind that this crucial first maneuver may be where your boat finds herself in irons. Or an unseen boat or swimmer may suddenly appear from behind another vessel, throwing off your calculations.

Here are some important things to remember in getting under way:

1. A sailboat cannot be steered until the sails are drawing and it's moving; therefore, only the lightest craft will be able to maneuver as soon as they **cast off,** or when the line holding them to mooring buoy or pier is released.

2. When casting off from a buoy, your boat will be effectively in irons — headed into the wind with the sails luffing. So your first tactics will be the same as those noted in the previous chapter for getting out of irons.

3. Remember to allow the boat to fall back from its mooring buoy a few feet before backing the jib, especially in a quick, lightweight boat. Otherwise you run the risk of taking off and overrunning the buoy or snagging the mooring line (which is usually permanently attached to the buoy).

4. Plan on sailing off on a beam or close reach if possible, as you'll then have the greatest maneuverability. If the harbor is very crowded, however, don't be ashamed to paddle out to open water before making sail. Every small sailboat should have a pair of paddles (See Chapter 11) and larger craft should have a motor.

As a general rule, when at a mooring your boat will automatically point into the wind. At the same time, however, the current, which is the horizontal movement of the water (See Chapter 12), may be carrying your boat in a different direction. With small sailboats, the effect of

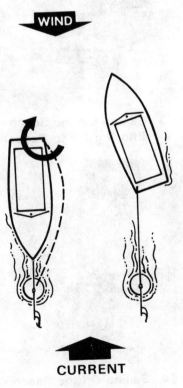

4-39 Current Vs Wind

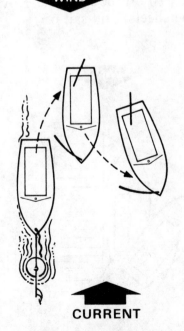

4-40 Using Current to Cast Off

wind overrides that of current; where the current is strong and the wind light, and when the boat in question is a deep-keel type, the current may have more effect than the wind, even to the point of forcing the boat to ride stern-first to the breeze.

In this case, there are two tactics you can choose between. First, you can lead the mooring line around to the stern, allowing the boat to swing end for end so her bow is again into the wind, then make sail and head off in the normal way, except that you'll drift forward instead of backward after casting off. Second, you can hoist only the jib and let it stream out over the bow. Cast off, sheet in the jib, and sail downwind until you are clear of the anchorage area, then head up into the wind and raise the mainsail. Most boats will sail reasonably well under either the jib or the mainsail, and many skippers use only one sail when the wind is strong (See Chapter 5).

Sailing away from a pier should not be too difficult as long as there's one edge of the structure that lines up more or less into the wind. If possible, lay your boat along an axis of pier or float so that the hull is in a closehauled position relative to the breeze **before** you cast off. Release the bow line first, let the bow swing away, then cast off the stern line. Now **harden in** (pull in the sheets) and sail off.

4-42 Sailing Off the Beach - Carrying Boat to Water's Edge

4-43 Sailing Off the Beach - Shoving Off to Deeper Water

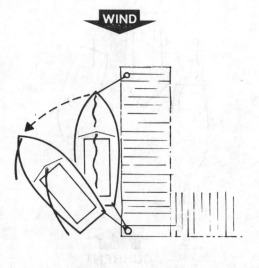

4-41 Leaving a Pier-Wind Ahead

4-44 Sailing Off the Beach - Sailing Through the Surf

If no side of the pier offers you a sailaway position, you'll just have to paddle or motor out to clear water before raising sail. It may be annoying, but it's a lot less embarrassing than being pinned helplessly against the float with your sails raised and no way to get off.

Sailing off a beach, one crewmember will usually have to stand about waist-deep in the water holding the boat in place until all is ready for sailing. Unless your boat is extremely maneuverable, don't try to stay a bit drier by sailing out of shallow water with the centerboard raised. When setting out from a standstill, the centerboard should be completely lowered.

Heading back to beach, pier or mooring is just the reverse of sailing away, with a few necessary exceptions. As always, the first item of importance is to plan the approach.

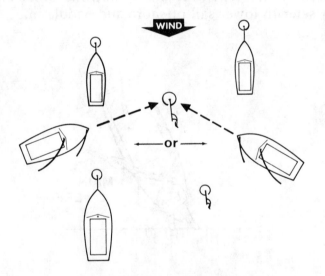

4-45 Approaching a Buoy

Coming into an anchorage, the best tactics call for retaining as much maneuverability as you can, consistent with reduced speed in case something does go wrong. Until you are very familiar with your anchorage, it may help to sail up to your buoy a few times from different directions, without trying to pick it up. This will not only provide good information on the best paths among the other anchored boats, but it will also make you think in terms of what to do should you sail up to the mooring and miss picking it up — something that happens to the best sailors sooner or later.

If the spacing of other boats allows, try to approach the mooring buoy on a close reach. Thus, you have good speed and good maneuverability. Make your approach — other conditions permitting — on whichever tack will allow you to fall away from the wind safely if you miss the buoy. You probably won't have enough momentum left to come about, but you should, by the time you know whether you'll make the buoy or not, have speed enough to head the bow away from the wind.

If your boat will handle reasonably well under mainsail alone, it's often a good idea to drop, remove and bag the jib before making your final approach to the buoy. This procedure will give you far better visibility forward in a critical couple of moments, and it will provide an unobstructed foredeck for the crewmember who must grab the mooring line or buoy: Not only is a Dacron or nylon sail very slippery underfoot, but it can also get muddied or torn if used for a carpet while mooring.

Your centerboard should be fully lowered for maximum maneuverability when making the final approach. At some point between one and three boat lengths from the mooring, head right into the wind and coast up to the buoy with the sail luffing and the sheet (or sheets) uncleated. Ideally, the boat should stop dead in the water with the mooring buoy in easy reach.

It sounds hard, but you may be surprised at how easy it becomes once you're used to your boat and familiar with her **carry,** the amount of distance she requires to lose momentum when headed into the wind from a close-hauled course. In addition, you can fudge a little just before the final approach, slacking the sheets and letting the sail luff if you're moving too fast, or heading off to gain a little speed.

What is tricky, however, is getting the mooring line aboard and made fast before the boat begins to move off in a new direction. Unlike an automobile, a boat won't stand still while you figure out a new approach to that parking spot. If you miss the mooring, you've got to be ready to do something else right away, and usually the safest tactic is simply to sail right clear, get your crew and gear sorted out, and start over from

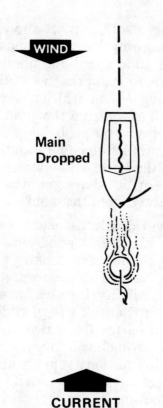

4-46 Mooring with Jib Alone

These remarks have been predicated on the usual mooring conditions, in which the wind direction is the dominant factor. As in leaving a mooring, it may sometimes be that the current is against the wind and stronger in its effects on the boat. When this happens, you may have to sail downwind to the mooring, in which case it may be easier to do so under jib alone, especially if that sail is smaller than the main.

Sailing to a pier involves much the same problem as coming up to a mooring, with the drawbacks being that only three sides of the pier, at most, will be accessible. Also, a pier or even a float is much more likely to damage a boat in case of collision than is a buoy. For relative beginners to sailing, it's probably not a good idea to sail into a slip or up to a pier unless the final shot can be made almost directly into the wind. When the pier is downwind, it's far safer to lower sail offshore and paddle in.

scratch. Trying to make a missed approach into a good one almost never works, and you're far better off to sail clear while you have the momentum and the room, then try again.

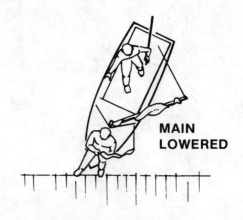

4-48 Approaching a Pier

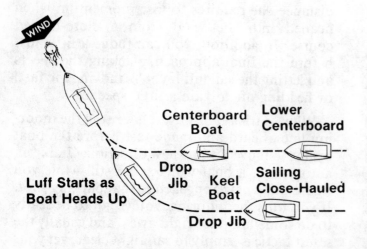

4-47 Mooring with Main Alone

When sailing to a pier, someone aboard the boat must be ready to fend off. In small boats up to 16 feet or so, it's practical to sit on deck and fend off with your feet — which should have boat shoes on them. Don't try to stop the boat's momentum with an arm or a leg while standing up. And if the boat is a large one, fend off with a fender — it will absorb much more shock than you can, and do it better, and in any case it's much more seamanlike to sacrifice a piece of gear than to risk injuring a crewmember.

4-49   Causes of Wind Shift in a Harbor

Sailing in a crowded harbor, be ready for sudden wind shifts which may be caused by large buildings ashore, high piers or even anchored boats. As in the case of approaching an unfamiliar anchorage, it often pays to sail close by your intended pier without committing yourself to the final approach, then return (if all is well) for the actual maneuver. Many small boats are advertised as being capable of being sailed "right up on the beach." With some of them, this may be true, but for most, a beaching at speed is an invitation to a wrenched rudder, a broken centerboard, or perhaps personal injury. Providing surf conditions will allow, it is far better to sail in close to the beach until the water is about waist-deep, then round up into the wind while one crew member goes overboard to hold a line attached to the bow. The person going over the side should be wearing a PFD (Personal Flotation Device) and sneakers and should know how to swim in case the water is deeper than waist-high.

If you must sail onto the beach, do so only when you have a very accurate idea of how steeply the shore shelves. Pull the centerboard or daggerboard all the way up (don't expect it to pop up by itself), and be prepared to flip up the rudder the instant before the boat touches shore, or the second you feel the rudder blade touch bottom, whichever is first.

All maneuvers with a small boat require practice to perfect. A boat's behavior in a five-knot wind may change considerably when the same boat is facing 10- or 15-knot breezes. One of the best ways to practice approaches to moorings or piers is to use an inflated air mattress or a plastic detergent bottle anchored to the bottom and practice making landings alongside from every possible sailing direction. With a full afternoon's experience in hand, you'll be far more confident and rightly so. And don't forget to change places with your crew from time to time. Not only will you have a happier and more satisfied sailing companion if you share the tiller, but you'll also have a crewmember who knows much better what the skipper's problems are — just as you'll better appreciate what the crew can and cannot do.

Chapter 5

Weather Forecasting and Heavy Weather Sailing

Boating people are, as a group, directly concerned with weather, and sailors have a special need to know about sea and wind conditions. Although many sailors tend to regard wind as synonymous with weather, the former is only one aspect of the latter, which also includes heat, pressure and moisture, all affecting the condition of the atmosphere. This chapter will deal with the essentials of sailors' weather on two levels, local and systemic; we will then consider some of the tactics to know and use when sailing in heavy weather. The information here won't make you a meteorologist or a Cape Horn skipper, but it should help, with practice, in making you able to tell what weather to expect and how to deal with it when it turns nasty.

What Makes Weather Work?

All weather takes place within the shallow envelope of gas we call the atmosphere. And all weather change is brought about by rise or fall of temperature. For the sailor, there are two kinds of weather — evidenced mostly in terms of wind — that he must deal with. The most immediate is **local weather;** specifically, how the local wind patterns operate and how to make best use of them. Intruding upon these local conditions is the larger effect of weather

systems, which may cover many thousands of square miles.

In very simplified terms, the large-scale movement of air around the earth is caused by air becoming heated from contact with the earth (or sea) near the Equator, then rising and diffusing

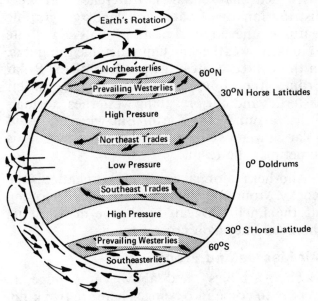

5-1 **Basic Wind Patterns**

itself around the globe while colder air from north and south replaces it. If the earth didn't spin, air circulation around it would be much

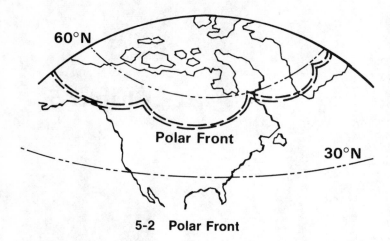

5-2   Polar Front

simpler. Because of the earth's rotation, the basic wind patterns are as shown, with prevailing winds that are generally quite reliable. In the continental United States, most of which is located between Latitudes 30° and 60° North, the prevailing winds are from the west — a fact that influences not only sailing habits, but also marina and harbor layouts. Although the majority of winds across our country blow from a generally westerly direction, there are many days when this isn't the case. Seasonal changes, differences in heat distribution over water and land, geographic features, uneven local heating — all contribute to making weather the unpredictable thing it is. In the United States, the position of the **Polar Front,** the boundary between the polar easterlies and our prevailing westerlies, normally lies around 60° North. But when the cold polar air moves south, violent weather is sometimes the result.

Another major cause of weather change is the Rocky Mountains, which cause the air moving off the Pacific Ocean to change many of its characteristics as it crosses them.

Air Masses and Fronts

The variables cited above cause huge air masses to come into being. There are two kinds — high-pressure masses, called **highs,** and low-pressure areas, known as **lows.** Each has its own characteristic behavior.

Highs are formed when air (for any of several reasons) cools, becomes more compressed, and

consequently sinks. In the northern hemisphere the circulation of air is clockwise around a high and the wind directions are both clockwise and outward from the high's center, as shown in the diagram. High pressure areas may cover immense stretches of the earth's surface — half the United States, under certain conditions — but they are usually a few hundred miles in diameter. Highs originating in the polar area move south and east. Fair weather is generally characteristic of a high, as are light winds and steady temperatures.

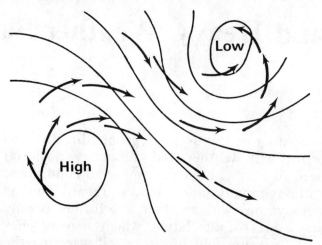

5-3   Air Circulation - Clockwise Around Highs Counter Clockwise Around Lows in the Northern Hemisphere

Low pressure areas, in most respects, are the opposite of highs. A low's center is constantly being filled with air moving into it in a generally counterclockwise direction (in the northern hemisphere). Winds are strong, but lows, like highs, generally move from west to east across our continent.

There are, however, semi-permanent high and low pressure areas. Off the West Coast of the United States is the **Pacific High,** somewhat larger in summer than in winter, and the **Azores High,** over the Atlantic, shows the same seasonal changes in size. In winter, a low frequently exists in the Aleutians, while in summer there is a low that extends from northeast Africa all the way to Indochina. The semi-permanent highs form largely over water, when the sea is cooler than the land.

Localized low pressure areas may also form under a **thundercloud formation,** where air is rising with great speed, or over very hot areas into which the cooler air flows as the heated air is elevated.

It can be useful to know where a low pressure area is in relation to you, since lows are usually the source of bad sailing weather. In the northern hemisphere, stand with your back to

**Present
Surface Wind**

5-4   Buys-Ballot's Law for Determining Low Pressure Area

the present wind; turn 45° or so to the right. This aligns you with the existing wind aloft, which blows in a somewhat different direction than the breeze at ground level. Under normal circumstances, where the true wind is not affected by highly localized conditions, the high pressure center is now to your right, the low center to your left. The pressure area to the west of you is, generally speaking, the one that will reach you, while weather to the east has already passed.

Besides highs and lows, it is useful to consider the great air masses, bodies of air in which conditions of temperature and moisture are the same or similar from one side to the other. Air masses take their names from their characteristics, and the masses which cross our country can be very different.

Although air masses change somewhat according to the surfaces they cross, they remain essentially the same. In the United States, there are two origins of such masses, called **Tropical** and **Polar.** Obviously the former type comes from southern latitudes, while the latter

originates in the north. But each may be further defined as **continental** — having formed over land — or **maritime,** having formed over the sea.

The air masses that affect us are:

Continental Polar (cP) — cold and dry

Maritime Polar (mP) — cold or warm, but moist

Maritime Tropical (mT) — warm and moist

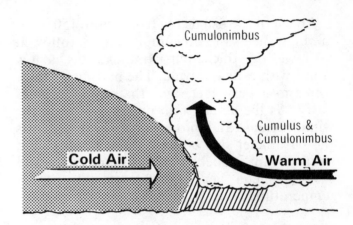

5-5   Collision of Cold and Warm Fronts Results in Bad Weather for the Sailor

Fronts form when air masses of different characteristics collide — the front being the barrier between two such masses. The front takes its name from the type of air which is arriving. That is, when an eastward-moving mass of cold air catches up with warm air, also moving east but not so quickly, a **cold front** is formed. Cold air, being more compact and heavier, pushes under the warm air mass and lifts it. This lifting causes unsettled or stormy weather along the front. The same thing happens with warm fronts, but in this case the warm air rides up and over the cold, and the storms which accompany a warm front are not so severe as those characteristic of a cold front. In either case, however, the weather along the front is not good.

It's very useful to know the normal sequence of weather as a front passes through. Although the time of passage will vary, it's possible to predict the weather sequence with considerable accuracy.

Cold fronts move at speeds from 10 to 50 knots, depending on the time of year — they are two or three times as fast in winter as in summer. If a cold front is moving fast, it may be preceded by a **squall line,** a roll of black, threatening clouds that may reach heights of 40,000 feet, with violent storms and even tornadoes. Wind shifts along the front will be sudden and velocities will increase dramatically. Behind the squall line are heavy rains, followed by clearing.

Ahead of the usual cold front about 150 miles are high sheets of Altocumulus cloud, followed by lowering, thickening Nimbostratus, a low cloud with rain and wind. The barometer falls, sometimes very fast, and the wind becomes gusty. As the actual front passes overhead, the winds increase and the barometer drops; then as the barometer hits bottom, the wind direction shifts abruptly clockwise, continuing gusty, and the barometer begins to rise quickly as the temperature falls.

A cold front is normally followed by some heavy rain, then clearing and gusty winds from west or northwest. At least a couple of days of clear, cool weather, often with excellent sailing winds, are in prospect.

The warm front is a different creature. Its cloud warnings — high, thin Cirrus — extend as much as 1,000 miles ahead, clouds representing warm air that has climbed up and over the retreating cold air mass. As the front advances (and it may take two days to arrive), clouds thicken and lower. The barometer starts a steady fall and the winds pick up. High-level **Cirrostratus** clouds become Mid-level **Altostratus** and rain or snow begins to fall, continuing until after the front passes. As this occurs, the winds shift clockwise and decrease. The temperature begins to rise and visibility is often poor. Behind the front is some **Stratus** and perhaps a little more rain. The barometer may rise and then fall slightly. After the front has completely passed, the skies will clear and winds will normally be from the southwest. Unfortunately, cold fronts frequently follow hard on the heels of warm fronts, so the duration of good weather may be short.

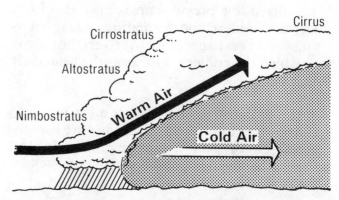

5-6 Warm Front Storm

5-7 Cumulonimbus Clouds - Note Anvil Shaped Cirroform Cap

One of the most useful tools in weather forecasting is the barometer, which measures the degree of air pressure at the instrument. As with any type of weather measurement, a single observation is of little use. A sequence of measurements will reveal a trend — most of the time.

Wind Direction	Sea-Level Pressure	Forecast	Wind Direction	Sea-Level Pressure	Forecast
SW to NW	30.10 to 30.20 and steady	Fair, with little temperature change, for 1 to 2 days.	E to NE	30.10 or higher; falling slowly	In summer, with light winds, rain may not fall for 2 to 3 days. In winter, rain within 24 hours.
SW to NW	30.10 to 30.20 rising rapidly	Fair, followed within 2 days by rain.			
SW to NW	30.20 or higher and steady	Continued fair with little temperature change.	E to NE	30.10 or higher; falling rapidly	In summer, rain probably within 12 to 24 hours. In winter, rain or snow within 12 hours and increasing winds.
SW to NW	30.20 or higher; falling slowly	Fair for 2 days with slowly rising temperature.			
S to SE	30.10 to 30.20; falling slowly	Rain within 24 hours.	S to SW	30.00 or below; rising slowly	Clearing within a few hours. Then fair for several days.
S to SE	30.10 to 30.20; falling rapidly	Increasing winds and rain within 12 to 24 hours.	S to E	29.80 or below; falling rapidly	Severe storm within a few hours. Then clearing within 24 hours-followed by colder in winter.
SE to NE	30.10 to 30.20; falling slowly	Increasing winds and rain within 12 to 18 hours.			
SE to NE	30.10 to 30.20; falling rapidly	Increasing winds and rain within 12 hours.	E to N	29.80 or below; falling rapidly	Severe storm (typical nor'easter) in a few hours. Heavy rains or snowstorm. Followed by a cold wave in winter.
SE to NE	30.00 or below; falling slowly	Rain will continue 1 to 3 days, perhaps even longer.	Hauling to W	29.80 or below; rising rapidly	End of the storm. Followed by clearing and colder.
SE to NE	30.00 or below; falling rapidly	Rain with high winds in a few hours. Clearing within 36 hours-becoming colder in winter.	NOTE: **Falling** or **rising rapidly** means a pressure change of .24 inches or greater within three hours. **Falling** or **rising slowly** means a change of approximately .09 inches or less in a three-hour period.		

5-8   Wind/Barometer Table (Eastern United States)

On this page is a table correlating wind direction and barometric tendency. With it and little else you can sometimes forecast local weather with tolerable accuracy. Other weather indicators are more subjective, but can frequently aid you in predicting local weather patterns. Here are some that have proven quite accurate over many years, in some cases many centuries:

Indicators of Deteriorating Weather

Clouds lowering and thickening

Clouds increasing in number, moving fast across the sky

Veils or sheets of gray cloud increasing on the western horizon

Clouds moving in different directions at different heights

Clouds moving from east or northeast toward the south

Barometer falling steadily or rapidly

Static on AM radio

Wind shifts from north to east and possibly through east to south

Strong wind in the morning

Temperatures far above or below normal for the time of year.

Indicators of Strong Wind

Light scud clouds alone in a clear sky

Sharp, clearly-defined edges to clouds

Yellow sunset

Unusually bright stars.

Indicators of Precipitation

Distant objects seem to stand above the horizon

Sounds are very clear and heard for great distances

Transparent, veil-like clouds thickening and lowering

Halo around sun or moon

Increasing south wind, with clouds moving from the west

Wind (especially north wind) shifts to west and then to south

Steadily falling barometer

Pale sunset

Red sky at dawn

No dew after a hot day.

5-9 Stratocumulus Clouds - Rain Warning

Indicators of Clearing Weather

Cloud bases rise

Wind shifts to west, especially from east through south

Barometer rises quickly

Gray early morning

Morning fog or dew

Indicators of Continuing Fair Weather

Early morning fog that clears

Gentle wind from west or northwest

Barometer steady or rising slightly

Red sunset

Bright moon and light breeze

Heavy dew or frost

Clear blue morning sky

Dull hearing, short range of sound.

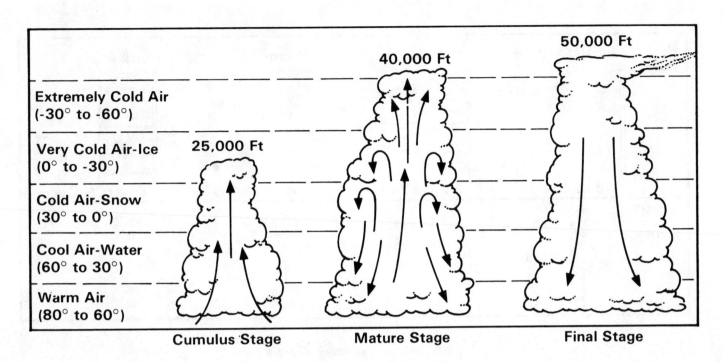

5-10   Thunderstorm Development

Thunderstorms and Squalls

The localized thundersquall is probably the one kind of weather most feared by experienced sailors. It need not be associated with major weather systems, as it can arise in a very short time, or it may lurk concealed in a hazy sky, and it can produce winds of shattering force. Add to that the fearful and often dangerous effect of lightning, and you have a natural demonstration that should inspire respect in any seafarer.

Causes of thunderstorms vary, but they are all characterized by a violent uplifting of air, sometimes to heights of 75,000 feet. There are usually three stages in the life cycle of an average thunderstorm. The early, or cumulus, stage occurs when a **cumulus cloud** — the detached, puffy cloud of summer fair weather — develops vertically from 15,000 to 25,000 feet. This means that the rising air currents within it may be cooled as much as 80° while ascending, to well

below freezing at the cloud's top. The air in the cloud is still warmer than the air outside.

5-11   Scattered Cumulus Clouds - Good Weather

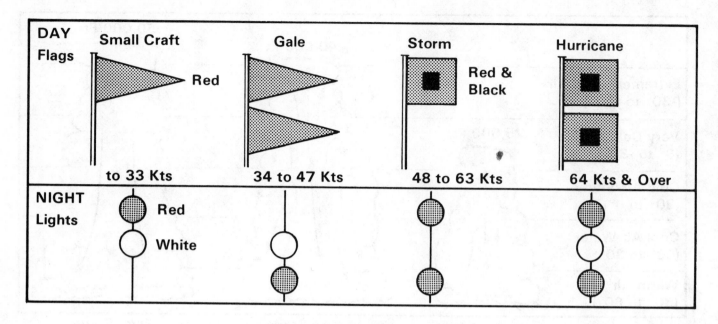

5-12   Warning Display Signals

In the second stage, when the cloud reaches a height of approximately 40,000 feet, its full vertical development, precipitation occurs and falling rain or hail cools the air inside, creating downdrafts and heavy rains. In the terminal third stage, the entire cloud becomes sinking air. With no ascending air to be cooled, rain stops. At this point, the cloud at the top of the thunderhead has been blown into the familiar anvil shape — the sign of an aging storm.

On most summer days, the cumulus clouds of afternoon have at least some potential for becoming thunderheads. As long as the boater keeps an eye on them, he or she can usually make for safety long before there's any danger. On the other hand, when visibility is limited by haze, as it sometimes is during ideal thunderstorm conditions, the formation of the towering, sharp-edged cloud — called **cumulonimbus** — typical of thunderstorms may be veiled by haze.

On such hot, muggy, hazy afternoons, the skipper should be alert for static on AM (not FM) radios, the sound of distant thunder, or the flicker of lightning. He or she should stay close to port, as the wind may die shortly before the storm itself begins.

5-13   Nimbostratus Clouds - Rain or Snow

5-14   Stratus Clouds
Overcast Sky

5-15   Altostratus Clouds -
Overcast Sky or Rain

5-16 **Cirrostratus Clouds - Cause Sun and Moon Halo - Maybe Rain**

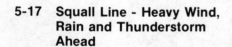

5-17 **Squall Line - Heavy Wind, Rain and Thunderstorm Ahead**

Weather Forecasts

During the boating season, most commercial radio stations regularly broadcast **marine weather forecasts** — meteorological information especially prepared for boating people. This information is highly localized, in most cases, and is usually updated several times a day. You should know the schedules of marine weather forecasts on your local stations, and should make a habit of listening to them, beginning at least the night before you plan to set sail.

In addition to the forecasts by regular commercial stations, there are also excellent weather reports available by phone from your local National Weather Service office, and the frequently updated Weather Service radio broadcasts on 162.55, 162.4 and 162.475 MHz on VHF-FM radios. These frequencies are normally just above the commercial VHF-FM band, so they will probably not be included on ordinary FM sets. The three weather channels are, however, available on special receivers or as receive-only frequencies on marine VHF-FM radiotelephones.

Whatever your source of weather information, you should make it a practice to secure an up-to-the-minute, marine weather forecast before setting sail even on a short hop across the harbor.

Emergency Handling in Squalls

Sooner or later, however, you're going to find yourself and your boat caught out when the wind is stronger than you'd like it to be. In such a case remember that your boat was almost certainly built to take a great deal of punishment and she will come through, as long as you keep your head and use proper sailing technique. There are two kinds of bad weather to consider — the first is the sudden and unexpected squall, the second is heavy weather that you expect.

Squalls can be unnerving simply because they give you little time to prepare. Even the fastest-moving squall line will nevertheless allow you the few minutes you need to get your boat in

shape to handle it. And always remember that a fast-moving squall has one great virtue — it's over in a hurry. Often a squall will last only a few minutes, seldom more than half an hour.

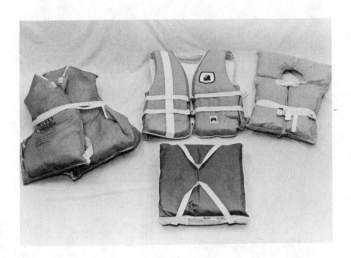

5-18 PFDs - Personal Flotation Devices

The first step when it becomes obvious that you're likely to be caught by a squall long before you can reduce sail is to have all hands put on their Personal Flotation Devices, the Coast Guard's technical term for what most people call lifejackets or lifevests (See Chapter Six). Not only should every crewmember have a lifesaving device of the proper size capable of supporting his or her weight, but everyone should wear it whenever there's any threat of bad weather. A good PFD will give the crewmember confidence, will conserve body heat, and will absorb the bumps that happen in rough weather.

The second step is to luff up into the wind and drop the sails and furl. A serious squall can pack winds up to 60 miles per hour, so don't take chances. Until you know the strength of the advancing storm, drop the sails and furl them securely. Drop the centerboard or daggerboard, if it isn't already lowered.

Secure all loose equipment, have a bailer or pump ready to operate, and tell the crew to keep their weight low in the boat. With these precautions you and your boat will be ready to deal with whatever is likely to come. If you're upwind from a beach or shore, it would be well to put your anchor out and set it (See Chapter Seven), to avoid being blown ashore.

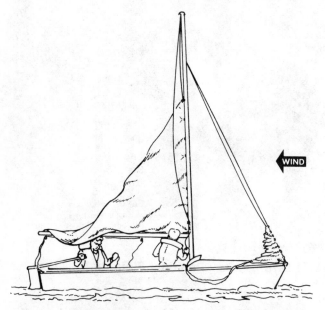

WIND

5-19   Luffing Up Into the Wind to Drop Sail

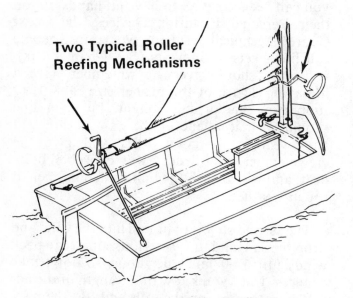

Two Typical Roller Reefing Mechanisms

5-20   Mainsail - Roller Reefing

If a squall moderates to where you can set sail, but the winds are still too strong to sail under main and jib, you can do one of several things. First and probably best is to **reef** your sails — reduce the area of the mainsail and/or jib.

5-21   Mainsail Roller Reefing at the Gooseneck With the Hand Crank in Place

5-22   Sailing With Roller Reefed Mainsail

There are basically two ways of accomplishing this on most modern sailboats. First is roller reefing, in which the boom is so designed that it can be rolled around its axis, with the sail tightly wound around it like an old-fashioned window shade. To roller reef a mainsail, put the boat on a close reach. Now ease the mainsheet just a little, so there's wind in the sail but not the full force of the breeze. Now, while one person eases the main halyard, the other works the crank that turns the boom.

Most roller reefing gear has the crank located at the forward end of the main boom, which usually means that one person can ease the halyard and turn the boom. In this case, the person at the helm should if possible grasp the mainsail leech and pull back, exerting a force parallel to the boom. This makes for a tighter, more even roll of sail.

If you roll a deep enough reef in the sail so that the lower batten becomes twisted, remove it — a wood batten can easily break under this kind of treatment, and even a flexible plastic batten does the sail no good when it's rolled up inside.

5-24 Sailing With Mainsail Jiffy Reefed

mets partway up the luff and leech (called the **luff cringle** and **leech cringle**) and then lash these lines tightly around the boom. In boats equipped with jiffy reefing, the luff cringle is secured to a hook welded to the gooseneck. The leech cringle reef line is also led through the outhaul, or a cheek block on the boom, to pull the clew of the sail both down to the boom and out along it.

In point reefing, individual lines hang down both sides of the sail in a line from leech cringle to clew cringle. These **reef points**, as they are called, are used to lash the unused foot of the reefed sail in a neat roll along the boom. Unlike luff and leech cringle lines, the reef points do not lead under the boom, but only under the foot of the sail — thus, if the reef points are evenly tied (with reef knots — See Chapter Seven), the pull along the sail's foot will be evenly transferred from slides to sail.

5-23 Reef Grommets

Some boats have a different form of reefing gear. Some sailors call it **point reefing** and other sailors call it **jiffy reefing,** but it is essentially the same operation. The boat is luffed up into the wind and the main dropped or partially lowered. The crew now run lines through grom-

A jiffy-reefed main, however, does not require reef points, and the unused foot of the sail may be left to hang without any problem. Jiffy or point reefing may also be used on a jib equipped with a boom, but most jibs cannot be reefed, which is why modern racers carry a large assortment of them to match many possible wind conditions. Increasing numbers of racing boats are being equipped with jiffy reefing jibs, but their use is not yet general. Jibs may, however, be equipped with **roller furling**, which is quite different from roller reefing.

5-25 Jib Being Roller Furled

A roller-furled jib is one in which the luff wire turns around its own axis, like roller reefing around a boom. But because of the way curvature is cut into a jib, a partially roller-furled headsail will not set properly. Roller

furling is, as the name says, a way of striking a sail entirely, not reducing its area partway. Since main and jib are usually balanced one against the other in terms of wind pressure, reefing the main usually entails switching to a smaller jib.

It is possible to reduce sail in a hurry simply by striking one sail or another, and furling it tightly. Which sail you choose will depend on how your boat balances and what point of sailing you are on.

In heavy weather, when you're not too sure of yourself or the boat, it's a good idea to put the boat on a reach first of all, before you attempt other points of sailing. A reach is not only the fastest point of sail, it's usually the safest as well — the boat is relatively stable and can head up into the wind, spilling the breeze's force from the sails, or head away as required, without changing tacks.

5-26 Full Jib - Mainsail Eased

If both sails are up, try sailing first with a full jib and a mainsail eased slightly so that it begins to flutter or backwind along the luff. The sail will still be helping to move the boat, but the heeling force of the wind will be considerably eased.

5-27 Sailing Under Jib Alone

5-28 Sailing Under Mainsail Alone

Now try sailing under jib alone, with the main tightly furled around its boom and the boom carefully lashed to prevent its breaking free. In a case where the main and working jib are approximately equal in size — the boat will probably maneuver well under the jib by itself, and you will be spared the worry of dealing with a swinging main boom in heavy winds.

On the other hand, boats with mainsails that are much larger than the jib will probably balance better if the main is left raised and the jib lowered, unsnapped and bagged (don't leave it on the deck, even tied down — it may easily escape over the side to act as an unwanted drag).

The only way to find which sail combination works best for your boat is to take her out and try the several variations open to you. The important thing is to try, where possible, to keep the proportion of sail areas ahead of and aft of the mast approximately the same. As the wind gets stronger, the relative amount of sail area forward of the mast may increase — the boat will probably balance better for it, a fact which will be reflected in the amount of **helm** — the pull felt by the person holding the tiller.

Most boats are designed to head up into the wind if the tiller or wheel is released. This is called **weather helm**, because the boat has a tendency, left alone, to swing up **to weather**, or windward. In mild amounts, weather helm is a safety factor, but in excess it can be both inefficient and tiring and over a period of time will weaken tiller handles and rudder fittings. The average modern sailboat is well balanced, but if you have problems with weather helm or its opposite, **lee helm** — the tendency for the boat to swing to leeward — See Chapter 9.

Knockdown and Capsize

When a boat is temporarily overpowered by the wind and heeled over till its mast is nearly level with the water, it is said to be **knocked down.** When a boat is laid over and has shipped so much water that it can't right itself, it is **capsized.** Many of today's small centerboard sail-

5-29 Beginning a Knock Down

5-30 Capsized

boats are designed to right themselves from a knockdown, even if there's a substantial amount of water in the cockpit. You can aid the process by releasing the sheets and using your weight to bring the boat back up.

In the case of a genuine capsize, especially with a non-self-righting boat, the situation may be more serious. Several steps should not only

be followed by the skipper, but they should also be thoroughly drilled into the crew.

1. Immediately after the capsize, count heads: Make sure all the crew have swum free from the boat.

2. Stay with the boat as long as it is floating, and put on PFDs, if you haven't already

5-31 Righting a Small Boat - Climbing on the Center/Dagger Board

5-32 Righting a Small Boat - Coming Up

5-33   **Righting a Small Boat - Climbing Aboard**

done so. If you are in this situation you should have already insisted that the crew don PFD's

3. Recover the loose gear that will be floating around the boat. Stuff it into a sailbag and tie the sailbag to the boat.

4. Get the sails down and off — at least down. This should allow the boat to come upright by itself. You may need to have some one help by pushing upward on the mast while you stand on the centerboard.

5. Once the boat is upright, lower the centerboard, plug the top of the centerboard trunk if it's open and bail the boat. You may have to swim alongside and scoop water out until the level is low enough for one crewmember — the lightest — to ease aboard and finish the job.

If after a couple of tries you see that it will be impossible to empty the boat and sail away, don't use up your energy and body heat by repeated attempts. Turn your attention to signaling for help. A horn sounded in repeated patterns of five blasts, a smoke signal by day or a flare by night, an International Orange distress flag — all are recognized signals of distress, and

all can be purchased in any marine supply store and carried in a waterproof bag (most are sold that way) in even the smallest daysailer. Many skippers equip each PFD with a mouth operated whistle attached by about 10 inches of lanyard.

If your boat must be towed home while full of water, make sure the towing vessel pulls your boat very slowly — two or three miles per hour, at the maximum. Not only are water-filled boats very unstable, but the water sloshing back and forth can easily gain such momentum it knocks

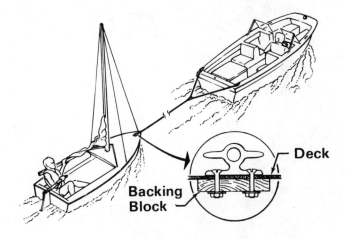

5-34   **Backing the Bow Cleat with a Backing Block. If the Boat is Full of Water Have it Towed Very Slowly**

the transom out. Make sure your boat has an extra-strong cleat or eye bolt on the foredeck, one that is bolted through the deck and through a backing board beneath. This kind of hardware will stand the great stresses of towing. One crewmember should stay aboard the swamped boat to steer and to keep weight aft, so she will ride better.

Man Overboard

When you have lost someone overboard you have a possible life/death situation on your hands. These are the things you must do or have your crew do at once, not necessarily in the sequence given but at once.

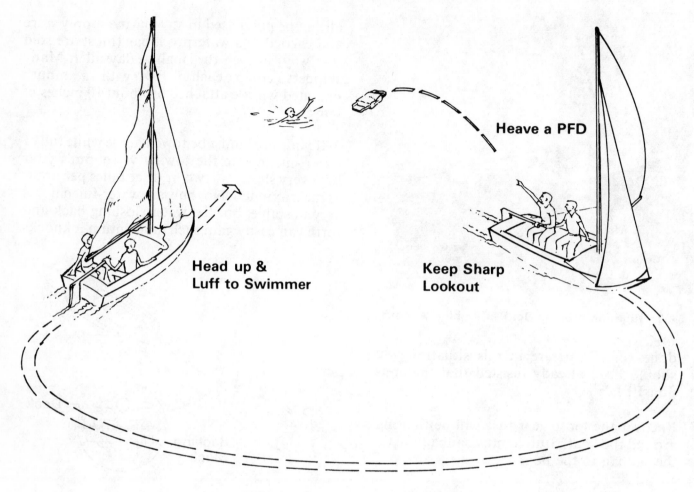

**5-35 MAN OVERBOARD - Heave a PFD, Keep
a Sharp Watch on the Victim, Head Up
and Luff to Him**

1. Don't lose sight of the victim. Give the cry: "Man Overboard!"

2. Heave a throwable personal flotation device (Type IV PFD) as close to the victim as possible without hitting him or her with it. One of a bright color (e.g., International Orange) is desirable. A soft PFD is not likely to injure. The PFD will help the victim to float; if the victim has sunk the PFD will mark the location. An observer should keep the victim in sight.

3. If the boat is under power, stop the propeller (disengage the gear or, if necessary, shut down the engine) until you are sure the rotating propeller will not strike the victim.

4. Get the boat under control. All too often someone goes overboard because the boat is out of control. It is a mistake to attempt a rescue before getting matters in hand on deck. Despite the urgent temptation to turn back instantly, be sure all the crew are on deck and know what's to be done, and that all the sailing gear is in control before making a rescue attempt. Don't take too long to do this.

5. Put the boat around to pick up the victim. Under nearly all circumstances it is better to jibe around than tack. Luff the boat up into the wind alongside of the victim, as close as you can get without endangering him or her.

Now, before attempting to recover the victim, secure him or her. At the moment of rescue

5-36 Assisting Overboard Victim

many people have ceased trying to keep afloat and have sunk before the eyes of their rescuers. Get a line under the victim's arms and secure it to the boat. Unless the person is injured, no other person should go over the side to help — you can almost always help better from the boat. The victim will be exhausted, scared, and probably so weighted down by clothing that he or she will be virtually helpless. In cold water areas the danger of hypothermia, the potentially fatal loss of body heat, makes it important to get the person aboard as quickly as possible. Ease the victim gently over the gunwale: usually the best way is to get the torso up over the side and secured, then to grab a leg and to heave it up onto the deck.

Remember that a sailboat has all kinds of gear to give you leverage if the victim's weight makes it impossible to bring him or her aboard unaided: winches, halyards, the boom, a sail lowered into the water to form a sling to contain the victim and then winched aboard.

Practice. Have "Man Overboard Drills" on your boat frequently. Unexpectedly throw a floating object (the "victim") over the side and call, "Man overboard!" Time yourselves from man overboard to recovery and then try to beat your time on the next try. You and your crew will become trained, experienced, and increasingly proficient.

Conclusion

No sailor is really competent until he or she has faced and matched heavy weather. While it is foolish to take chances, neither should you underestimate yourself or your boat. The best way to find out what heavy weather is all about is to hitch a ride aboard the boat of someone you know to be a top skipper and observe what he or she does, asking questions anytime the actions aren't obvious. Sooner than you think you should arrive at the point where you have a healthy respect for the awesome force of the sea, but not an irrational fear of it.

BEAUFORT WIND SCALE

Beaufort number	Seaman's description of wind	Velocity m. p. h.	Estimating velocities on land	Estimating velocities on sea	Probable mean height of waves in feet	Description of Sea
0	Calm	Less than 1 ...	Smoke rises vertically.	Sea like a mirror	....	Calm (glassy)
1	Light air	1-3	Smoke drifts; wind vanes unmoved.	Ripples with the appearance of scales are formed but without foam crests.	½	Rippled
2	Light breeze	4-7	Wind felt on face; leaves rustle; ordinary vane moved by wind.	Small wavelets, still short but more pronounced; crests have a glassy appearance and do not break.	1	Smooth
3	Gentle breeze ...	8-12	Leaves and twigs in constant motion; wind extends light flag.	Large wavelets. Crests begin to break. Foam of glassy appearance. Perhaps scattered white caps.	2½	
4	Mod. breeze	13-18	Raises dust and loose paper; small branches are moved.	Small waves, becoming longer, fairly frequent white caps.	5	Slight
5	Fresh breeze	19-24	Small trees in leaf begin to sway; crested wavelets form on inland water.	Moderate waves, taking a more pronounced long form; many white caps are formed. (Chance of some spray.)	10	Moderate
6	Strong breeze ..	25-31	Large branches in motion; whistling heard in telegraph wires; umbrellas used with difficulty.	Large waves begin to form; the white foam crests are more extensive everywhere. (Probably some spray.)	15	Rough
7	Moderate gale ..	32-38	Whole trees in motion; inconvenience felt in walking against wind.	Sea heaps up and white foam from breaking waves begins to be blown in streaks.	20	Very rough
8	Fresh gale	39-46	Breaks twigs off trees; generally impedes progress.	Moderately high waves of greater length; edges of crests break into spindrift. The foam is blown in well-marked streaks along the direction of the wind.	25	High
9	Strong gale	47-54	Slight structural damage occurs.	High waves. Dense streaks of foam along the direction of the wind. Sea begins to roll. Spray may affect visibility.	30	
10	Whole gale	55-63	Trees uprooted; considerable structural damage occurs.	Very high waves with long, overhanging crests. The surface of the sea takes a white appearance.	35	Very high
11	Storm	64-73		The sea is completely covered with long white patches of foam lying along the direction of the wind. Everywhere edges of the wave crests are blown into froth. Visibility affected.	40	
12	Hurricane	74-82		The air is filled with foam and spray. Sea completely white with driving spray; visibility very seriously affected.	45 or more ..	Phenomenal

5-37 Beaufort Wind Scale

Chapter 6

Navigation Rules and Legal Requirements

The hazard of collision at sea has existed ever since the world's second boat was built. Throughout maritime history nations have been working toward a uniform set of regulations under which vessels approaching each other might proceed safely to avoid collision.

The United States has adopted the 1972 International Regulations for Preventing Collisions at Sea. These are commonly called the International Rules or the 72 COLREGS.

The Inland Navigational Rules Act of 1980 became effective in most applicable waters on Dec. 24, 1981. This new set of Inland Rules supersedes the old Inland Rules, the Western Rivers Rules, the Great Lakes Rules and parts of the Motorboat Act of 1940.

Why are there two sets of rules? Well, just as most states have generally similar traffic codes but with special regulations for local conditions, so it is with the two sets of nautical rules of the road. The International Rules (72 COLREGS) are chiefly designed for use on the high seas and similar bodies of water. The Inland Rules provide special regulations for crowded waterways, rivers, Vessel Traffic Services, lakes, and other conditions which the International Rules do not cover.

The Commandant of the U. S. Coast Guard establishes demarcation lines which mark the boundaries between where the International and Inland Rules apply.

Navigation Rules, International — Inland (COMDINST M16672.2), published by the U. S. Government Printing Office for purchase, contains both sets of rules, including annexes and demarcation lines. Demarcation lines are also printed on charts.

General Principles

The International and Inland Rules parallel each other but there are important differences. The purpose of the Rules of the Road is to prevent collisions at sea. Remember, the steering and sailing rules come into play when vessels are approaching each other so as to involve risk of collision.

As you can see from the following definitions, a sailboat is a "power-driven vessel" if the engine is in use. All rules for power-driven vessels (maneuvering, sound signals, lights) apply to sailboats using their engines.

A *power-driven vessel* means any vessel propelled by machinery.

A *sailing vessel* means any vessel under sail provided that propelling machinery, if any, is not being used.

Underway means that a vessel is not at anchor, or made fast to the shore, or aground.

Restricted visibility means any condition in which visibility is restricted by fog, mist, falling snow, heavy rainstorms, sandstorms or other similar causes.

Conduct in Any Condition of Visibility

Every vessel must maintain a *proper lookout* and always proceed at a *safe speed* so that she can take proper and effective action to avoid collision. In determining a safe speed, consideration must be given to such things as the state of visibility; the traffic density, including concentration of fishing vessels, etc.; background lights (at night), the state of wind, sea and current, and the proximity of navigational hazards; the vessel's draft in relation to the available depth of water; and other factors, including operational radar, if fitted.

Every vessel must use all available means to determine if *risk of collision* exists. Such a risk *exists if* the *compass bearing* of an approaching vessel *does not appreciably change*. Therefore, if the direction from which an approaching vessel stays the same, or nearly so, as the vessel gets closer, there will be a collision unless action is taken. Mariners call this a "constant bearing and decreasing range" and recognize it as critical to their vessels' safety.

In taking action to avoid collision any alteration of course or speed should be large enough to be readily apparent to another vessel observing visually or by radar. Avoid a succession of small alterations of course and speed; it is difficult to detect them from a distance and the other vessel might misunderstand, which is dangerous.

International and *Inland Rules differ* slightly on the subject of *Narrow Channels.*

Both sets of rules state that vessels proceeding along a narrow channel or fairway must keep to the starboard side of the channel. Vessels of less than 20 meters or a sailing vessel must not impede the passage of a vessel that can safely navigate only within a narrow channel or fairway. No vessel may cross a narrow channel or fairway if it impedes the passage of a vessel which can safely navigate only within that channel or fairway. Vessels, if circumstances permit, must avoid anchoring in a narrow channel.

The *Inland Rules* have something to add to the subject of narrow channels concerning power-driven vessels operating in narrow channels or fairways on the Great Lakes, Western Rivers, or other specified waters. If downbound with a following current, such vessels have the right-of-way over an upbound vessel and will initiate the signals for maneuvering (which will be described later).

Traffic Separation Schemes

Traffic Separation schemes are covered under Rule 10 of the 72 COLREGS. A vessel of less than 20 meters in length or a sailing vessel must not impede the safe passage of a power-driven vessel following a traffic lane.

Vessel Traffic Service
(Inland Navigational Rules)

"Each vessel required by regulation to participate in a vessel traffic service shall comply with the applicable regulations," says Rule 10 in the first statement ever in any rule dealing with vessel traffic services. It would be unusual to find pleasure craft participating in a vessel traffic service; it is most important, however, to understand the Coast Guard's system for monitoring ship traffic.

Vessel Traffic Services (VTS) have been established by the Coast Guard to reduce danger of collision in certain areas where ship traffic is heavy. VTS consists of one or more of three distinct components, depending on the area: (1) all have a Vessel Movement Reporting System (communications); (2) some have a Traffic Separation Scheme (TSS); and (3) some have either Radar or Closed Circuit Television (CCTV) Monitoring (surveillance) of selected areas.

Vessel Traffic Services have been established in the ports of New Orleans, Houston/Galveston, San Francisco, Valdez, and in Puget Sound and its approaches. One has been under construction in New York Harbor. Some Canadian waters used frequently by American yachts have an equivalent — Vessel Traffic Management System (VTMS).

If you are sailing in waters where there is a VTS you must learn its location and to recognize any buoys marking a traffic separation scheme if any. You should never travel the "wrong way" in any one-way lane or anchor in a traffic separation scheme. If you must cross a lane, do so at right angles to it. Realize that you are sailing where a ship is most likely to pass.

It is a good idea to listen to the radio communications between ships in the system and the Coast Guard's Vessel Traffic Communications Center for information about any ship in your proximity. VTS does not invite radio communications from pleasure boats. **Any contact with the Coast Guard is normally made on Channel 16.**

the **Distress, Safety, and Calling frequency.** In an extreme situation VTS may be reached as illustrated. See Chapter 13.

Other Vessel Traffic Services are located at St. Mary's river, Michigan, Berwick Bay, Louisiana, and Louisville Kentucky.

VTS LOCATION		VHF CHANNELS									
		5	6	11	12	13*	14	16	18	22	67*
HOUSTON/ GALVESTON	ⓐ			◆	◆	●					
NEW ORLEANS	ⓑ			◆	◆	●	◆	●			●
NEW YORK	ⓒ			◆	◆	●	◆	●			
SAN FRANCISCO					●	◆		●	●		
PUGET SOUND	ⓓ	◆				●	◆	●			
VALDEZ			●			◆		●		●	

Channel 13 is the Bridge-to-Bridge frequency in all areas except New Orleans and the Intracoastal Waterway, which use Channel 67.

LEGEND

◆ = VTS WORKING FREQUENCY

● = VTS-MONITORED FREQUENCY

Notes:

ⓐ Houston, Channel 11; Galveston, Channel 12; boundary of separation, Exxon Baytown.

ⓑ Channels 13 and 16 traffic monitored between Huey P. Long Bridge at mile 106.0, Above Head of Pass (AHP), and Baton Rouge, at mile 243.0 (AHP). (VTS Operating at reduced capability; call VTS New Orleans, 504-589-2772, for current operational information.)

ⓒ Temporarily suspended

ⓓ Channel 5 implementation pending

6-1 Vessel Traffic Service—Locations and Frequencies

Conduct of Vessels in Sight of One Another — Sound and Light Signals

There are three situations which involve risk of collision: *Overtaking,* meeting *Head-on,* and *Crossing.* The rules for Head-on and Crossing situations are different for power-driven vessels and sailing vessels, as will be discussed later. The rules point out which is the stand-on vessel (the one having the right-of-way) and which the give-way vessel (the one which must yield the right of way) in each encounter.

When one of two vessels is to keep out of the way, the other, the stand-on vessel, must maintain course and speed; the stand-on vessel may take avoiding action as soon as it becomes apparent that the vessel required to give way is not taking appropriate action.

The *give-way vessel* must, under the rules, take early and substantial action to keep well clear, when

directed by the situation to keep out of the way of another vessel.

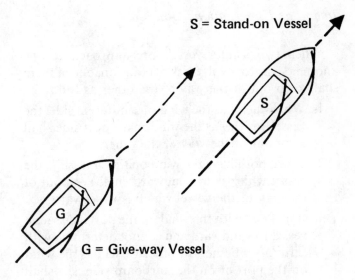

S = Stand-on Vessel

G = Give-way Vessel

6-2 The Overtaking Situation

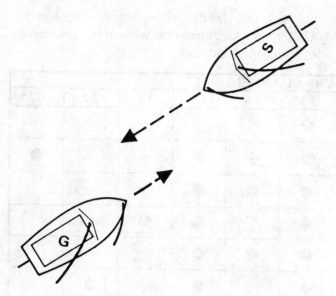

6-3 The Meeting Situation—Head On or Nearly So

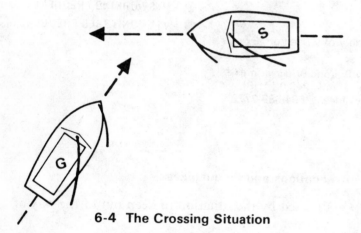

6-4 The Crossing Situation

Inland and International Rules for Sailing Vessels

When two sailing vessels are approaching one another so as to involve risk of collision, one of them shall keep out of the way of the other as follows:

1. When each has the wind on a different side, the vessel which has the wind on the port side shall keep out of the way of the other.

2. When both have the wind on the same side, the vessel which is to windward shall keep out of the way of the vessel which is to leeward.

3. If a vessel with the wind on the port side sees a vessel to windward and cannot determine with certainty whether the other vessel has the wind on the port or on the starboard side, she shall keep out of the way of the other.

4. For the purposes of these rules the windward side shall be deemed to be the side opposite to that on which the mainsail is carried. On square-rigged vessels, it shall be deemed to be the side opposite to that on which the largest fore-and-aft sail is carried.

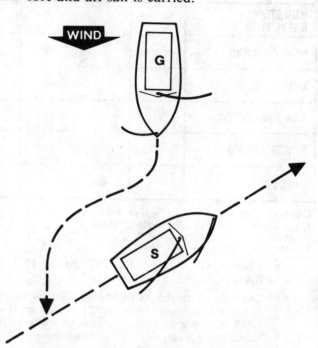

6-5 The Give-Way Vessel Must Keep Clear of the Stand-On Vessel

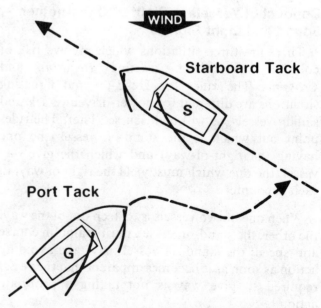

Starboard Tack

Port Tack

6-6 A Sailboat on Starboard Tack has Right-of-Way Over a Sailboat on Port Tack

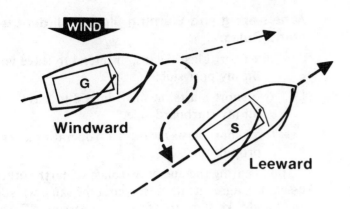

6-7 The Windward Sailboat Must Give Way to the Leeward Sailboat on Same Tack

6-9 Stay Clear of Large Vessels at all Times

Rights of Way of Vessels

Power-driven vessels underway must keep out of the way of:

vessels not under command;

vessels restricted in ability to maneuver;

vessels engaged in fishing (with nets, lines, trawls and other apparatus which restricts maneuveribility); and

sailing vessels.

Sailing vessels underway must keep out of the way of:

vessels not under command;

vessels restricted in ability to maneuver; and

vessels engaged in fishing (as above).

Sound Signals — General Principles

Sound signals described in both sets of rules are normally made by whistles and bells (and, sometimes, gongs). Historically, power-driven vessels were "steam vessels" with steam whistles; sailing vessels, of course, did not have steam whistles; consequently there are no maneuvering whistle signals for sailing vessels although there are sound signals for *all* vessels, whether underway or at anchor, in or near areas of restricted visibility.

The term *short blast* means a blast of 1 second's duration.

The term *prolonged blast* means a blast of from 4 to 6 seconds' duration.

A vessel 12 meters or more in length must be provided with a whistle and a bell. A vessel of less than 12 meters in length is not obliged to carry such sound signaling appliances but must be provided with some other means of making an efficient sound signal.

Rules Governing sound signals for maneuvering are different under each set of rules. Sound signals under the 72 COLREGS for head-on, crossing and overtaking (except in narrow channels) situations are *signals of action:* only the vessel actually altering course sounds a signal and the vessel not altering course does not answer. Sound signals under the Inland Rules for head-on, crossing and overtaking

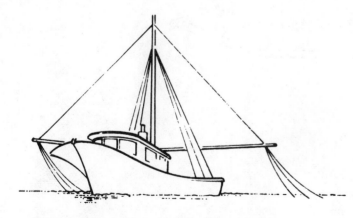

6-8 Commercial Fishing Vessels, While Fishing, Have the Right-of-Way Over Sail and Power Boats

situations are *signals of intent;* one vessel signals intended action and the other responds. These signals will now be explained.

Maneuvering and Warning Signals — Danger/Doubt Signal — Both International and Inland Rules

When vessels in sight of one another are approaching each other and, from any cause, either vessel fails to understand the intentions or actions of the other, or is in doubt whether sufficient action is being taken by the other to avoid collision, the vessel in *doubt* must immediately indicate such doubt by giving *at least five short and rapid blasts* on the whistle. The doubt signal is sometimes called the danger signal.

Maneuvering and Warning Signals Under the International Rules:

— one short blast means, "I am altering my course to starboard."
— two short blasts mean, "I am altering my course to port."
— three short blasts mean, "I am operating astern propulsion."

These signals are sounded only when the action is being taken.

Maneuvering and Warning Signals Under the Inland Rules:

— one short blast means, "I intend to leave you on my port side."
— two short blasts mean, "I intend to leave you on my starboard side."
— three short blasts mean, "I am operating astern propulsion."

Upon hearing the one or two blast signal the other vessel, if in agreement, must sound the same whistle signal and take steps to effect a safe passing. "Cross signals" are not permitted under the rules. (Two

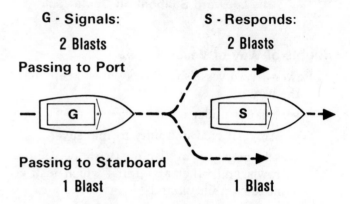

6-10 The Overtaking Situation - Inland Rules

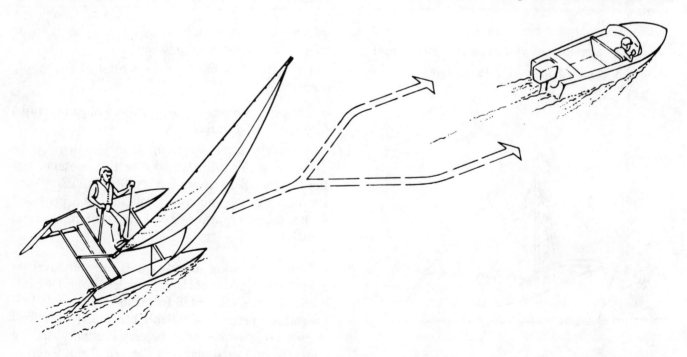

6-11 When a Sailboat is Overtaking Another Boat the Sailboat is the Give-Way Vessel, No Matter How the Other Vessel is Propelled

blasts are never answered with one blast, for example). If in disagreement or doubt, the other vessels responds with the doubt signal (5 or more short and rapid blasts).

The Overtaking Situation

Any *vessel overtaking* any other must keep out of the way of the vessel being overtaken. (Notice that this includes sailboats which are overtaking.)

A vessel is deemed to be *overtaking when coming up* with another vessel from a direction more than *22.5 degress abaft her beam.* At night only the stern-light of the vessel being overtaken would be visible but neither of the sidelights. If in doubt about whether it be an overtaking situation the overtaking vessel should assume that it is and act accordingly.

The International Rules give, in effect, consideration to two types of overtaking, according to whether (1) maneuvering in a narrow channel or fairway (as explained below); or (2) maneuvering elsewhere than in a narrow channel or fairway (when the usual signals of action explained above are used).

Under the *International Rules* vessels in sight of one another in a narrow channel or fairway must use these signals in the overtaking situation whenever the vessel ahead must take action to permit safe passing.

A vessel overtaking indicates intention by the following whistle signals:

— two prolonged blasts followed by one short blast to mean, "I intend to overtake you on your starboard side."

— two prolonged blasts followed by two short blasts to mean, "I intend to overtake you on your port side."

The vessel about to be overtaken indicates agreement by:

— one prolonged, one short, one prolonged and one short blast, in that order.

When either vessel fails to understand the intentions of the other or doubts whether sufficient action is being taken by the other to avoid collision, the vessel in doubt must give at least five short and rapid blasts on the whistle.

Under the *Inland Rules,* a power-driven vessel intending to overtake another power-driven vessel indicates intention by the following whistle signals:

— one short blast to mean, "I intend to overtake you on your starboard side."

— two short blasts to mean, "I intend to overtake you on your port side."

The power-driven vessel about to be overtaken shall, if in agreement, sound a similar signal or, if in doubt, sound the danger signal (at least five short and rapid blasts on the whistle).

The Head-on (Meeting) Situation

The International and Inland Rules for maneuvering are identical in wording, but the whistle signals are different, as will be discussed.

When two power-driven vessels are meeting on reciprocal or nearly reciprocal courses so as to involve risk of collision, each must alter course to starboard so that each will pass on the port side of the other. At night it is a head-on situation when a vessel sees the other vessel's (white) masthead lights in a line or nearly in a line or both (red and green) sidelights.

When a vessel is in any doubt whether a head-on situation exists she must assume that it does exist and act accordingly.

Sound Signals — Meeting or Crossing

Under *International Rules,* when vessels are in sight of one another, a power-driven vessel underway when maneuvering as required by the rules, must indicate that maneuver by whistle signal:

— one short blast to mean, "I am altering my course to starboard."

— two short blasts to mean, "I am altering my course to port."

— three short blasts to mean, "I am operating astern propulsion."

When either vessel fails to understand the intentions of the other, or doubts whether sufficient action is being taken by the other to avoid collision, the vessel in doubt must give at least five short blasts on the whistle.

Under *Inland Rules,* when power-driven vessels are in sight of one another and meeting or crossing within half a mile of each other, each vessel underway must use whistle signals. Either vessel may indicate the maneuver:

— one short blast to mean, "I intend to leave you on my port side."

— two short blasts to mean, "I intend to leave you on my starboard side."

— three short blasts to mean, "I am operating astern propulsion."

Upon hearing the one or two blast signal, the other vessel, if in agreement, is required to sound the same signal (never a "cross signal"). If in doubt about the safety of the proposed maneuver she must sound the danger signal (at least five short and rapid blasts on the whistle).

The Crossing Situation

Both International and Inland Rules state that when two power-driven vessels are crossing so as to involve risk of collision, the vessel which has the other on her starboard side must keep out of the way and, if circumstances admit, avoid crossing ahead of the other vessel.

The *Inland Rules* add that on the Great Lakes, Western Rivers, or other specified waters, a vessel crossing a river must keep out of the way of a power-driven vessel ascending or descending the river.

Conduct of Vessels in Restricted Visibility — Sound Signals

The term "restricted visibility" was defined earlier in this chapter. It is important to realize that this section of the rules applies to all vessels not in sight of each other when navigating *in or near* an area of restricted visibility. A vessel in broad daylight could be surprised by a large ship suddenly emerging from a nearby fog bank.

There is a special provision in the rules for the vessel which detects by radar alone the presence of another vessel. The law requires this vessel to take action in ample time if a change of course becomes necessary. When the other vessel is forward of the beam (and not being overtaken) the change of course should not be to port. When the other vessel is abeam or abaft the beam, the change of course should not be toward the other vessel.

Sound Signals in Restricted Visibility are identical under both sets of rules.

In or near an area of restricted visibility, whether by day or night, signals must be used as follow:

A power-driven vessel making way through the water sounds one prolonged blast at intervals of not more than two minutes.

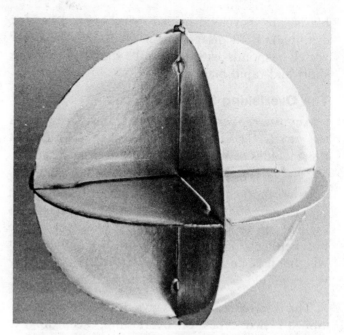

6-12 A Radar Reflector Helps Make Your Boat "Visible" to Ships and Boats With Radar

A power-driven vessel underway but stopped and making no way through the water must sound, at intervals of not more than two minutes, two prolonged blasts in succession with an interval of about 2 seconds between them.

A vessel not under command, a vessel restricted in ability to maneuver, a *sailing vessel,* a vessel engaged in fishing, or towing or pushing another vessel, sounds one prolonged followed by two short blasts in succession, every two minutes.

A vessel at anchor, at intervals of not more than 1 minute, rings the bell rapidly for about 5 seconds. Inland Rules do not make this requirement of vessels 20 meters or less in special anchoring areas.

It is helpful to know that a vessel of 100 meters or more in length sounds the bell in the forepart of the vessel and, immediately after, sounds the gong in the after part of the vessel.

A vessel at anchor may, in addition, sound one short, one prolonged and one short blast in succession to give warning of her position and of the possibility of collision to an approaching vessel.

A vessel aground gives the bell signal (and, if required, the gong signal) and, in addition, gives three separate and distinct strokes on the bell immediately before and after the rapid ringing of the bell.

A vessel of less than 12 meters in length is not obliged to give the above-mentioned signals but, if she does not, is obliged to make some other efficient sound signal at intervals of not more than 2 minutes.

Signals to Attract Attention

If it is necessary to attract the attention of another vessel, any vessel may make light or sound signals that cannot be mistaken for any signal authorized elsewhere in the rules, or may direct the beam of her searchlight in the direction of the danger. One should take care not to blind another vessel's operator by shining a light at the steering station.

Lights

The rules concerning lights are to be complied with from sunset to sunrise in all weathers. When these lights are being exhibited no other lights may be exhibited if they can be mistaken for the lights otherwise specified in the rules or if they interfere with the keeping of a proper lookout.

Here are some of the lights discussed in this chapter:

Masthead Light

a *white* light
placed over the *fore and aft centerline*
showing an unbroken light
over an *arc* of horizon *225 degrees* so as to show the light
from right *ahead to 22.5 degrees abaft the beam*
on *either side* of the boat.

Sidelights

a *green* light on the *starboard side,*
a *red* light on the *port* side.
each showing an unbroken arc of light
over an *arc* of the horizon of *112.5 degrees* so as to show the light from right *ahead to 22.5 degrees abaft the beam*
on the *respective side* of the boat.
(On boats less than 20 meters in length, sidelights combined in one lantern are to be placed as nearly as practicable to the boat's fore and aft centerline.)

Sternlight

a *white* light
at the stern
showing an unbroken light
over an *arc* of the horizon of *135 degrees*

so as to *show* the light *67.5 degrees from right aft on each side of the boat.*

Towing light

a *yellow* light with the *same characteristics* as the sternlight.

All-round light

a light showing an unbroken light over an *arc* of the horizon of *360 degrees.*

Flashing light

a light flashing at regular intervals of *120 or more flashes per minute.*

Special flashing light (Inland Rules)

a *yellow* light
flashing at regular intervals
of *50 to 70 flashes per minute*
placed forward on the fore and aft
centerline
of a *tow*
showing an unbroken *arc* of the horizon of not less than *180 nor more than 225 degrees*
to show from right ahead
to *abeam* and no more than 22.5 degrees abaft the beam
on either side of the vessel.

The positioning and technical details of lights and shapes are in Annex I of each set of Rules; technical data are not within the scope of this course.

The intensity of prescribed lights must be such that they be *visible* from the minimum *distances* in nautical miles as shown.

Lights for Power-driven Vessels Underway

A power-driven vessel underway is required to exhibit a masthead light forward. *(Inland Rules* provide an exception for vessels of less than 20 meters in length in that they need not exhibit this light forward of amidships although it must be as far forward as practicable.)

A power-driven vessel of 50 meters' length or more must exhibit a second masthead light abaft of and higher than the forward one; a power-driven vessel of less than 50 meters' length is not obliged to exhibit such a light but may do so.

A power-driven vessel must also exhibit sidelights and a sternlight.

Inland Rules state that a power-driven vessel of less than 12 meters in length may exhibit an all-round white light and sidelights instead of the mast-

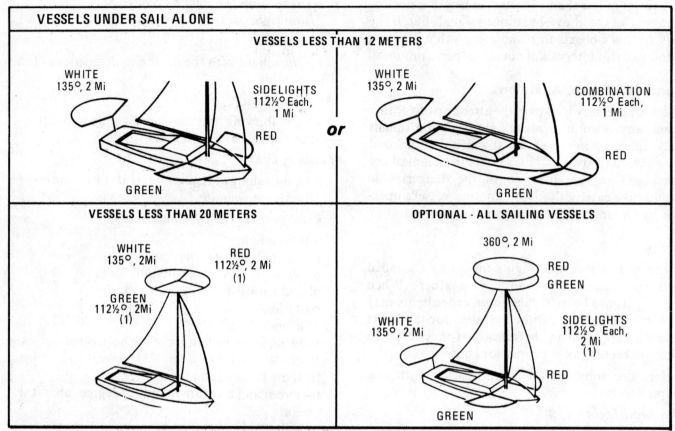

International Lights may be used under Inland Rules by ALL Vessels

Note: (1) Range of Visibility may be 1 Mile for Vessels Less than 12 Meters

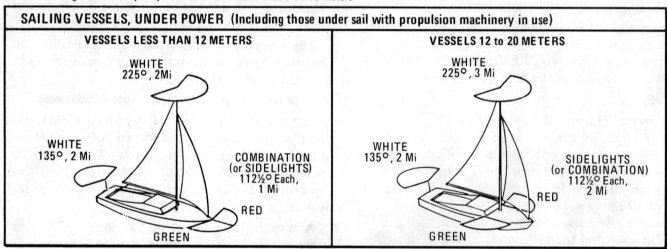

6-13 Light Configuration Chart

CONVERSION TABLE

Metric Measure	U.S. Custommery/ Imperial Measure (Approx.)	Metric Measure	U.S. Custommery/ Imperial Measure (Approx.)
20M	65.6 ft.	4.0M	13.1 ft.
12M	39.4 ft.	2.5M	8.2 ft.
7M	23.0 ft.	2.0M	6.6 ft.
6M	19.7 ft.	1.5M	4.9 ft.
4.5M	14.8 ft.	1M	3.3 ft.

head lights and sternlight described above. An additional provision of the Inland Rules states that a power-driven vessel operating on the Great Lakes may carry on all-round white light in lieu of the second masthead light and sternlight described above. The light is carried in the position of the second masthead light and be visible at the same minimum distance of visibility.

Lights for Sailing Vessels Under Sail Only and Vessels Under Oars

A *sailing vessel* must exhibit sidelights and sternlight.

A sailing vessel less than 20 meters in length may combine the sidelights and sternlight in one lantern carried at or near the top of the mast where it can best be seen.

A sailing vessel underway may, in addition to sidelights and sternlight, exhibit at or near the top of the mast, where best seen, two all-round lights in a vertical line, the upper red, the lower green; these may not be used in conjunction with the combined, three-color lantern described in the preceding paragraph.

LIGHT TYPE	VISIBILITY MIN DISTANCE — MILES			
	1	2	3	5
MASTHEAD		●	▲	◆
SIDE	●	▲◆		
STERN		●▲◆		
ALL-ROUND		●▲◆		
TOWING		●▲◆		
SPECIAL FLASHING (Inland Rules Only)		●▲◆		

VESSEL LENGTH

● *Less than 12 Meters*

▲ *12 Meters but Less than 20 Meters*

◆ *20 Meters but Less than 50 Meters*

6-14 Lights—Distance of Visibility

A sailing vessel of less than 7 meters' length must, if practicable, exhibit sidelights and sternlight but, if she does not, must have ready at hand an electric torch or lighted lantern showing a white light to be exhibited in sufficient time to prevent collision. A *vessel under oars* may exhibit the same lights just described for sailing vessels and in the same manner.

A *reminder* — sailboats with propulsion machinery in use must comply with the requirements for power-driven vessels.

Other Lights ——— Special Vessels

Air-cushion vessels are now being seen in many areas. Underway, in the non-displacement mode, they move at a rapid speed and their heading, as judged from their lights, could be quite different from their track over the water. Therefore, the Rules require that, in addition to the lights prescribed for power-driven vessels, they exhibit an *all-round flashing yellow* light where it can best be seen when operating in the non-displacement mode.

Here are some other lights you should recognize. These lights are shown in addition to the running lights for sailing and power-driven vessels described above if underway.

Power-driven vessel *towing astern:* 2 masthead lights (in a vertical line) instead of one; 3 if tow exceeds 200 meters. Getting between a tug and its tow is almost always fatal.

Fishing vessel trawling (dragging): 2 all-round lights in a vertical line, upper green, lower white.

Vessel *not under command:* 2 all-round red lights in a vertical line.

Vessel *constrained by her draft (72 COLREGS only):* 3 all-round red lights in a vertical line.

Distress Signals

When a vessel is in distress and requires assistance, signals to be used or exhibited either separately or together are listed in the Annex IV of each set of Rules.

Exemptions (Inland Rules)

Many boats carry lights in conformity with the Rules which were superseded by the Inland Navigational Rules Act of 1980. Therefore, many (not all) boats of less than 20 meters in length built or being built before Dec. 24, 1980 are permanently exempted from being changed if used in the waters where the former rules applied. See Rule 38.

ANNEXES (Inland Navigational Rules)

There are five annexes to the Inland Navigational Rules Act of 1980. Annexes I through III contain technical information. Annex IV and Annex V contain new requirements as follow:

ANNEX IV adds to the list of DISTRESS SIGNALS a high intensity white light flashing at intervals from 50 to 70 times per minute.

ANNEX V Pilot Rules require the operator of each self-propelled vessel 12 meters or more in length to carry on board and maintain for ready reference a COPY of the Inland Navigational Rules.

PENALITIES (Inland Navigational Rules)

Whoever operates a vessel in violation of the Inland Navigational rules Act of 1980 is liable to a civil penalty of not more than $5000 for each violation. (Notice that the operator, not the owner, is named responsible if they are not one and the same; it follows that an operator chartering a boat is held liable under the law, not the chartering firm which owns the boat).

International Rules' Requirements Legal Where Inland Rules Apply

All vessels complying with the construction and equipment requirements of the International Regulations are considered to be in compliance with the Inland Rules.

A Final Note

Certain things should be noted because they are *not* mentioned in the rules:

Nothing in the rules ever imposes a requirement to place your own vessel in danger. If any action called for under the rules seems to do so, remember that the Responsibility Rule provides for a departure from the Rules to avoid immediate danger. In such circumstances you would have to decide whether the danger/doubt signal would be appropriate.

Legally Required Equipment

Under federal law, certain equipment is required to be aboard every boat. Some of these items apply to powerboats only and may be omitted on a sailboat with no engine aboard.

However, most sailboats will have at least an auxiliary engine and so will need this equipment.

Over and above the bare minimum legal requirements some additional equipment should be on board. The Coast Guard Auxiliary offers a free Courtesy Marine Examination to all boat owners. This includes checking all the legally required equipment and a few additional safety items. If your boat passes this examination, it will be issued a decal showing that it has passed. If it fails to pass, you will be told privately in what ways it is deficient so that you can take corrective action. No report will ever be issued to any law enforcement agency concerning any deficiencies. The table shown on page 6-15 gives a brief summary of the various legal requirements and the extra items required for the award of this decal — **The Seal of Safety.**

While no attempt will be made in this book to discuss these various requirements in detail, a few brief comments are in order.

1. PERSONAL FLOTATION DEVICES (PFDs). One PFD is required for every person aboard. If the boat is less than 16 feet in length, any Coast Guard approved PFD is acceptable. If the boat is 16 feet or longer, the PFD must be of a **wearable** style (Type I, II, or III). In addition, at least one **throwable** PFD (Type IV) must be aboard any boat 16 feet or longer. Wearable PFDs must be kept **readily** available while throwable PFDs must be **immediately** available.

2. FIRE EXTINGUISHERS. These must be Coast Guard or UL approved and of a marine type. At least one must be aboard every power boat (more if over 26 feet in length) and should be located where it will be readily available in case of fire. The requirement for carrying a fire extinguisher is waived for a powerboat under 26 feet in length with an **outboard** motor only and with no closed compartments where gasoline fumes might accumulate.

3. IDENTIFICATION AND NUMBERS. All boats with any type of mechanical propulsion must be numbered — usually assigned

by the state of principal use. They must be in plain, vertical block characters at least 3 inches high, of a color in contrast to the hull's, separated by spaces or hyphens as needed, and reading from left to right on both sides of the vessel's forward half. Registration papers or document must be aboard whenever the boat is in use.

6-15 Registration Numbers Properly Displayed

4. WHISTLE OR HORN. A whistle or horn is required aboard every powerboat 16 feet or longer. Smaller boats must still give whistle signals as required. A boat 40 ft. to less than 65 ft. must have a power operated whistle or horn.

5. BELL. A bell is required aboard every boat 26 feet or longer. Smaller boats must still give bell signals as required.

6. ACCIDENT REPORTS. While it is not an equipment requirement, every boater should be aware that reports must be made within 48 hours to the appropriate agency (usually the state) in every case of death, disappearance, or injury requiring treatment beyond first aid, and for property damage in excess of $200 within 10 days. These are federal limits; Some individual state requirements may be more stringent.

7. DISCHARGE OF OIL. Federal law prohibits the discharge of oil or oily waste from any vessel and vessels 26 feet or longer are required to have posted a placard warning of this prohibition.

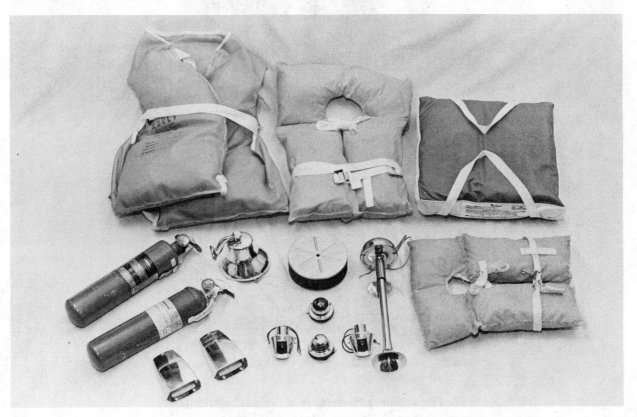

6-16 Legal Requirements Are Minimum Safety Requirements

VISUAL DISTRESS SIGNALS. All recreational boats 16 feet or more are required to be equipped with visual distress signalling devices at all times when operating on coastal waters. Also, boats less than 16 feet are required to carry visual distress signals when operating on coastal waters at night. Completely open sailboats without engines are excepted, as are boats propelled manually. Also, excepted are boats in organized races, regattas, parades, etc. Visual Distress Signals must be Coast Guard approved, readily accessible, serviceable and, for those applicable, bearing a legible, unexpired date.

9. MARINE SANITATION DEVICES (MSD's). Each vessel with an installed toilet must have attached to it either: 1) a marine sanitation device (MSD) certified by the Coast Guard; or 2) a holding tank. Operating a boat with a non-approved MSD is illegal in the navigable waters of the U.S., including the "territorial sea" ("three mile limit"). In addition, certain bodies of freshwater have been declared no-discharge areas. To comply, all installed toilets must be certified by the Coast Guard or designed to retain waste onboard for pumpout at a land site. All non-approved overboard discharge toilets must be removed or permanently disabled, but there is no requirement to install toilet facilities on vessels not currently having them. These regulations do not affect portable toilets on vessels.

6-17 A Safety Harness is a "Must" Particularly in Foul or Heavy Weather

	Less than 16'		16' Less than 26'		26' Less than 40'		40' Less than 65'	
	Legal	CME	Legal	CME	Legal	CME	Legal	CME
PAPERS — In order & on person or boat	◆	●	◆	●	◆	●	◆	●
NUMBERING — Block type of contrasting color	◆	●	◆	●	◆	●	◆	●
BELL —					◆	●	◆	●
PERSONAL FLOTATION DEVICE — Approved type, adequate number	◆	●	◆	●	◆	●	◆	●
VENTILATION — Cowls & Ducts to closed areas	◆	●	◆	●	◆	●	◆	●
FLAME ARRESTER(S) — On carburetors of inboard engines	◆	●	◆	●	◆	●	◆	●
FIRE EXTINGUISHER(S) — Approved type, adequate size & number	(1)	●	(1)	●	◆	●	◆	●
HORN OR WHISTLE		●	◆	●	◆	●	(2)	●
LIGHTS — Navigation & Anchor	(3)	●	(3)	●	(3)	●	(3)	●
FUEL TANKS Properly secured & vented		●		●		●		●
CARBURETOR DRIP PAN — Under updraft carburetors	◆	●	◆	●	◆	●	◆	●
ELECTRICAL INSTALLATION — In good condition & fused		●		●		●		●
DISTRESS FLARES — For emergency signalling	(4)	●	(4)	●	(4)	●	(4)	●
GALLEY STOVE — Marine type, properly installed		●		●		●		●
MANUAL PUMP OR BAILER —		●		●				
ANCHOR AND LINE — Suitable size & adequate line		●		●		●		●
MARINE SANITATION DEVICE	(4)		(4)		(4)		(4)	

Notes: 1. Not required on boats of open construction, powered by outboard

2. Power operated

3. Legal requirements call for display of lights when needed. However, their installation on the vessel is not mandatory.

4. See page 6-14

Legend: ◆ = Legal Requirements

● = CME Requirements

6-18 Legal Requirements and Requirements For the Seal of Safety

Chapter 7

Sailing Seamanship

Where the able seaman aboard a square-rigged sailing vessel of the 1800s might have to be familiar with literally dozens of knots and splices, today's weekend sailor only needs to know a few basics about ropework and seamanship generally. Although it's legitimately a subject by itself, anchoring is so closely connected with rope and line handling that we'll consider it in this chapter.

Anchoring and Mooring

Basically an anchor is a hook. Its point or points (flukes) dig into the sea bottom while a line connects it to the boat. The whole process seems so simple, but in fact several elements in the equipment and in the anchoring process are critical, and if they fail, the boat can drift to disaster.

There are several common types of anchors in use throughout the United States today. Probably the most popular is the Danforth and other makes derived from it. Known collectively as "lightweight burying anchors," all the Danforth-types have a pair of long, wide flukes that pivot at one end, where they are connected to a pipe-shaped stock. The amount of pivot of the flukes is very important, as it controls the angle between the flukes and the shank, to which the anchor line is attached; a proper angle

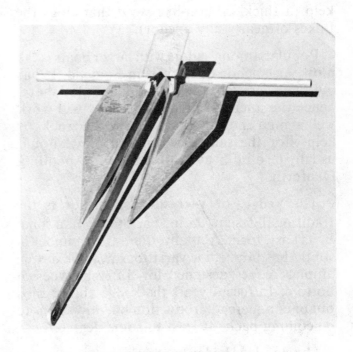

7-1 Danforth Anchor

between shank and flukes insures that the sharp-pointed flukes will dig in deeply and quickly, instead of skidding along the bottom.

Danforth-style anchors are lightweight for their size and holding power (see the table at the end of the chapter). They are most often employed where the sea bottom is sand, mud or just

7-2   Yachtsman's Anchor

7-3   Plow Anchor

about anything except rocks, gravel, coral or kelp (a thick, ribbon-like weed that clogs the flukes of nearly any anchor).

Popular among sailors with larger boats is the **plow,** an anchor developed in England. It has but one oversize fluke shaped like a plowshare, hence the anchor's name. The plow will work well in mud and will sometimes work in rocks or kelp. For the same size boat, a plow should usually be a bit heavier than the corresponding Danforth.

The **kedge,** or **yachtsman's,** anchor is the traditional design, dating back to Roman times in its basic form. Actually, there are a number of subtle but important variations in fluke design among kedges designed for different types of bottom. In recent years the kedge almost died out of commercial production but now seems to be coming back, at least to some degree.

The standard kedge has two opposed, curving flukes, so that only one can dig in at a time. There is a relatively long shank at right angles to the flukes, and then a folding stock at the anchor's upper end. A kedge anchor can dig into types of bottom that defy other flukes, but considerably more weight in the anchor itself is required to make the design function — for normal use, one pound of anchor per foot of boat length. Since one fluke is exposed after the anchor is dug in, it's easy for the boat to swing

around, foul the anchor line, and jerk the anchor free.

Kedge anchors are popular with tradition-oriented sailors and with those whose anchorages include large patches of rocky or kelp-ridden bottom. Since most sailing areas include anchorages with varying types of bottom, most cruising sailboat owners carry two different types of anchor, to be ready for anything. In all but the smallest daysailers it is also convenient to have an everyday, or **working,** anchor and one a size heavier, the **storm** anchor.

The anchor itself is only one part of the whole **ground tackle** system. The prudent skipper will shackle a length of chain — 12 to 20 feet or more — to the anchor ring. This not only precludes chafe at a point where it is most likely to occur, but also, by its weight, aids the anchor in dig-

7-4   Anchor Fouled

ging in. To the chain is attached, with a shackle and an eye splice, the anchor **rode,** usually nylon line tied to the boat. Check the chart of your sailing area for anchorages, and try to carry a rode at least 10 times longer than the high-tide depth of the deepest anchorage you expect to use. If this is impossible, a 100- or 150-foot rode should be adequate for most circumstances.

When a boat is at anchor, she normally has no motive power of her own. She will respond to the force of the current or the wind or both. Different kinds of boats react differently to these forces. Deep-draft keel boats, with a great deal of underbody, will often swing according to the current, while shallow centerboarders will respond primarily to wind pressure. When wind and current are in different directions, this can cause problems for dissimilar boats anchored close together, as they may swing into each other.

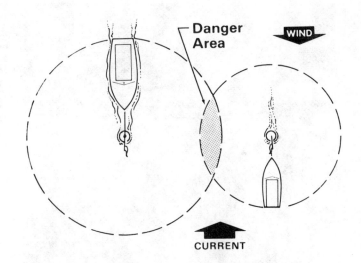

7-5 Anchoring Too Close

Anchoring

Generally speaking, when there is a choice it's best to anchor among boats of a size and type similar to your own. Try to calculate roughly the swinging circle of nearby craft — you can always ask other skippers, if they're aboard. If you know the depth of the anchorage (you can mark the depths in advance on **your** anchor line with plastic tags) and the amount of line a boat has out, it's easy to figure her swinging circle. Do bear in mind, too, that in anchorages the first boat has priority, and you must keep clear if you're a late arrival.

Having selected your anchorage, you should set up the boat and her gear for the final approach. If your anchor is stowed in **chocks** or otherwise carried on deck ready for use, undo the lashings and make sure that the anchor line is clear to run out. It's a good idea to lower and furl the jib before your approach, to give you a clear foredeck.

Bring up as much anchor line as you expect to use and coil it loosely on deck so it will run out easily. The coil should be **capsized** — upside down — so that the end of the rode closest to the anchor is on top.

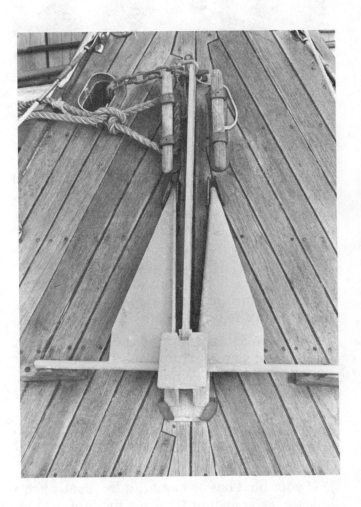

7-6 Anchor Stowed on Foredeck Chocks

7-7 Anchor Stowed on Bow Rail

7-8 Plow Anchor Stowed at Bow

When you've reached the spot where you want to anchor, head up into the wind until all momentum is lost. When the boat stops moving forward, lower the anchor hand-over-hand from the bow. Don't throw it and don't drop the coil of rode over in one lump. You'll feel the anchor touch bottom, at which point make a mental note of how deep the water is. Now, as the boat drifts backward, have one crewmember lower and furl the mainsail while the other pays out the anchor line until approximately five to seven times the water depth has been used.

Take a quick turn around the deck cleat and let the boat's momentum snub the anchor line and dig in the hook. You can tell if the anchor is holding by grasping the rode forward of the bow. If the boat is dragging, you'll feel the anchor bouncing along the bottom. You can also sight on objects ashore, to see if their positions change relative to the boat.

If your boat has an engine, it frequently helps in setting the anchor to give a burst of reverse, once the anchor is down and the rode is fully extended. If the anchor refuses to bite in,

retrieve it. Chances are a rock or clump of seaweed has fouled the flukes. If, after several attempts, the anchor still won't set, try another place in the anchorage.

If you anchor among rocks, it's a good idea to buoy the anchor, by tying a light line to the lower end of the anchor and running the line to a lightweight buoy or float. If the anchor's flukes get stuck under a large rock, you can then draw it out backwards. When using this type of **trip line,** it will have to be paid out independently of the anchor rode, to avoid one line fouling the other.

Permanent Mooring

A permanent mooring is a ground tackle system designed to remain in place for whole seasons at a time. Mooring anchors are generally cast iron mushrooms, so named because of their appearance. A mushroom (except in the smallest sizes) is an uncomfortable device to carry aboard, and its relative holding power is not great compared to modern lightweight anchors. It does have a couple of outstanding advantages for permanent installation. First, even a very heavy mushroom is extremely cheap (relatively speaking), and second, a dug-in mushroom will resist pulls from any side.

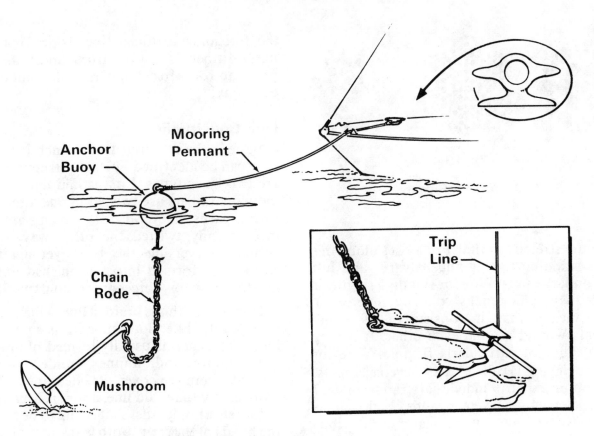

7-9 Buoys for Mooring and Trip Lines

Normal mooring rigs today employ a heavy mushroom (see the table) shackled to a length of chain approximately equal in length to three times the high water depth in the anchorage. At the far end of the chain is a buoy, often made from polystyrene. To the buoy is attached the **mooring pennant**, a heavy, nylon rope with a large eye spliced in the extreme end. The only thing to be extra careful of, when setting up a mooring rig, is that the buoy has a metal rod running through it, to take the strain of the boat at one end and the mushroom at the other. Most mooring buoys are so reinforced, and one can tell at a glance. In some cases, a small pickup buoy, additional to the mooring buoy, is made fast to the loop in the pennant, so the crewmember on the bow can see and grab the pennant more easily.

Line for Sailors

In today's sailboats, there are only four kinds of line in general use, and each is suited for certain applications.

Nylon is a manmade fiber distinguished by its great strength, imperviousness to rot, and stretchiness. Because of this last factor, nylon is used where stretch is either unimportant or an asset for taking up sudden shocks. Anchor rodes, mooring pennants and dock lines are generally nylon.

Dacron is similar to nylon in most respects, except that it is not nearly as stretchy. For this reason, Dacron (called Terylene in England) is used for sheets and halyards, where stretchiness is a definite liability.

Polypropylene is weaker than either nylon or Dacron, and is so slippery that knots tied in it frequently work loose. It has, however, one asset that neither of its stronger cousins possesses: It floats. For dinghy towlines, pickup lines to mooring pennants and other applications where buoyancy is more important than strength, polypropylene is useful.

Steel Wire, which you may not consider a rope, is employed where maximum strength and

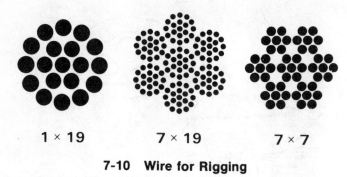

1 × 19   7 × 19   7 × 7

7-10   Wire for Rigging

minimum stretch are vital. For most sailors, this means standing rigging and halyards and luff wires on large sails. Wire for standing rigging is called **1x19**, (spoken as "one by nineteen"), which means that it consists of 19 equal elements wound around each other. It is very strong, but not particularly flexible. Wire for running rigging is called **7 x 19** (seven elements, each composed of 19 individual strands) or **7 x 7** (seven elements, seven strands each); it is slightly weaker but a great deal more flexible. Nearly all wire is made from stainless steel.

Some rope of **Manila** is still available in marine outlets. While much cheaper than any of

the foregoing artificial fiber ropes, manila, a natural fiber, is not as strong and is also very prone to rot. Most skippers find manila a false economy.

Line Construction

Besides the material from which it is made, rope can be identified by its construction. There are two basic types. First is **laid line**, in which individual fibers are twisted in one direction to form yarns, several of which are then mechanically twisted the other way to form strands. Reversing the twist yet again, the strands are formed into the finished line, and most such line is three-strand construction.

Opposed to this is **braided line**, which appears superficially like clothesline in its smooth surface, but which is usually formed of an outer, braided cover and an inner, braided core quite separate from the cover. Braided line is slightly more costly than laid line, and it is usually used for sheets or halyards, as it is said to be easier on the hands of the crew. Both laid and braided line may be combined with 7x19 or 7x7 wire to form rope-and-wire halyards. The wire is long enough to reach from the fully-hoisted sail to

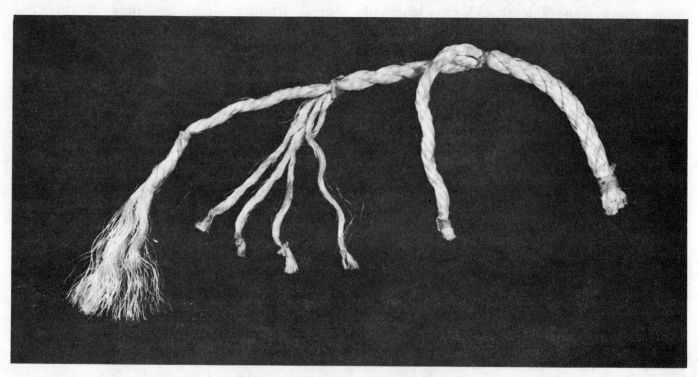

7-11   Three Strand Laid Line

7-12   Braided Line

the winch, plus at least three turns around it. The rope end, called a **tail**, is used merely to get the sail up to where the wire takes the load.

Basic Knots

It is still possible to become master of dozens of useful or decorative knots, but for most sailors it is far easier and more efficient to learn a few basic knots and learn them well. The following are all basic and applicable aboard most boats, power or sail.

7-13   Figure Eight Knot

Figure Eight is employed whenever it is useful to have a thick segment, called a **stopper**, at the end of a line. Most seamen put a figure eight in the end of each sheet, to keep it from running accidentally through the sheet block.

7-14   Square Knot

Square Knot (also called a **Reef Knot**) was developed, as the alternative name suggests, in reefing. If your boat has point reefing, use a **slippery** square knot — like a shoelace knot with a single loop — to tie each pair of reef points together. A square knot will serve for connecting any two lines of the same diameter.

7-15   Sheet Bend, Double Sheet Bend and Slippery Sheet Bend

Sheet Bend is for connecting two lines. It is better than a square knot because it is ·not as likely to over turn and it will work when the two lines are different in diameter. For extra security, try a **Double Sheet Bend.**

7-18 Completed Clove Hitch

7-16 Bowline

Clove Hitch is for temporarily making a line fast to a piling. It should never be unattended, as it can easily work free under continued, sharp tugs. By making a simple overhand knot with the end of the line around the standing part, the clove hitch's security is greatly increased.

Bowline (pronounced boe-lin) is one of the most useful knots ever invented. Practice it until you can tie it with your eyes closed. A bowline is used whenever a temporary loop is wanted in the end of a line.

7-19 Fisherman's Bend

Fisherman's Bend (also known as **Anchor Bend**) makes a good, temporary attachment of a line to an anchor. It is better for this purpose than a bowline, because the loop around the anchor ring, where chafe may occur, is double and is also drawn tight, to minimize sliding friction.

7-17 Starting the Clove Hitch

7-20 Overhand Knot

None of these knots is likely to stick in your mind until you have practiced it over and over again and have actually used it in earnest. Always try to make a point of using the appropriate knot for a given purpose.

A good knot is said to have two outstanding characteristics: It is easy to tie and, even more important, easy to untie. Unfortunately, all knots have one bad feature — they weaken the rope in which they are tied, subtracting as much as half the strength is some cases. When a permanent loop or connection between two similar lines is desirable, it's far better to employ a splice, which only weakens rope by perhaps 10% when properly executed.

Splices

There are only two splices of interest to the average boatman and -woman: The **eye splice** is for making a permanent eye or loop in the end of a rope, and the **short splice** is for permanently joining two ropes of identical diameter.

When learning to splice, it's a good idea to equip yourself with a length or two of manila line about 3/8″ in diameter (rope size is nearly always given in terms of diameter in this country). Manila is stiffer than nylon or Dacron and holds its construction better during the twists and pulls of splicing. As you become more skillful, try the same thing with Dacron and nylon.

7-21 The Short Splice

You'll also need some waterproof tape — electrician's tape will serve, but you should carry a roll of sailor's waterproof tape in your ditty bag (see Chapter 11) as well. If you're working with new, stiff rope, a **fid** (a sailor's tool for separating strands of rope) will also be handy. Now you're ready to make a short splice.

Unlay one end of your rope about six inches.

This means undoing the line into its three component strands. Tape the end of each strand to keep it from untwisting and tape the point at which you want the unlaying to cease. Now do the same for the other end of the rope.

"Marry" the two untwisted ends so that one strand of rope A alternates with one of rope B. Tape one set of strands in place.

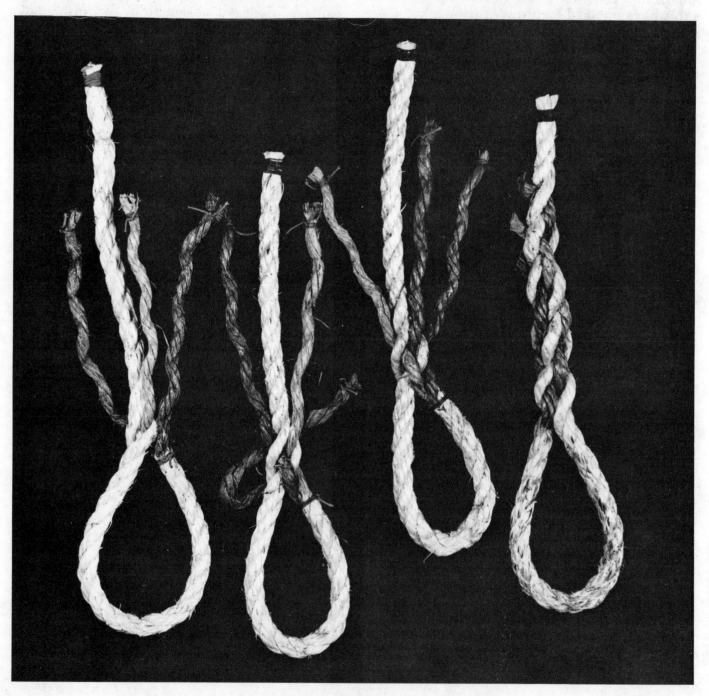

7-22 The Eye Splice

Now take one of the loose strands and lead it over the taped neck of the opposite rope. Open a space between strands of the opposite rope and push the strand through as far as it will go — but don't pull it tight just yet.

Now do the same thing with the other two strands, working each one through an adjoining opening and pulling it through.

Pull all three tucked strands tight one by one.

Make a second set of tucks like the first. Be sure that you keep the alternations between strands of ropes A and B even.

Make a third set of tucks and pull them tight.

Untape the free set of strands and perform the same three-tuck operation with them.

When you're done, cut off the ends of the strands to within about a quarter-inch of the main rope. Roll the completed splice under your foot.

With practice, you'll find you can achieve great neatness and speed, but it does take time.

The eye splice is a little harder than the short splice. It's basically the same idea, except you're making the tucks back into the standing part of the original rope. Unlay and tape the line as before. Now form the eye to the size you'll want and lay the unlaid end along the standing part with one of the strands arbitrarily chosen to be the first tuck.

Open the strands of the standing part with your fid and insert the first end strand, pulling it through.

Take the next strand to the right of the first, as shown, and insert that, pulling it through.

Turn the whole splice over — this is very important — and lead the remaining strand between the only two standing part strands left. Do this slowly and be sure you have it right. As soon as it's done, you'll know just by looking.

Now continue with the remaining two sets of tucks, trim off the ends, and you're done.

When you splice artificial fiber line, which has less friction among the strands than does natural fiber line, you should take five full series of tucks instead of three. This makes a somewhat lumpy-looking splice, but one with maximum strength, which is of course the most important thing.

Seizing

As you can tell from reading these instructions and looking at the illustrations, this kind of splice can only be made in laid line. To splice braided line, one substitutes core for core and cover for cover. It's not really necessary, however, as one may form a semi-permanent loop by the technique of **seizing** the two parts of the line together.

To do this, you need a sailmaker's palm — a kind of super-thimble — large needle and thread of the same material as the line you are seizing.

Form the loop to the size desired. Now lay a series of tight, even turns of thread lashing the two parts of the line together.

When the turns of thread have formed a lashing about equal in length to the diameter of the rope being used, sew the thread through the two parts of the line two or three times.

Now make a second series of turns with the thread between the two parts of the main rope. Draw these turns as tight as possible.

Sew through the main part of the rope, tie a figure eight in the end of the thread and cut it off.

Although not quite as neat as a splice, a seizing is very strong and can be unmade. It can also be done with laid line.

Whipping and Finishing

Some of the most unattractive and un-seamanlike things visible on many boats are the tattered, frayed ends of line with overhand knots tied in the ends to keep further unlaying at bay. The end of every line aboard your boat should be neatly finished off, both to preserve the line itself and to make it easier for the rope to run through tight places like chocks and blocks.

There are several ways to finish the end of a nylon or Dacron line, but the easiest with lines

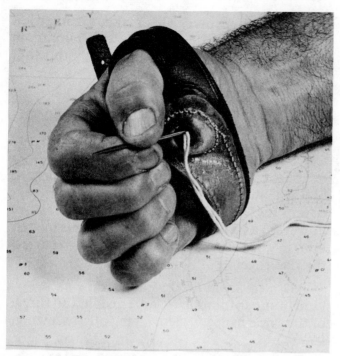

7-23   Sailmaker's Palm and Needle

7-24   Eye Splice in Braided Line

of 3/8″ diameter or less is simply to hold a match to the end until the fibers melt and fuse. Use a freshly-cut end for a neat job.

For a temporary end, simply take four or five tight turns of waterproof tape, or buy one of the many commercial products and treat the end — usually by dipping into a plastic liquid that hardens instantly.

With larger lines, and for sailors who enjoy ropework, a technique called **whipping** may be employed. It's not unlike seizing, except that only one piece of line is dealt with.

With Dacron or nylon thread, lay a series of tight turns around the end of the main rope, about half or three-eighths of an inch from the very end of the fibers.

When the whipping turns form a lashing about equal in length to the diameter of the main rope, sew through the strands. Lay the thread in the spiral groove formed by the strands of laid line, or diagonally along braid.

After making three sewed retaining threads, as shown, tie off the end of the thread. Besides being decorative, a whipping like this is very functional.

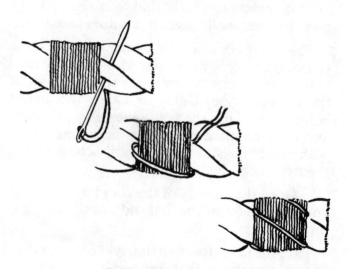

7-25   Whipping

Coiling

Learning to coil a line properly is the mark of a good sailor. The so-called **flemish coil,** which looks like a doormat and which many uninformed people associate with good seamanship, is nothing but a decoration and is virtually useless as a coil.

Coiled line should be formed in loops as large as practical, because the sharper a bend one

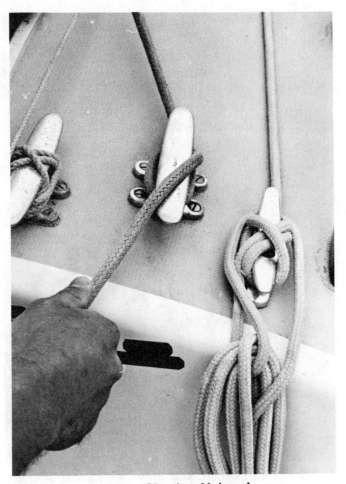

7-26 Cleating Halyard

makes in a line, the greater the chance of fracturing the fibers inside. When coiling a halyard or sheet, form the loops with one hand, then transfer them to the other hand, which holds the coil.

To secure a coiled halyard, simply take the short length between the coil and the halyard cleat and lead it through the coil as a doubled piece of line.

Twist it two or three times, as shown, and then loop the doubled piece over the upper horn of the cleat. This will hold the coiled halyard neatly and securely in place.

If there isn't room or the proper fitting for this, you may tuck the coil between the halyard just above the cleat and the mast itself. While neatness is desirable, it is important that the coiled line should be capable of being easily released in a hurry.

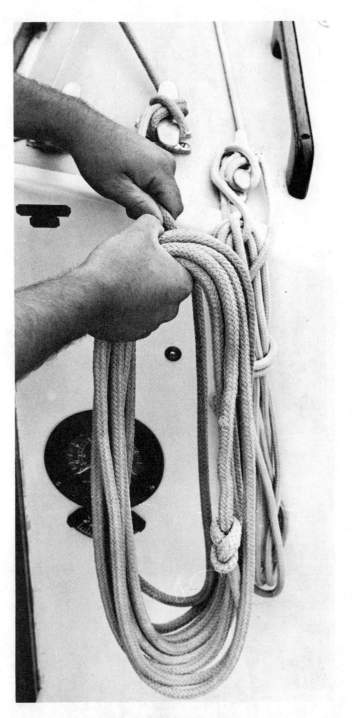

7-27 Cleated Halyard and Coiling Line for Stowing

Coiled line stowed below may be hung from hooks with small loops of light line, as shown. While not as impressive as some fancy methods of hanging a coil, this way works just as well.

When hooks aren't available, one may lash a coil with its own end.

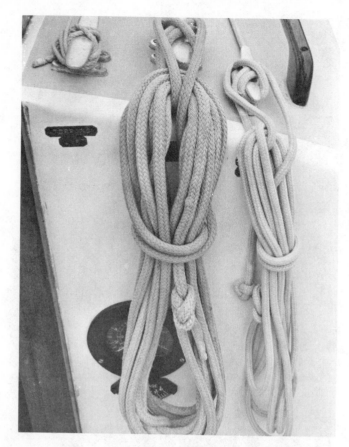

7-28 Halyards Properly Secured

Artificial fiber line may be stowed wet without damage, but it should not be exposed needlessly to strong sunlight for great lengths of time. This means that sheets especially should be taken down below or tucked inside sail covers. It will materially prolong the rope's life, especially in more tropical areas.

7-30 Lines Coiled and Stowed by Loop of Coil

7-29 Line Coiled and Stowed

7-31 Lines Coiled and Stowed with Hitch

7-32 Halyard Coiled and Stowed Between Mast and Self

Belaying and Tying Up

Making a small boat fast to the fittings found in the average marina isn't hard. Like everything else to do with boats, however, there are more and less effective ways of doing it.

The two most commonly-seen attachment points for boats are cleats and pilings. Making a line fast to a cleat is simple, if it's done right. Take a full turn around the base of the cleat, then lead the line up and around one horn, and finally make a hitch, as shown, around the other horn. The important thing here is that first full turn, which allows you to undo the hitch while the cleated line is still under load.

The clove hitch, described in detail above, is the standard way of making fast to a piling. If the line is to be left without someone to keep an eye on it, do make the small extra effort of tying a hitch around the standing part of the line.

7-33 Cleated and Flemished Mooring Line

If a boat is tied up alongside a pier, it will normally require only two lines for a short stay. One, the **bow line**, leads forward from the bow to a cleat or piling ashore; the **stern line** leads to another fitting aft of the boat. If your boat is large — more than about 25 feet — or if she is to be left for awhile, **spring lines** are also useful.

The **bow spring** leads aft from the boat's forward cleat to a pier fitting located about amidships, while the **stern** or **aft spring** leads from the same pier fitting aft to the boat's stern cleat.

Some saltwater areas have a significant **tidal** range. If your boat is tied to a fixed pier in such an area you will have to use mooring lines of length appropriate to the predicted rise or fall of the tide.

Good fenders are an important part of tying up properly. It's not an exaggeration to say that nearly all boats have fenders that are too small. The easiest way to make sure yours are large enough is to measure the ones most used on boats the size of yours, then get at least three fenders one size larger.

7-34 Mooring Hitch (Clove) on Piling

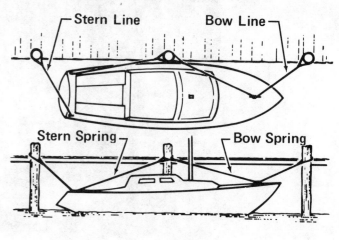

7-35 Tying Up

Table of Suggested Anchor Sizes

Boat length	Anchor weight in pounds		
	Danforth	Plow	Kedge
under 17′	4	5	10
17′-20′	8	10	12-15
21′-25′	8	15	15-20
26′-30′	13	15	25
31′-40′	22	20	30-35

(for storm anchor, use one size larger in each case)

Working Loads of Ground Tackle Elements*

Nylon rode		Galv. chain		Galv. shackle	
size	load	size	load	size	load
5/16"	570 lbs.	3/16"	1,400 lbs.	3/16"	670 lbs.
3/8"	800 lbs.	3/16"	1,400 lbs.	1/4"	1,000 lbs.
7/16"	1,100 lbs.	3/16"	1,400 lbs.	5/16"	1,500 lbs.
1/2"	1,670 lbs.	1/4"	4,350 lbs.	3/8"	2,000 lbs.
5/8"	2,400 lbs.	1/4"	4,350 lbs.	7/16"	3,000 lbs.

*Working load of rope is 1/5 of breaking strength; working load of chain is 1/2 of breaking strength; working load of shackle is 1/6 of minimum strength: given shackle size is 1/16" less than pin diameter.

Mooring Rig Sizes

Boat length	Anchor	Chain	Shackle	Pennant
under 16'	75 lbs.	3/16"	1/4"	3/8"
17'-20'	100 lbs.	1/4"	5/16"	7/16"
21'-25'	150 lbs.	5/16"	3/8"	1/2"
26'-30'	200 lbs.	3/8"	1/2"	5/8"
30'-40'	250-300 lbs.	7/16"	1/2"	3/4"

(Note: Mooring buoy can be of any convenient size, but must be capable of lifting the weight of chain from bottom to itself. A 12" diameter polyethylene-filled buoy will support up to 24' of 3/16" chain or 15' of 1/4" chain. A 16" diameter buoy of the same material will support up to 35' of 3/8" chain; an 18" buoy will support 60' of 3/8" chain.)

Table of Anchor Rode Sizes
(laid nylon line)

Boat length	Rode diameter	Strength (average)
under 14'	5/16"	2,800 lbs.
15'-20'	3/8"	4,000 lbs.
21'-25'	7/16"	5,500 lbs.
26'-30'	1/2"	8,250 lbs.
31'-40'	5/8"	12,000 lbs.

Chapter 8

Engines For Sailboats

Why a Sailboat is a Poor Powerboat

No matter how swift and nimble they may be under sail, most sailing craft handle poorly under power. There are a number of technical reasons for this, but the overriding one is that sail propulsion calls for a different kind of hull than engine-driven boats require, and on sailing vessels, the engine is usually described, with accuracy, as an auxiliary — the main powerplant is the sailing rig.

Compared to a powerboat of equal displacement, or weight, a sailboat generally has a very small engine. A cruising ketch 30 feet long, with a displacement of 10,000 lb., will probably carry an auxiliary of 30 hp. A powerboat of similar size will have an engine three times as powerful, and even larger if it's a high-speed planing boat.

Sailboat Propellers

Sailboat engines are designed — by and large — to turn a large propeller at a rather slow speed. For this reason, many auxiliary engines are geared down, so that the propeller turns at something like one-third the speed of the engine itself. The propeller may be one of several types. On cruising sailboats, where high performance under sail isn't a factor, the propeller is usually three-bladed and large. The skipper accepts the drag penalty under sail in order to have reasonably good performance under power.

8-1 Three Blade Propeller

The sailing cruiser with some pretensions to speed under sail has a two-bladed propeller. While not as efficient for powering as a three-bladed wheel of similar diameter, the two-bladed prop can be made to lie vertically in the space just ahead of or behind the rudder, for minimum drag.

Racing sailboats frequently use a folding propeller. When moving through the water with

8-2　Two Blade Propeller

8-4　Folding Propeller - Closed

8-3　Folding Propeller - Open

the engine off, the prop folds into a flower-bud shape, but when the engine is on and in gear, centrifugal force from the spinning propeller shaft opens the blades and holds them in place, moving the boat forward. Except for boats that will be raced frequently, the folding propeller is inefficient for simple propulsion and makes close-quarters maneuvering under power difficult.

Requirements of an Auxiliary Engine

Ideally, a sailboat engine should meet certain criteria, but only recently have small internal combustion engines been developed that perform reasonably well all that is asked of them.

A primary requirement is that a sailboat engine should be compact, using up — with its fuel tank, battery, and wiring system — as little space as possible. In a daysailer, the engine should be light in weight, as it should be in any unballasted boat. It should still, however, be unobtrusive, as the average sailor is hardly fond of his engine, and only wants to hear from it when he needs it.

Most sailboats have very primitive electrical systems, at least until one considers vessels in the 30-foot-and-over range. The engine itself is the primary source of ship's electrical power, there being no separate generator. Thus, the auxiliary should be capable of turning out sufficient extra electricity to light the running

8-5 Spark-Proof Main Switch and Switch Panel

lights, anchor light, interior lighting system, and perhaps to operate a radiotelephone, depth sounder or radio direction finder.

Compared to powerboat skippers, sailors are frequently not interested in or attentive to their boats' motors. Therefore, a sailboat auxiliary must be very reliable, as it will get little attention and will often be installed in a compartment too damp and inaccessible for anything else. Dampness is of course the major enemy of internal combustion engines, especially those gasoline engines with complex electrical systems. Many of the best inboard engines aboard sailboats derive from the power used to push small agricultural equipment, such as tractors, where slow-turning motors with simple, rugged construction are equally desirable.

Above all, a sailboat engine must be safe. No gasoline engine is safe in and of itself. Sailboat engines can be made rugged enough and fool-proof enough to forestall the accidents that arise from neglect. And more and more owners of larger sailing craft are turning to diesel power. In large part, this movement is happening because of the evolution of the diesel into a relatively lightweight engine, but probably the majority of skippers going to diesel power do so because of the relative safety of diesel fuel.

Types of Engines Available

It is safe to say that the majority of engine-equipped sailboats, like the majority of powerboats generally, are pushed by outboard motors. The standard outboard is a high-speed engine turning up 5,000 rpm. or more, which would seem to make it a poor choice for a sailboat, but the outboard has so many attractive features for many sailing craft that it's possible to overlook certain mechanical drawbacks.

Ouboard engines are normally found powering sailboats from the smallest up to about 27 or 28 feet (and light-weight multihulls considerably larger). As a general rule, outboards up to about five hp. are adequate for daysailers' auxiliary engines, while motors from 10 to 15 hp. are used for small cruisers.

8-6 Outboard Mounted on Transom

Outboards can be mounted on sailboats' transoms, as they are on powerboats, and where a sailboat's design permits this location, it offers several advantages. First, the engine, which of course incorporates its own steering, is easy to operate from a transom mount, having been designed for it. Second, the outboard may be tilted up for sailing or when the boat is moored, which makes for sailing efficiency in the first case and for a better-maintained lower unit in the second. Third, the motor is most accessible on the transom, whether for repair or for removal.

8-7 Outboard Mounted in Well

On some boats, however, the shape of the stern prohibits transom mounting or makes it practically inaccessible. Such boats often have outboard wells — usually a lazarette compartment with a hole in the bottom for the outboard lower unit, and a reinforced crossbar for the motor mounting clamps. An outboard well often looks better than a transom mount, but it frequently requires that the motor stay in the water at all times, except if the whole unit is unclamped and removed. In addition, many lazarette-type wells are rather poorly ventilated, causing the engine to run roughly and sometimes to choke on its own exhaust.

One minor inconvenience of an outboard is that it usually requires a fuel of gasoline and lubricating oil mixed in a fairly precise proportion. In order to be sure of having oil when it's needed, many skippers carry an extra can or two — which is fine, except that a can of oil is intended to mix with exactly a given volume of gasoline, usually one six-gallon tank. The unlikelihood of running out of gas with the fuel dock in reach makes many skippers carry either partially full cans of oil or — better — two gas cans, both of which should be of the proper design for the engine.

Until recently, only outboards of 25 hp. and up were electric-start and thus provided with generators to charge the boat's battery. Recently, however, three of the four major outboard manufacturers have extended electric-start to engines of approximately 10 and 15 hp., the sizes most popular for small cruisers. The generating capacity offered by these outboards is not great, but it's usually enough to keep the boat's 12-volt battery up during the season, even allowing for generous interior lighting and frequent use of the running lights. Self-powered anchor lights, depth sounder, spotlight and radio or RDF are still indicated, however.

An outboard's major feature is its portability. Not only can it be removed during and after sailing, but it can also be taken to a mechanic, if necessary, rather than paying for a mechanic to come to it. The modern, medium-size electric-start 10 or 15 weighs about 75 lb., exclusive of battery or fuel tank. This means that an average adult can carry it at least the length of the pier to the family car. Smaller outboards are correspondingly lighter.

Today's outboards are far, far more reliable than the predecessors of even a few years ago, but it must be admitted that pushing a sailboat is not the best thing for the standard outboard. Two common problems with outboard auxiliary engines are spark plug fouling at low speeds and cavitation.

Most outboards are made to run economically and efficiently at three-quarter throttle or better. Unfortunately, many sailboats achieve hull speed in flat water at about half throttle. Running an outboard for extended periods at half throttle or less is an invitation to fouling the spark plugs. While making the fuel-air mixture leaner (less fuel, more air) may help, a certain amount of fouling is built into the situation. The only answer is to get a motor that's small enough so it needs to be run near full throttle to attain hull speed in calm water — which is when you'll be running the engine, anyway.

This solution is only partial, for it means that in rough, windy conditions your engine won't be powerful enough to help the boat a great deal. It is true, however, that most sailboats are as maneuverable under sail as under power, or in many cases more so. Learn to dock under sail, even in adverse winds, and save the engine for getting home in flat calms.

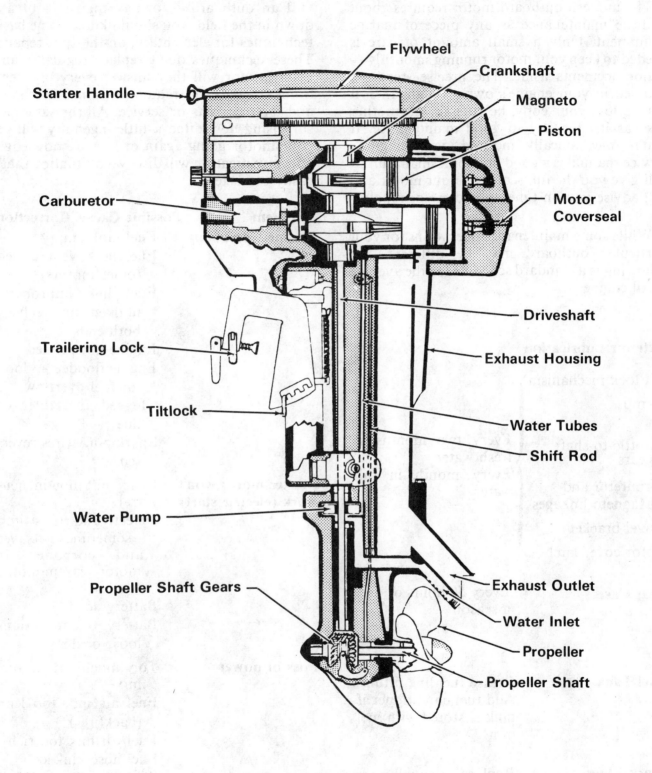

Flywheel

Crankshaft

Starter Handle

Magneto

Piston

Carburetor

Motor Coverseal

Driveshaft

Trailering Lock

Exhaust Housing

Tiltlock

Water Tubes

Shift Rod

Water Pump

Propeller Shaft Gears

Exhaust Outlet

Water Inlet

Propeller

Propeller Shaft

8-8 Cutaway of Outboard Engine

Outboard Maintenance

The modern outboard motor requires about as little maintenance as any piece of marine equipment. Only a small amount of care is needed to keep your motor running smoothly — major accidents aside. The precise steps are detailed in your engine's owner's manual — if you've lost your copy, be sure to get another one, as it's the key to good maintenance. If you're mechanically inclined, your engine's service manual is a good buy for a small sum. It will give you the full scoop on your motor and will advise you on tune-up and major repairs.

While some maintenance operations for your particular outboard may be different, the following is a standard schedule for the average small engine.

Exterior Lubrication

Tilt lock mechanism

Clamps

Throttle-to-shaft gears

Carburetor and Magneto linkages

Swivel bracket

Motor cover latch

Every two months in fresh water
Every month in salt water

Gear Case   Every 50 hours or once a season

Fuel Tank   Grease fuel line fittings. Add fuel conditioner if tank is stored with fuel in it.

Spark Plugs   Replace annually or sooner as required.

Outboard Trouble Shooting

If an outboard — or any engine — breaks down in the field, you should know some basic techniques for elementary, on-the-spot repairs. These techniques don't replace regular maintenance, nor will they answer every problem: Some breakdowns require a trained mechanic and factory parts or service. All the same, it's surprising how often a little ingenuity will get your motor going again or how a knowledgeable investigation will discover a situation that's easily corrected.

Problem	Possible Cause/Correction
Engine won't start	Fuel tank empty
	Fuel tank vent closed (older motors)
	Fuel line improperly hooked up - check both ends
	Engine not primed
	Engine flooded — look for fuel overflow
	Clogged fuel filter or line
	Spark plug wires reversed
Starter motor won't work (electric start)	Gear shift not in neutral
	Defective starter switch - sometimes gets wet and corrodes if motor is mounted too low
	Battery dead
	Battery connections loose or dirty
Loss of power	Too much oil in fuel mix
	Fuel/air mix too lean (backfires)
	Fuel/air mix too rich
	Fuel hose kinked
	Slight blockage in fuel line or fuel filter
	Weed or other matter on propeller

Motor misfires	Spark plug damaged
	Spark plug loose
	Spark plug incorrect
Poor performance on boat	Wrong propeller
	Engine improperly tilted relative to transom. Engine should be vertical when boat is under way
	Bent propeller — usually accompanied by high level of vibration
	Improper load distribution in boat
	Heavy marine growth on boat bottom
	Cavitation

Gasoline-powered inboard engines, once the most popular in small and medium size cruising sailboats, have largely been replaced by outboards aboard smaller boats and by diesel inboards for larger auxiliaries. Still, there is a sizable number of skippers who prefer inboard gasoline engines, whether because of their familiarity or because of the unpleasant smell frequently associated with diesels — a smell that can be minimized or eliminated in a proper fuel installation, properly maintained.

Although inboard engines aren't usually seen in boats under about 25 feet overall, very small gasoline-powered engines — single-cylinder, five-hp. models — do exist. A single-cylinder inboard, whether gasoline or diesel, is often a fairly noisy and vibratory engine, and unless it is a question of a special installation, a two-cylinder outboard of the same horsepower will generally be more reliable, and a good deal lighter.

Ventilation

The installation of a gasoline engine and fuel system is of vital importance, both for safety and efficiency. The accompanying illustrations detail the ventilation arrangements approved for auxiliary engines using gasoline as a fuel — these ventilation requirements apply to fuel tanks when electrical wiring is installed in the same compartment. In most cases, a sailboat's engine and gas tank will be in essentially the same compartment, so a common set of ventilators can be used.

The minimum acceptable ventilation system to meet Coast Guard regulations calls for one intake and one exhaust ventilator for each engine/fuel compartment. A normal safe practice is that the intake vent must be so positioned that its cowl or scoop faces forward, in clear air, and that its ducting, which should be of sturdy, temperature-resistant tubing, be at least three inches in diameter, and extend downward, without kinks or obstructions.

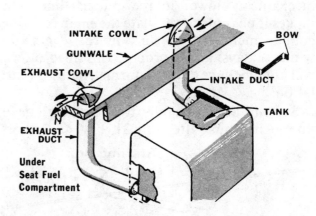

8-9 Example of Ventilation Arrangement for Small Boats Built Before July 31, 1980

The exhaust vent, with its cowl facing aft, should be of similar construction and size. Its ducting should extend to the lowest portion of the bilge, except that in boats — keel boats for the most part — fitted with bilge pumps, the ducting should not go so far down that its opening will be obstructed by normal accumulations of bilge water.

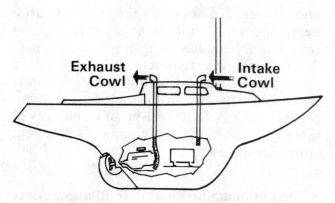

8-10 Example of Ventilation Ducts

Obviously, the ducts should be so located that vapors from the exhaust duct cannot flow back into the intake. On a sailboat, it is wise to use removable vent cowls that can be capped in rough weather. The cowls are best mounted — all other things being equal — on the cabin top, free if possible from where they will be caught by sheets or other lines. There should be no narrowing or obstruction anywhere in the system; but it is also a good idea to install, if possible, a mechanical blower in the exhaust line. This makes it possible to ventilate the engine and fuel compartment before starting the engine on windless days, and a properly-installed blower will not block the duct for normal, natural ventilation.

See end of this chapter for boats with gasoline engines built after July 31, 1980 and others.

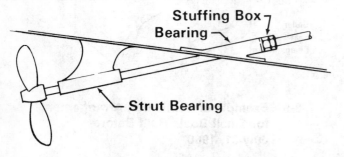

8-11 Stuffing Box

Maintenance Requirements

Other installation requirements for an inboard engine include accessible propeller shaft bearings, especially the one located where the propeller shaft goes through the hull. This bearing, called a **stuffing box,** does require oc-

casional adjustment so that the shaft can turn easily while admitting as little water as possible. The engine should be placed as close to horizontal as possible — something that is frequently overlooked. Lubrication systems within the engine may fail or operate badly if the engine is seated with its forward or aft end too high.

Propeller Location

The propeller location — forward or aft of the boat's rudder — will be an aspect of design over which the skipper has little control, once he's bought the boat. Generally speaking, a prop forward of the rudder will steer the boat somewhat more effectively. If a fixed, two-bladed propeller is used, the propeller shaft should be marked to show when the two blades are in an up-and-down position relative to the rudder. This will be the most efficient sailing position, from the viewpoint of minimizing prop drag when under sail alone. With a folding propeller, it's obviously of no consequence.

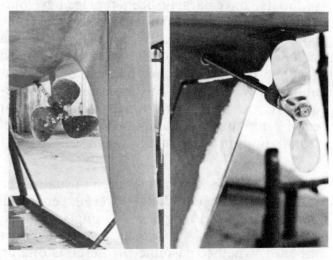

**8-12 Propeller Forward of Rudder
and Propeller Aft of Rudder**

The engine's accessibility is of course a matter of some importance. The more accessible the better, but an engine box in the middle of the cabin can be both a nuisance and a source of noise and smell. A prospective owner would be wise to insist on an inboard installation that allows access to the carburetor, fuel line and filter, oil fill and spark plugs — as a minimum.

The standard small inboard gasoline engine used in sailing craft has a number of characteristics you can count on — some good, some bad. To begin with, most small engines in the 5-50 hp. size range operate at relatively slow speeds and provide good power and reasonable economy. A 30-hp. inboard's gasoline consumption will normally equal that of a 10-hp. outboard, not even counting the cost of the oil.

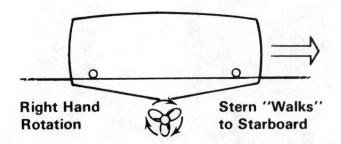

Right Hand Rotation   **Stern "Walks" to Starboard**

8-13 Propeller Rotation Effect on Stern

Nearly all inboards are installed so the propeller shaft is in line with the rudder, and most have the propeller just forward of the rudder. Nearly all small gasoline engines are right-hand-turning. A right-hand-turning propeller, as viewed from the stern looking forward, turns in a clockwise direction to move the boat forward. This means that the boat has a tendency to edge to port when moving either ahead or astern. Going forward, the clockwise-turning prop "walks" its way to starboard, pulling the stern along with it and, by extension, pushing the bow to port. With the engine in reverse, the propeller turns counter-clockwise, with the opposite effect. The stern is pulled to port as the boat backs. In many cases, this effect is very marked in reverse, and makes the boat virtually unsteerable; no matter which way the wheel or tiller is turned, the boat backs irresistibly to port.

The generating capacity of a small to medium size inboard is not unlimited, but it should suffice to run all the yacht's lights, plus radio direction finder, depth sounder and VHF-FM radiotelephone. Ideally, the boat should have two 12-volt batteries, one for starting and one for accessories, both charged by the engine's generator or alternator. The batteries should be hooked up to a master switch that allows current to be drawn from either one or both at once. Batteries should be installed as low as possible, because of their weight, yet above the level of the bilge. Batteries must be secured in their own container against the most violent heeling the boat may encounter, and they should also be protected by a cover or shield from accidental short-circuiting caused by dropping a tool across the terminals. The battery box should also be ventilated, as rapid charging builds up gas concentrations.

Inboard Trouble Shooting

A gasoline-fueled inboard engine is basically the same as an outboard, but it has some problems that are peculiar to its method of installation. The following suggestions should cover most engines, but it should be emphasized that your best guide for trouble shooting and maintenance is the owner's manual.

Problem	Cause/Solution
Starting motor will not operate	1. **Low or dead battery:** turn off all electrical equiment and wait for about 30 minutes. While waiting for the battery to recoup enough power to turn the engine over, remove and clean the battery cable connections and then re-clamp them.
	2. **Defective starter switch:** inspect connections for tightness, broken wires or bare wire touching engine. Take a test lamp (see **Tools** below) and place one lead to the ground post of the battery

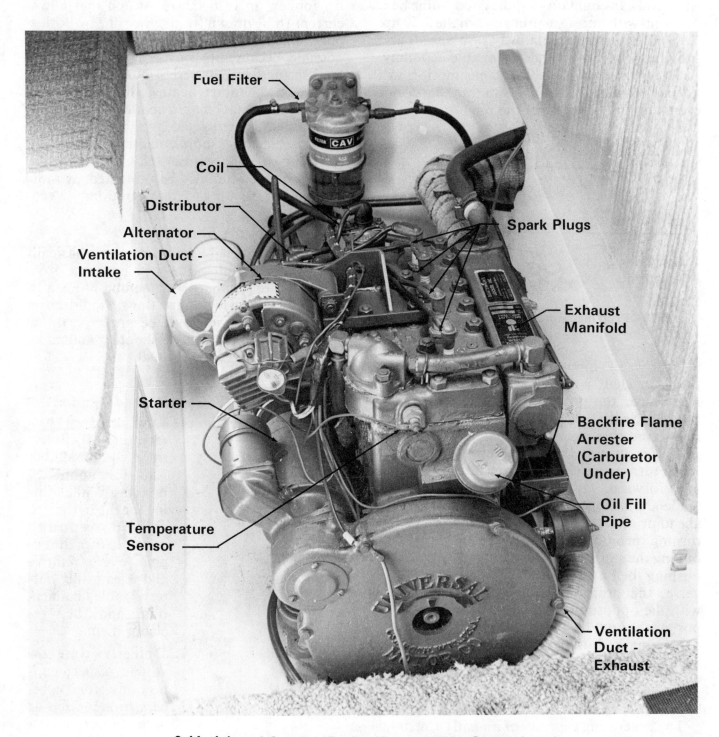

Fuel Filter

Coil

Distributor

Alternator

Ventilation Duct - Intake

Spark Plugs

Exhaust Manifold

Starter

Backfire Flame Arrester (Carburetor Under)

Oil Fill Pipe

Temperature Sensor

Ventilation Duct - Exhaust

8-14 Inboard Gasoline Engine Mounted in its Compartment

(usually the negative post, but always the one bolted to the engine frame or block) and the other lead to the primary terminal (small wire) on the distributor. When the engine is turned over, by hand or starter, the test lamp will light when the ignition switch is in the "on" position and working properly.

Starting motor works, but engine will not start

1. **Primary electrical circuit:** Look for corroded, dirty, damaged or loose connections in the wires from the junction box to the ignition switch, the wire to the coil and to the distributor.

2. **Secondary circuit:** Look for broken or damaged wires to spark plugs and from the coil to the distributor cap. Check for moisture on the wires or spark plugs that would cause the spark to be grounded.

3. **Ignition:** Check distributor points to see if they open and close as the engine is cranked. In the maximum open position, the opening should be about .02 inches — about the thickness of a matchbook cover.

Inspect the distributor cap to ensure that the contact button is in place and, if spring loaded, free to move so it can touch the rotor.

4. **Spark test:** Hold a spark plug wire about 1/4" from the engine while cranking the engine with the ignition on. (Do not hold a bare wire). The capacitor discharge ignition system utilizes an extremely high voltage which would require the use of nonconducting pliers or a testing tool which has been specifically designed for this purpose. If a spark occurs, problem is probably in the fuel system or with the plugs themselves. If there is no spark, remove the secondary wire from the distributor cap to the coil and try the spark test again. If you get a spark this time, the trouble is between the coil lead and the spark plugs — that is, the distributor cap, rotor contact, plug wires and spark plugs.

Starting motor operates, spark is good, but engine will not start

1. **Out of fuel:** Always refuel in plenty of time, preferably when tank is still one-third full. Planning a round trip

with no fuel stops, make sure the outbound leg is one-third the boat's cruising range or less.

2. **Fuel not reaching fuel pump:** Check the fuel filter or sediment bowl. If it is not filled with fuel and if the tank is full, the gas line shut-off may be closed or the line may be clogged. Disconnect the inlet side of the pump and blow through the line.

3. **Fuel not reaching carburetor:** Make sure the filter screen is clean. If there is an additional filter beside the fuel pump, check that, too. Disconnect the outlet line from the fuel pump to the carburetor, turn off ignition, and see if fuel flows out when the engine is cranked.

4. **Fuel not reaching cylinders:** Remove spark plugs and see if they are moist. If the plugs are dry, the problem may be in the carburetor. Check the main jet adjustment and open it more if possible.

5. **Choke not closing properly:** Operate manually.

6. **Engine flooded:** Open the throttle all the way; put choke in non-choke position (open); turn ignition on; crank engine several times.

More and more owners of cruising sailboats are turning to diesel power, because of its safety, its dependability and its operating economy. Although diesels are still far more expensive to buy than equivalent-horsepower gasoline engines, and although they are heavier than gas engines, diesels are now available in most boats from about 27' up. Diesel horsepower sizes are much the same as those of gasoline-powered engines, and auxiliaries in larger cruising vessels may be 60 hp. or even larger. Because diesels have a dual horsepower rating, it is sometimes a little difficult to know just what to expect from a given engine. The **maximum continuous horsepower** is what the engine will put out hour after hour, and is the figure of most interest to the consumer. **Maximum intermittent horsepower** is a higher rating but can be sustained for only brief periods of emergency speed.

Diesel installation and operation is much the same as for gasoline engines. Because one need not ventilate a diesel for safety reasons, many skippers do not provide the kind of venting they would for a gas engine. This is a mistake, as a diesel requires considerable quantities of fresh air to operate properly. A diesel's only great drawback, purchase price aside, is its smell — more correctly, the smell of its fuel. Many people find it considerably more unpleasant than gasoline, but a proper installation, good maintenance and careful fueling procedures can minimize odors. Most small diesels are left-hand-turning (counter-clockwise), so the stern will move to port — and the bow to starboard — when in forward gear. In reverse, the stern moves to starboard.

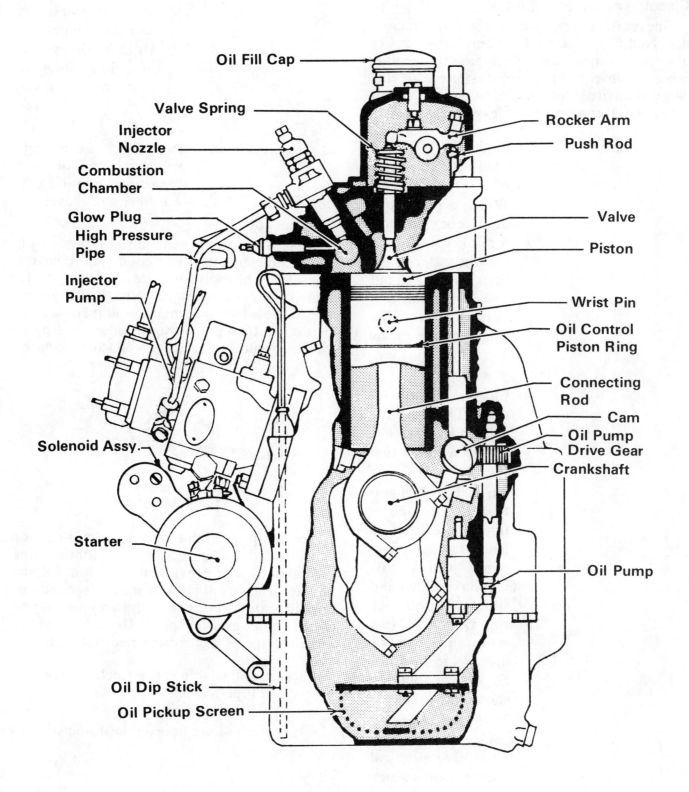

Oil Fill Cap

Valve Spring

Injector
Nozzle

Combustion
Chamber

Glow Plug
High Pressure
Pipe

Injector
Pump

Solenoid Assy.

Starter

Oil Dip Stick

Oil Pickup Screen

Rocker Arm

Push Rod

Valve

Piston

Wrist Pin

Oil Control
Piston Ring

Connecting
Rod

Cam

Oil Pump
Drive Gear

Crankshaft

Oil Pump

8-15   Cutaway of Diesel Engine

Diesel Trouble Shooting

One reason a diesel is so reliable is that it lacks the complex electrical system required to provide a timed spark to a gasoline engine. Since electricity and the dampness of the nautical environment are incompatible, a simple electrical system means fewer breakdowns.

Fuel problems

1. **Tank empty.**
2. **Shut-off valve closed.**
3. **Water in fuel:** Open drain cock in bottom of fuel filter. If there is water in the filter, drain it all out and prime the fuel system with the prime pump or by cranking the engine.
4. **Clogged or dirty filter(s):** There are usually at least two filters in a diesel fuel system.
5. **Air leak in fuel system:** Check connections in the fuel lines from tank to fuel pump. Check gaskets on fuel filter and strainer housing or cap. Disconnect fuel return line and allow fuel to flow until no air bubbles show in the fuel.
6. **Fuel not reaching engine:** Some engines have electrical fuel shut-offs which operate when the engine is shut down. A short may have closed the switch. Dis-

connect it and try to start the engine.

7. **Air in fuel lines:** Use the prime pump to build up fuel pressure and try to restart.

Electrical problems Probably associated with starter motor. See "Starting motor will not operate" above.

A Basic Tool Kit

A sailor's tools are generally associated with rigging adjustment. It is a good idea to have a separate set of tools for your boat's engine. In many cases, your owner's manual will suggest special tools for your engine, and many manufacturers offer a prepackaged set of spare parts for their engines — an extra well worth having.

8-16 Test Lamp

Test lamp: available in hardware stores or easily made by purchasing a socket for the bulbs used aboard your boat and two six-foot lengths of wire. Uncover about one inch of each end of the wires; attach one end to the lamp socket and use the other as a test prod. Use a bulb of the same voltage as your boat's electrical system.

Wrenches: Adjustable end wrench (crescent)
Pipe wrench
Box end wrench set
Pliers: Slip-joint adjustable (insulated) pliers
Vise grips
Wire cutting pliers
Needle nose pliers
Screwdrivers: Assorted regular and Phillips head
Hammer
Hacksaw
File

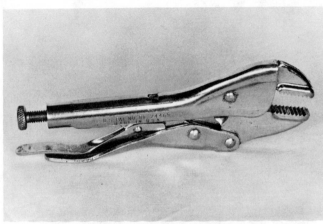

8-17 Vise Grip Pliers

Spare Parts

Points for distributor
Condenser
Coil
Spark plugs
Fan belt (and belts for all engine's
    power take-offs)
Fuel pump
Fuel filter for diesel engines
Fuel injectors for diesel engines
Waterproof tape
Hose clamps

Ventilation Systems —
Boats Built After July 31, 1980

Both (1) powered and (2) natural ventilation requirements have been in effect since July 31, 1980, for boats builts since that date. Some boat builders have been in compliance since July 31, 1978. If you are building a boat, check with the Coast Guard for details.

1. Any compartment on a boat containing a permanently installed gasoline engine with a "cranking motor" (e.g., starter) must have a power ventilation system and a label close to the ignition switch and in plain view of the operator: WARNING — GASOLINE VAPORS CAN EXPLODE. BEFORE STARTING ENGINE OPERATE BLOWER FOR 4 MINUTES AND CHECK ENGINE COMPARTMENT BILGE FOR GASOLINE VAPORS.

2. Other engine and/or fuel compartments may require natural ventilation.

All ventilation regulations, as in the past, require the operator to maintain them.

Boats with gasoline engines not under these newer regulations must comply with the requirements discussed elsewhere in this chapter.

Chapter 9

Tuning and Variant Rigs

In Chapter Four, we discussed basic rigging technique. In order to make your boat sail at peak efficiency, however, merely having the mast more or less upright isn't enough. Since most beginners' boats have rigid, or non-bendy, masts, let's look at the proper tuning of that type of rig.

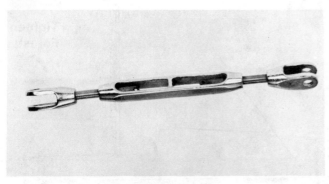

9-1   Turnbuckle

The average small sloop has between four and six lengths of wire comprising its standing rigging system. There are the fore- and backstays, the masthead, or upper, shrouds on each side, and perhaps lower shrouds. In larger craft, there are more elements to the rigging system, but the principle remains the same — every piece of standing rigging exerting tension on the mast must be balanced in some manner, usually by another piece of wire leading to the same spot on the mast. Tightening the various pieces of standing rigging to make a balanced

system is called **tuning the rig,** and of course the devices most used in exerting tension on the stays and shrouds are turnbuckles.

Setting Up Rigging

In remembering how to set up the rigging, it may be worth while bearing in mind the old adage, "the higher the wire, the tauter it is:" Masthead shrouds are set up most taut, and stays and shrouds terminating below the masthead are correspondingly slacker. The important thing, when first tensioning the fore - and backstays and the upper shrouds, is to set them up evenly, so the mast is straight as you sight upward along the mainsail luff track or groove. If you can, get off the boat and look directly over the stern, checking that the spar is straight in the boat, tilted neither to port nor starboard. Chances are the mast should angle aft a little — this is called **rake,** and the degree is usually specified in your owner's instruction. If no literature exists to tell you how many degrees aft to rake the mast, ask some skipper knowledgeable in your class to help you set the rig up the first time.

Normally, start with the lower shrouds being taut enough that there is no visible slackness. Bear in mind that the function of the lowers is to keep the bottom half of the spar from buckling when the load of a wind-filled sail pulls it to one side. When there is no side load on the mast, there should be no stress on the lowers.

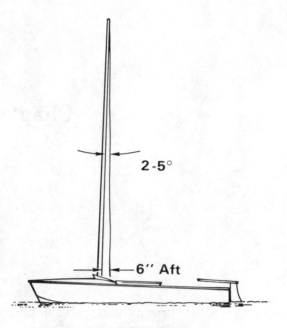

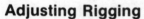

9-2 Mast Rake

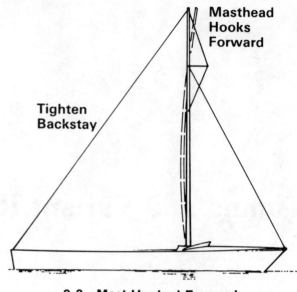

9-3 Mast Hooked Forward

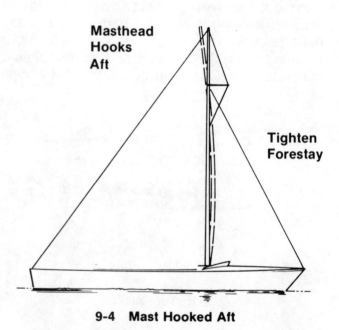

9-4 Mast Hooked Aft

Adjusting Rigging

Now raise the sails, cast off and sail out to some area where there isn't any disturbing traffic. Both main and jib luffs should be taut enough so there is no sign of scalloping. Put the boat on a close-hauled course on either tack and check the mast (it may be necessary to do this from another boat the first time): Should the spar be straight as you sight upward, everything is fine. However, it's more likely that one of the following problems will exist.

1. Mast hooks forward. The forestay is too taut or — more likely — the backstay is not taut enough.

2. The mast hooks aft. The forestay is too slack or the backstay too taut.

3. The mast hooks to windward. The windward side upper shroud is too taut or the windward lower is too loose.

4. The mast hooks to leeward. The windward upper is too slack or the windward lower is too taut.

When adjusting turnbuckles, do so a little at a time. The forces created by the turnbuckle can be considerable. Remember to turn the center section of the turnbuckle, holding the upper part to keep it from turning as well. There should always be as much turnbuckle screw showing above the center section as below it.

Once the mast is straight on the original tack, come about to a close-hauled heading on the opposite tack, and repeat the adjustment. Do

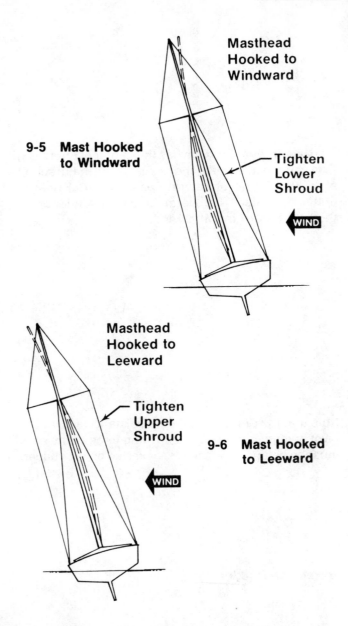

9-5 Mast Hooked to Windward

Masthead Hooked to Windward

Tighten Lower Shroud

WIND

Masthead Hooked to Leeward

Tighten Upper Shroud

9-6 Mast Hooked to Leeward

WIND

on which sails, clothing or skin might snag. A roll of waterproof tape — sold in any marine supply store — should be a part of your ditty bag (See Chapter 11).

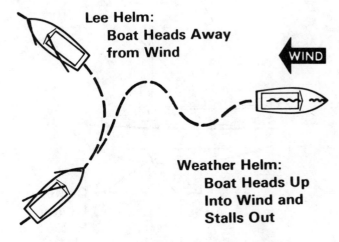

Lee Helm: Boat Heads Away from Wind

WIND

Weather Helm: Boat Heads Up Into Wind and Stalls Out

9-7 Lee Helm vs Weather Helm

Lee and Weather Helm

The average, modern small sailboat is remarkably well balanced, compared to boats of equivalent size from previous periods. Even so, certain adjustments may be required to create the optimum balance of which the boat is capable.

What we mean, when we talk about balance in reference to a sailboat, is the boat's ability — or lack of it — to sail a straight course without pressure on the tiller. A perfectly balanced boat would sail straight with no hand on the tiller when the sails were properly set for the direction and force of the apparent wind. Obviously, waves and weight distribution in the boat can upset the most neutral balance. Not so obviously, totally neutral balance is not normally considered an asset in a boat.

For most skippers, a perfectly balanced helm feels dead and unresponsive. Since most helmspeople sit on the up or windward side of the boat, a degree of imbalance that causes the tiller to pull against them is most comfortable. If you doubt this, try it yourself: sit first on the low

this until the spar is vertical on either close-hauled tack as well as at rest. You should begin each day's sail by checking the straightness of the mast. Although the stretch of stainless steel shrouds and stays is negligible, the wire has a certain amount of slack in its construction and will loosen a bit, especially early in the sailing season.

When the standing rigging is adjusted to your satisfaction, pin the turnbuckles with cotter pins or rings, to keep them from backing off. Be sure to bend the sharp ends into the turnbuckle to avoid protruding snags. After you've done so, tape over any remaining sharp edges or points

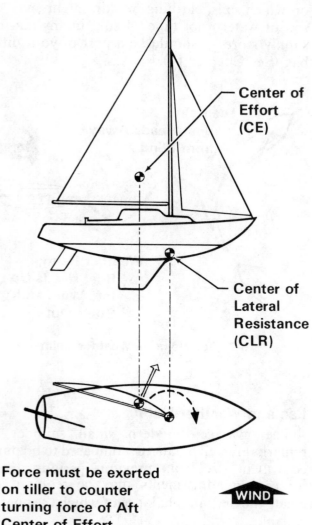

Center of
Effort
(CE)

Center of
Lateral
Resistance
(CLR)

A boat with weather helm has the Center of Effort (CE) (The combined effort of the headsail and main) acting aft of the Center of Lateral Resistance (CLR) of the hull underwater. The overall effect is a tendency for the boat to turn into the wind.

Note that the Center of Lateral Resistance acts as the pivot point about which the turning force of the sails must be balanced by the force exerted on the rudder.

**Force must be exerted
on tiller to counter
turning force of Aft
Center of Effort**

WIND

9-8   Effect of Weather Helm on Rudder

side and try pushing against the average tiller; then switch. Unless you are quite unusual, you'll find the slight pull of a normal helm gives you a better feel of how the boat is progressing through the water.

If you let go of the tiller in an average boat, she will round up into the wind more or less quickly — a centerboard boat will often spin right up, while a long-keeled vessel may take 10 seconds or so. Turning to windward — or to **weather**, to use the old term — when the tiller is released is the mark of a boat with **weather helm**. A slight amount of weather helm is not

only advantageous for steering, it is also a safety factor, as the boat will head up into irons and stall out if an emergency causes the skipper to let go of the tiller.

Some boats have weather helm all the time, and some have it only under certain conditions, as we shall see later. Other boats have the opposite condition, the tendency to head away from the wind when the tiller is released, and this is called **lee helm**. Lee helm is generally considered a negative attribute in a boat, as it makes for tiring steering and is a potential danger. When the tiller is released, a boat with lee helm will head off the wind and into a jibe.

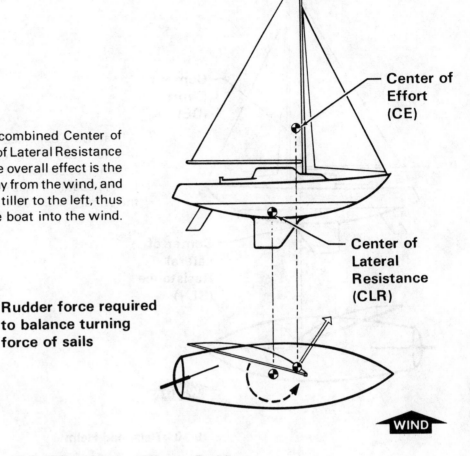

A boat with Lee Helm has the combined Center of Effort (CF) forward of the Center of Lateral Resistance (CLR) of the underwater hull. The overall effect is the tendency for the boat to turn away from the wind, and must be corrected by moving the tiller to the left, thus creating a force which turns the boat into the wind.

Center of Effort (CE)

Center of Lateral Resistance (CLR)

Rudder force required to balance turning force of sails

WIND

9-9 Effect of Lee Helm on Rudder

Correction of Weather Helm

Causes of excess weather helm may be temporary or permanent. If your boat's tiller requires uncomfortable amounts of pull under way, or if your rudder is at an angle to the transom greater than about five degrees, your craft probably has too much weather helm.

Temporary causes of weather helm may be any one of the following:

1. Jib too small or mainsail too large for conditions.

2. Jib not trimmed enough or main trimmed in too much.

3. Mast raked too far aft.

4. Centerboard too far down and forward.

5. Too much weight forward in the boat.

6. Boat heeled too much.

The cures for the causes of temporary weather helm are, of course, implicit in the problems themselves. If none of the foregoing remedies works, then the weather helm may stem from something more basic to the boat. Causes of permanent weather helm include:

1. The foretriangle is too small. (The foretriangle is the area contained within the forestay, the mast and the deck).

2. The mainsail is too large.

3. The mast is stepped too far forward.

4. The centerboard drops too far down.

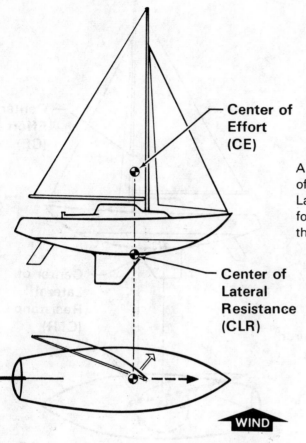

Center of Effort (CE)

Center of Lateral Resistance (CLR)

A boat with a balanced helm has the combined Center of Effort (CE) acting close enough to the Center of Lateral Resistance (CLR) that there is little tendency for the boat to either head up into the wind or fall off the wind.

WIND

9-10 Balanced Helm

It may or may not be worth trying to fix these problems. In most small boats, 2 and 4 can be remedied, while 1 or 3 might be a good reason to sell the boat.

Correction For Lee Helm

Lee helm, too, is either permanent or temporary. Temporary causes tend, reasonably enough, to be the opposites of what creates weather helm:

1. Jib too large or main too small for conditions.

2. Jib overtrimmed or main not trimmed enough.

3. Mast raked too far forward.

4. Centerboard not dropped enough.

5. Too much weight aft.

Permanent lee helm problems are again the opposites of conditions causing permanent weather helm:

1. Mainsail too small or jib too large.

2. Mast stepped too far aft.

3. Centerboard too small.

Mainsail Trim

Trim, or shape adjustment, of the mainsail under way is accomplished by tension on the three corners of the sail or by bending the mast. Let's look at how and why the main is trimmed in this way. The basic adjustment comes from the halyard, which regulates luff tension and — if the main boom is on a sliding gooseneck — sail height off the deck. Sailing close-hauled, the mainsail luff is normally quite taut, but as the

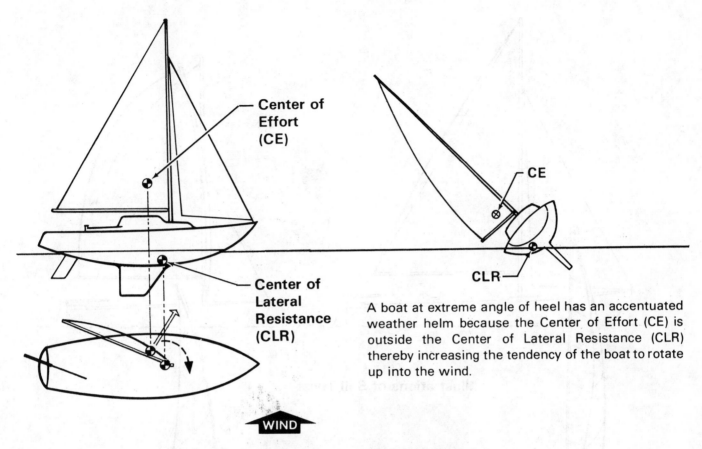

Center of
Effort
(CE)

Center of
Lateral
Resistance
(CLR)

CE

CLR

A boat at extreme angle of heel has an accentuated weather helm because the Center of Effort (CE) is outside the Center of Lateral Resistance (CLR) thereby increasing the tendency of the boat to rotate up into the wind.

WIND

9-11   Effects of Extreme Angle of Heel

boat comes onto a reach and then a run, the sail is more effective if it's fuller or more rounded. Easing the halyard is one way of gaining fullness.

To flatten the sail again, or to lower it on the mast, in case of strong winds, the downhaul under the gooseneck is used. To get really hard tension along the luff, the main is frequently raised as high as it will go with the halyard, after which tension is applied to the gooseneck downhaul. On mains without a sliding gooseneck, the same effect can be obtained with a **Cunningham** — a grommeted hole in the mainsail luff slightly above the foot. A hook in the Cunningham is pulled downward to exert stress on the luff and flatten the sail.

The third adjustment point is the outhaul. Normally taut, the sail's foot is slackened when sailing off the wind by easing the outhaul. This

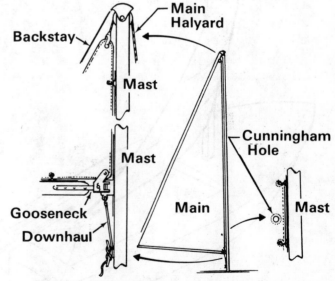

Backstay

Main
Halyard

Mast

Mast

Gooseneck
Downhaul

Main

Cunningham
Hole

Mast

9-12   Points of Mainsail Adjustments

and easing the halyard cause the main to bag somewhat, creating a more efficient downwind shape.

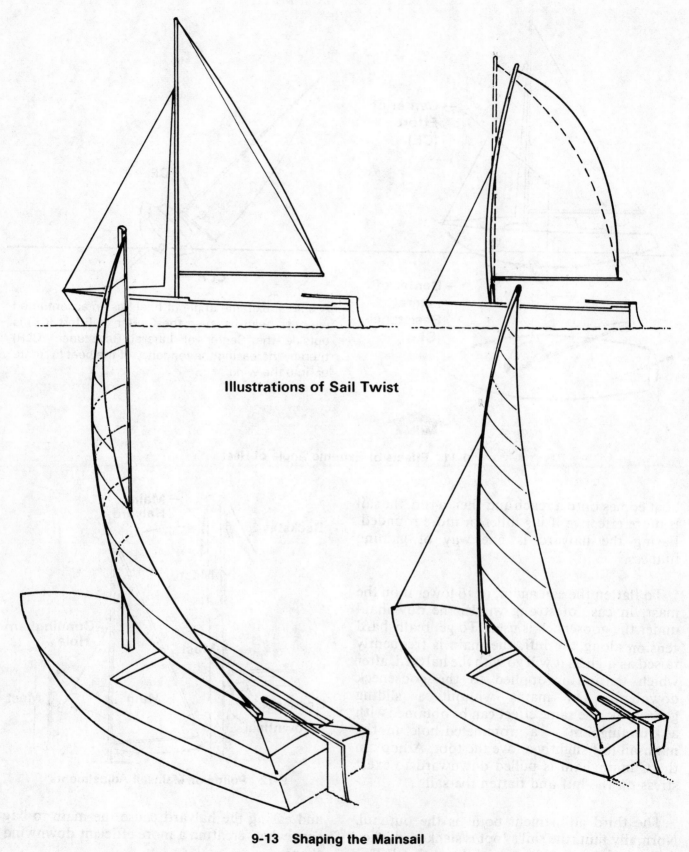

Illustrations of Sail Twist

9-13 Shaping the Mainsail

Adjusting Backstay

On some boats, the backstay tension can also be regulated underway, either by a sophisticated hydraulic tensioner or by something as simple as putting a wrench to the backstay turnbuckle. Tightening the backstay, especially on a boat whose forestay runs only partway up the mast, puts a bow in the spar, flattening the mainsail for upwind sailing. Off the wind, the backstay is eased, the mast straightens, and the main becomes fuller. It's worth mentioning that a sail and spar must be properly designed for bending and flattening in this manner: Trying to bow a rigid spar will just damage it.

Boom Vang

Off the wind, a boom vang — a tackle from the boom down to deck or gunwale — is used to hold the boom down and increase sail area, and rigged to prevent (hence the term **preventer**) an

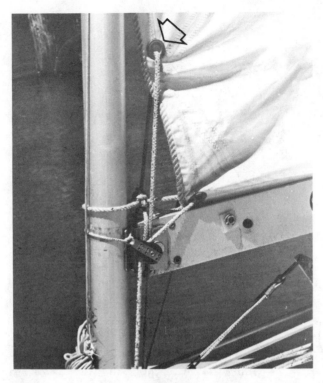

9-14   Cunningham Rig

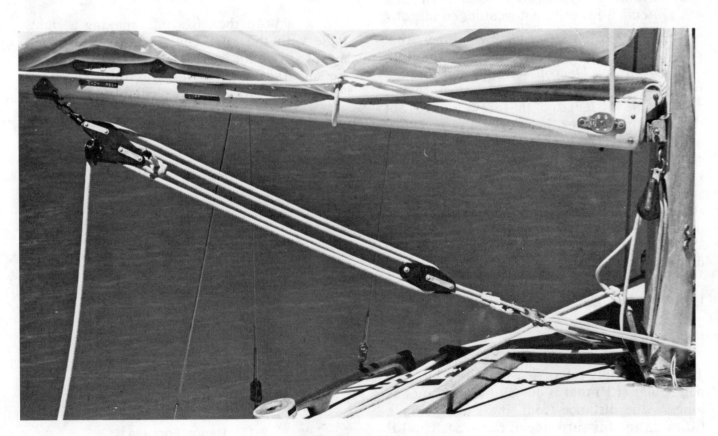

9-15   Boom Vang

accidental jibe when running directly before the wind. Some boats have permanent vangs rigged from the underside of the boom to a point at the base of the mast. A four or five part tackle can exert tremendous force on a boom, so it's a good idea to go easy with the vang, using just enough pressure to bring the boom down parallel to the water.

One disadvantage of a vang set to the gunwale is that it must be cast off with each jibe and attached to the other gunwale. An accidental jibe using this type of vang would possibly result in a damaged or bent boom.

Light-Weather Sails

In addition to the average sloop's working sails — her mainsail and jib — she may have any number of light-weather sails. The most common of these is perhaps the **Genoa jib.** By definition, a Genoa is simply a jib that overlaps the mast. Genoas come in all sizes and shapes and in many cloth weights. An offshore racer may have as many as half a dozen such sails, each intended for different weather conditions.

Genoas are often described by numbers that refer to their size and to the weight of the cloth — nearly always Dacron — from which they are made. A #1 Genoa is the largest, with a luff running the full length of the forestay and a foot that greatly overlaps the mast and extends just about back to the cockpit. A #2 Genoa is only slightly smaller, but is made from perceptibly heavier cloth. It's hoisted when the wind is strong enough possibly to stretch the #1 out of shape. A #3 is smaller and heavier still, and the numbers usually run as far as #5, which is rather short on the luff but which still has the considerable overlap characteristic of Genoas.

Luff Perpendicular (LP)

A Genoa is also sometimes described by its **luff perpendicular,** a term derived from racing. Thus, we may hear a sail called "a 150% Genoa." This term simply refers to a sail with a luff perpendicular (LP) that is one-and-a-half times as long as the distance from the boat's jib tack fitting to the forward side of the mast. The **LP** measurement itself is the straight line from the

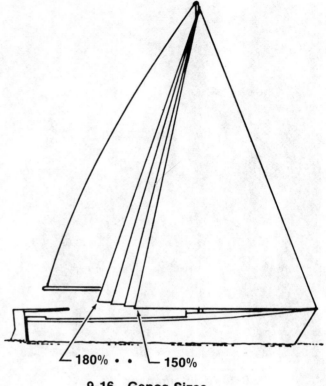

9-16   Genoa Sizes

Genoa clew to the sail's luff, making a right angle with the luff. The standard #1 Genoa, because of handicap rules, is a 150%, but there are sails that come as large as 180% (or even larger — the only limit is the length of the boat).

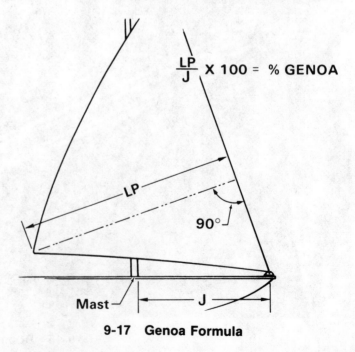

$$\frac{LP}{J} \times 100 = \% \text{ GENOA}$$

9-17   Genoa Formula

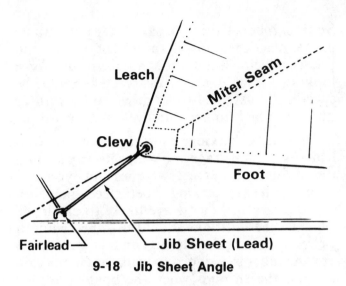

Leach

Miter Seam

Clew

Foot

Fairlead

Jib Sheet (Lead)

9-18 Jib Sheet Angle

A Genoa's sheets usually lead to a block which is mounted on a sliding car. The car rides in a track running fore and aft on the deck or gunwale. This arrangement allows a proper lead for nearly any size of Genoa, simply by moving the car forward or back along the track. The same sheeting rules apply to a Genoa as to a working jib. When you hoist the sail, pull the clew aft and take a line extended slightly downward from the sail's miter seam for your initial Genoa sheet lead. Set the block at the corresponding position on the track. Now sail the boat close-hauled and observe the Genoa's foot and leech. If the foot appears loose while the leech is stressed, it means the sheeting point is too far forward. If the leech is loose and the foot taut, the Genoa sheet block should be moved forward. When the leech and foot appear equally tensioned, luff the boat slowly up into the wind. The Genoa should begin to ripple all along its luff, and if it does, your sheet lead is correct. If the ripple appears first at the head of the sail, then the leech is still a bit too loose, and vice versa if the sail luffs first toward its foot.

The sheet block on the opposite track should be set to match the first one. This will usually be the correct setting, but some slight adjustment may be required. This just means that your boat is imperceptibly out of shape, or the two tracks do not quite match, and is nothing to worry about. In many cases, the Genoa sheet is led from the sail's clew through the block to a winch

mounted on the cockpit coaming. This mechanical aid is required because of the amount of pull a Genoa can create. If your Genoa has a very long foot, or if the winch is mounted well forward in the cockpit, you may be faced with a

9-19 Jib Sheet Block

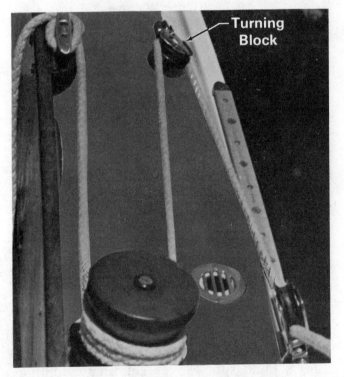

Turning Block

9-20 Genoa Turning Block

sheet that leads rather abruptly upward from the sheet block to the winch. In this case, you will need a **turning block** at the aft end of the track, so the sheet comes to the winch at the flattest possible angle. The turning block must be extra strong, as it will be taking stresses nearly twice those on the sheet block. If you doubt this fact, ask any high school physics student.

For maximum efficiency, many Genoas are cut to be so-called **deck sweepers:** The sail's foot

9-21 Genoa Window

9-22 Window in Main

Some skippers have their sailmaker put a transparent plastic window in the foot of the sail, and this is a help. But there's no substitute for a lookout, and one of the crew should be specifically assigned to sit down to leeward or up by the tack to keep an eye out forward.

Tacking with a Genoa sometimes offers problems, as the sail drags and whips its way around the shrouds. After a few times out, you will know from exasperating experience which deck or rigging attachments are likely to catch the Genoa. These fittings should be taped smooth or relocated if possible. In some large boats, a crewmember is assigned to walk the Genoa clew around the shrouds when the boat tacks, but hopefully you won't require this.

There are three variants of the Genoa worth knowing about. These sails exist for special conditions which are fairly common in many parts of the United States, but which may or may not exist where you are.

9-23 Lapper

is in contact with the deck for nearly its whole length. When close-hauled, this kind of sail can cause a blind spot for the helmsman running from dead ahead to amidships on either side.

Lapper: The cross between a working jib and a Genoa. Its luff runs nearly the length of the forestay, but its foot only just overlaps the mast, hence the name.

9-24 Reacher

9-25 Drifter

Reacher: As big in area as a Genoa, but of lighter fabric, the reacher is usually a 180% LP sail with a very high foot. As the name suggests, it is used for reaching and is normally sheeted right aft to the transom or sometimes to a block at the end of the main boom.

Drifter: For very light airs, when most non-racers will turn on their auxiliary engines. The drifter is cut like a big Genoa, but is made of very light nylon. It often has no snap hooks along the luff, being made fast only at head, tack and clew.

The Spinnaker

The light-air sail called the spinnaker is the queen of the racing sails. Shaped like a triangle with two convex sides, the spinnaker is often cut from brightly-colored nylon in individualistic patterns. It is a sail that's often maddening to set, fly or lower, but no serious racing boat would be without one, if the sail plan and class rules allow it.

9-26 Radial Head Spinnaker

Although there are a number of different ways to arrange the cloths of a spinnaker, for the purposes of this book just a few are shown. The sail with cloths parallel and horizontal across the bottom half of the sail, and an arrangement of triangular cloths at the top, is called a **radial head.** It's commonly used for broad reaching and running. The spinnaker that appears to have a three-pointed star superimposed on it is a **starcut.** Relatively flatter and smaller than a radial head, the starcut is used downwind in heavy weather or for beam and close reaching in normal conditions.

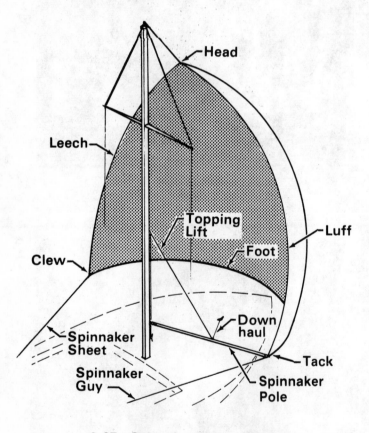

9-27 Spinnaker Nomenclature

The spinnaker's nomenclature employs the same words that are used to describe any triangular sail, but the terms are defined differently. The lower edge of the sail is the foot, and the two sides are the leeches — until the sail is set, as we shall see. Likewise, the two lower corners are the clews and the upper corner is the head.

Unlike the sails we have been talking about so far, a spinnaker is set **flying** — that is, it's connected to the boat by its halyard and the lines from its clews, not along any one of its edges. A spinnaker, also known as a **chute** (like parachute), is made of ultra-light nylon with reinforcing patches and grommets at the corners. The head grommet often has a swivel attached to it.

Once the sail is raised, it assumes a position in front of the mainsail. The chute rides outside all shrouds and stays — an important point to remember. The sail's windward side becomes its **luff** and the lower corner on that side is now called the **tack.** The windward side is extended by a **spinnaker pole,** which fits to the sail's tack grommet or to the **spinnaker guy,** the controlling line on the pole side of the sail. (The other line is called the **spinnaker sheet.**)

Sheet and guy run back to blocks which may be located either at the quarters or — in very beamy boats — along the Genoa track and thence to sheet winches. These are either the same winches that control the genoa sheets or, on racers, a separate pair. The Genoa is seldom carried along with the spinnaker. The spinnaker pole is held at its inboard end to a track running partway up the forward side of the mast (or, in small boats, to a simple eye on the mast). The pole is usually double-ended, with identical spring-loaded jaws at each end and eye fittings for the line that suspends the pole — the **spinnaker pole topping lift,** to give it its full name — and the line that holds down its outer end is called the **spinnaker pole downhaul.**

The pole topping lift runs to a halyard block about halfway up the mast and then down to a cleat on the mast itself, while the downhaul runs forward to a turning block on the foredeck and back to the mast. Thus, the pole's height and attitude relative to the water can be adjusted from the middle of the boat. With its five attendant lines — halyard, sheet, guy, lift and downhaul — the spinnaker adds considerable complexity to any boat.

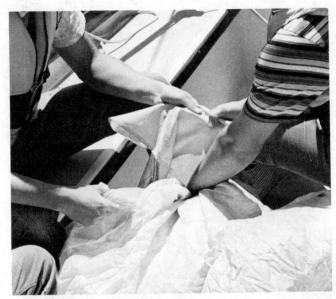

9-28   Packing the "Chute" (Spinnaker)

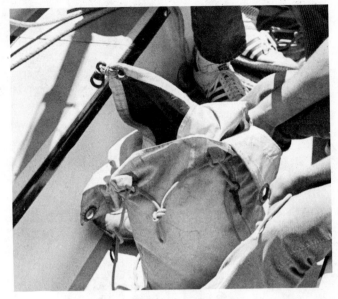

9-29   Spinnaker Bagged

Setting A Spinnaker

To set a spinnaker, pick first a day with light but steady winds and an area with little or no traffic. It's a good idea to have an experienced sailor along, and a minimum crew of three is usually necessary until you become experienced. First, the sail is arranged to be set from its bag, or from a bag-like container called a turtle. Spread the spinnaker out on a smooth clean surface, such as a dry lawn. Gather one edge in scalloped handfuls until the head and one clew grommet are together. Now do the same with the other two edges. Carefully stuff the ungathered middle of the sail into the bag, then insert the bunched edges on top, so the three corner fittings of the sail are showing at the top of the sail bag.

On the boat, take the spinnaker bag forward and make it fast to the deck by the strap across its bottom. Underway on a broad reach, the sail bag should be located well toward the bow on the lee side of the foredeck, just under the foot of the jib (which is now set).

Run the spinnaker sheet and guy forward to the bag from their turning blocks. Make sure that sheet and guy are outside all shrouds, stays and lifelines. **This is crucial.** Now attach the sheet and guy snap shackles to the clew fittings on the spinnaker.

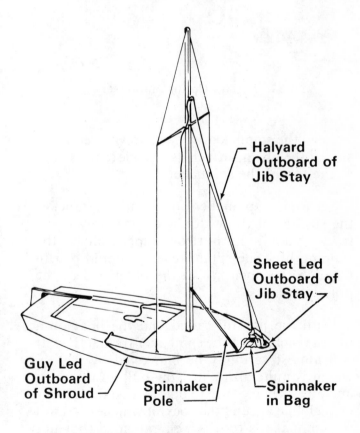

Halyard Outboard of Jib Stay

Sheet Led Outboard of Jib Stay

Guy Led Outboard of Shroud

Spinnaker Pole

Spinnaker in Bag

Note: Main Boom and Mainsail eliminated for clarity

9-30   Spinnaker Rigging

9-31 **Setting Up for Spinnaker**

9-32 **Hoisting Spinnaker**

Lead the spinnaker halyard down over the lee side of the jib and attach its shackle to the swivel at the top of the spinnaker.

Set up the spinnaker pole so it is parallel to the surface of the water, about halfway up its track, held in its horizontal position by the topping lift. The spinnaker guy should be run through the open jaw at the outer end of the pole.

With the jib still raised and the boat on a broad reach, hoist the spinnaker from its bag. It will almost certainly be blanketed by the jib, which is quite all right. Now pull on the sheet and guy — being sure to take at least three turns of each line around the cockpit winches — until the spinnaker's foot is well extended (but not stretched). The chute may now fill by itself, but drop the jib in any case. Adjust the spinnaker pole topping lift and downhaul to bring the spinnaker pole parallel to water. If the spinnaker is not filling properly at this point, make further adjustments with the spinnaker sheet,

easing or trimming it to keep the chute full.

There is perhaps no sailing as exhilarating as moving well under a good spinnaker, but on gusty days, the big sail can take charge and drive the boat out of control. Until you are well used to the chute, leave it in its bag on days when reefing is a consideration. If a sudden gust does overtake you with the spinnaker up, simply let the sheet run until the spinnaker will no longer hold air. As a vital safety point, never put figure eight stopper knots (see Chapter 7) at the end of a spinnaker sheet, guy or halyard: The sail should always be capable of being fully released if necessary.

As the boat is headed further up into the wind, the spinnaker pole must be trimmed further forward and the sheet further aft. With most spinnakers, the sail cannot be carried when the apparent wind is forward of the beam, but some starcuts can be effective on a very close reach. A Genoa is both easier and safer, however, and is often just as effective or even more so.

A moment's thought will tell you that it's impossible to tack with spinnaker up. You can, however, jibe the boat. It is easier than it looks.

With the boat on a dead run, detach the spinnaker pole at its inner end from the mast and reattach it to the spinnaker sheet.

9-34 Shifting Spinnaker Pole

9-33 Jibing With Spinnaker

Now detach the pole from the spinnaker guy and snap it to the mast fitting. Adjust the pole downhaul to bring spinnaker pole parallel to water. As all this is taking place, jibe the mainsail. And there you are. Just remember that after the jibe, the sail's nomenclature changes: The line to which the pole end fitting is snapped is now the guy, the other line has become the sheet, and the respective corners of the spinnaker are the tack and the clew.

9-35 Jibe Complete - Pole Needs Adjustment

9-36 Dropping Spinnaker

Variant Rigs

Although most small boats are sloops or cat-rigged craft, you'll see a number of vessels with slightly different rigs. The sloop or single-sail rig is probably best for the beginner, but it's interesting to understand what makes other types of boats go and why variant rigs exist.

The most common two-masted yachts are **ketches** and **yawls**. The classic definition of each is:

9-37 Ketch

Dropping the spinnaker should be easy, as long as you don't allow the lines to become fouled. The halyard especially should always be carefully coiled (see Chapter 7) once the sail is raised. Head the boat off on a broad reach, raise the jib, and the spinnaker should collapse behind it. Reach under the foot of the jib until you can grab the spinnaker clew and pull the sail into the boat, while slacking off the halyard.

If the chute doesn't die when the jib is raised, simply change headings a bit until it does. Try to keep the spinnaker from falling in the water and beware of any sharp-pointed or edged fittings that might tear this very delicate sail. Take it below and bag it immediately.

Ketch: A two-masted sailing vessel in which the forward mast, called the **mainmast**, is the larger, and the after mast, the **mizzen**, is stepped forward of the rudder post.

Yawl

A yawl, on the other hand, is really a sloop with a small balancing sail well aft. Many yawls race — and the yawl is essentially a racing rig — with or without the mizzen. Off the wind, both ketch and yawl can set a **mizzen staysail,** a large, light-air sail that is set flying from the mizzen masthead and sheeted to the end of the mizzen boom. The staysail's tack is on deck, more or less amidships at the foot of the mainmast — thus it's a sail that's often as large as the mainsail, and far easier to control than a spinnaker, as it is entirely within the boat.

The mizzen sail itself is often dropped when the staysail is up, and it is little or no use when close-hauled in any case. When running, a ketch's mizzen will often blanket the mainsail, unless it can be set on the opposite side of the boat.

9-38 Yawl

Yawl: A two-masted sailing boat with a large mainmast and a small mizzen aft of it. The mizzen mast of a yawl is stepped aft of the rudder post.

While these definitions are accurate as far as they go, they are not terribly helpful in identifying a ketch from a yawl at a distance, or in suggesting why these are really two quite different types of boats.

Ketch

A true ketch is a genuine two-masted boat in which the sail area of the jib and the mizzen combined are approximately equal to the area of the mainsail; in modern ketches, the jib is usually somewhat larger than the mizzen. The rig came about because, beyond a certain point, a sail becomes too big for one person to handle, even with mechanical aids like winches. Dividing the sail area makes for less aerodynamic efficiency but easier handling, which is why a ketch is usually a cruising boat, and is seldom seen in lengths under about 30 feet.

9-39 Cutter

Cutter

Also seen from time to time is the single-masted **cutter,** whose spar is stepped anywhere from 40% to 50% of the deck length back from the bow. A cutter normally sets three sails — the main, which is smaller than on a sloop of comparable size; the **forestaysail (staysail** for short), which is often self-tending and set on a staysail boom; and outside and forward of it, the jib, which is often a high-cut sail set on a **tack pendant,** a length of wire running from the jib tack to the deck.

A cutter has several advantages over a sloop: In stormy weather, the jib can be dropped or roller-furled (see Chapter 5) and the boat sailed with main and staysail. To tack this abbreviated rig, one simply puts the tiller over — each of the two boomed sails is self-tending. In light weather, the cutter can drop its staysail and set from the jibstay a truly immense drifter or reaching jib. Disadvantages of the cutter are extra cost and more things to break or go awry.

Schooner

The schooner is a rig associated with America, although it did not originate on this side of the Atlantic. Most schooners today — the few remaining — are two-masted vessels of some size with the mainmast aft and the smaller foremast forward. A three-masted schooner's masts are the fore, main and mizzen. The schooner is a complex and inefficient rig except off the wind, and having its largest sail aft, the mainmast usually winds up blocking the cabin. Its proponents argue that a schooner is the fastest of the rigs on a reach, which may or may not be true, and is easy to handle short-handed.

Most schooners are gaff-rigged on the main and foremasts, though some have marconi mainsails and gaff foresails, and there are other arrangements possible. Off the wind, a schooner may set a big **fisherman staysail** in the space between fore and main. No matter how inefficient she may be compared to a modern sloop, a schooner driving along on a reach is a splendid sight.

9-40 Schooner

Chapter 10

Trailer Sailing

The average small sailing cruiser meanders along at about four knots. Ten hours of sailing, given a decent wind, and you're 40 miles from where you started. Or look at the price of marina accommodation for a small sailboat — even assuming the berths are available. By fitting your boat with a trailer, you can start your sailing vacation 500 miles from your usual cruising grounds, visit places you'd normally never see, avoid the costs and hazards of marinas — and, at the season's end, store the boat alongside your home, where you can work on her through the winter months, as the weather allows.

Trailer sailing has become increasingly popular in recent years. Its techniques are firmly based on those developed by outboard skippers, and much of the equipment was devised for owners of 16- to 20-foot power skiffs with one or two big motors clamped to the transom. The skills that serve them are largely adaptable to sailboats, but they must be revised for quite different kinds of boats.

The Trailerable Boat

The first requirement is a suitable boat, with one of the few absolute limiting factors being width. For trailering without a special permit, the maximum width of the rig is eight feet. Most manufacturers and designers will go out of their

10-1 Trailerable Keel - Centerboard Hull

way, when a design's natural beam is approximately eight feet, to make sure that it falls within the trailerable limit. Although boats over 30 feet have been built with an eight-foot beam, the maximum length of most trailerable sailboats is under 25 feet. Most centerboard daysailers are easily trailerable.

It's obvious that hull shape is also a major factor. The ideal hull from a trailering point of view is flat-bottomed or gently rounded, with no protrusions, and this kind of hull is virtually required if you're going to launch at a municipal ramp or off a beach. Even the vestigial keel of a standard cruising centerboarder can pose considerable problems when selecting a trailer. The rollers on the trailer are often designed for the much flatter conformation of an outboard hull, and it may not be possible to adjust them high enough to support your boat properly. If in doubt, get in touch with the dealer who handles your boat, and if he doesn't know, have him ask the manufacturer. Chances are that a standard brand of trailer was in the designer's mind when he drew the plans for the boat. All else failing, it's possible to replace the rollers of a standard trailer with bunks or bolsters, which may be as simple as segments of 1″ x 6″ or 1″ x 8″ padded with carpeting. It makes launching more difficult, but it will work.

The Trailer

Width and length aside, highway requirements for a trailer to be towed at high speeds are fairly serious. These requirements fall into two general categories — what's legally necessary, and what is derived from common sense. Legal requirements are still changing rapidly in many areas, as more and more states turn their attention to the dangers inherent in trailering. Consult your state police and your motor vehicle bureau for up-to-the-minute information.

Your trailer will probably require license plates and lights. If possible, get a rear light and license plate set that's demountable, so you can remove them before backing the trailer into the water. Lights like this normally clamp to the boat's transom. No lighting system made can resist repeated immersion, despite what a manufacturer may claim. You'll also require turn indicator lights and, if your rig nears the eight-foot maximum, side lights as well. Pay special attention to the electrical plug and socket arrangement connecting the car's light system to the trailer. The wiring should be under no stress, should be as weatherproof as possible, and should not sag or loop so it can get caught in machinery or drag along the ground.

Brake requirements vary greatly from state to state, but the American Boat & Yacht Council recommends that trailer manufacturers offer brakes of some sort for all wheels of trailers designed for a gross weight of 1,500 lb. or more.

10-2 Typical Electrical Connector

Legal requirements can be met in many areas by any one of the three common brake systems — **electrical, hydraulic** or **surge.** The first two are integrated into the tow vehicle's own system, and are accepted anywhere. The surge brake, which is activated by the trailer's own momentum and which is not under the driver's control, is outlawed in an increasing number of states. Your trailer's brakes should operate automatically when the towing car's service brakes are applied, and should continue to operate even if the trailer separates from the tow car.

Towing Hitches

Like brakes, towing hitch attachments come in three common types. In ascending order of capacity, they are the **bumper hitch,** which fastens directly to the tow vehicle's bumper and which is illegal in many states; the **frame hitch,** which bolts to at least two of the towing vehicle's structural members — frame or unitized body/bumper; and the **weight distributing hitch,** a complicated mechanical device that uses leverage on both car and trailer to distribute the load evenly and keep the towing vehicle even with the ground. A frame hitch can be used for gross trailed weights — trailer and load — up to 3,500 lb. or so, beyond which a weight distributing hitch is virtually mandatory.

The key point in the hitch itself is the ball and socket connector between the towing vehicle and the trailer, respectively. For some reason, there are two sizes of towing balls — 2″ diameter and 1 7/8″ — and they are not interchangeable. They are also close enough in size so that you can't expect to eyeball the difference. Too large

10-3   Tongue in Position to Engage Ball

10-4   Locking Ball in Cup

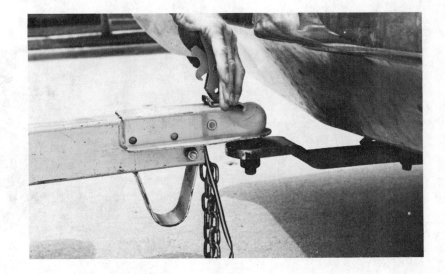

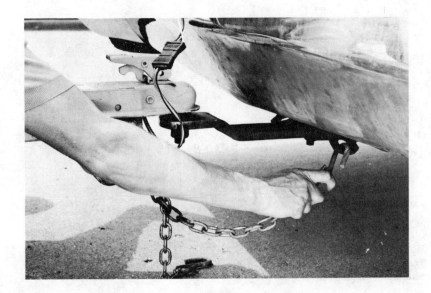

10-5   Attaching Safety Chain

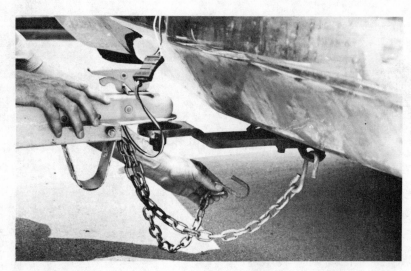

10-6   Crossing Second Chain Under First

10-7   Hookup Complete

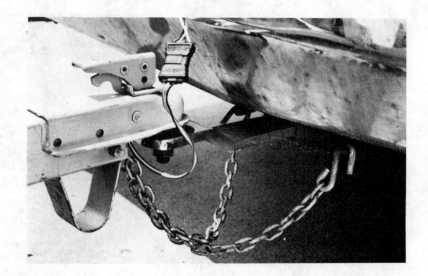

10-8   The Winch

10-9 Outboard Chained to Transom and Drain Plug in Place

a ball won't fit the socket; too small a ball can spring free from the socket's automatic clamp. The American Boat & Yacht Council recommends use of the 1 7/8" ball for gross loads up to 2,000 lb., and the larger ball for heavier weights. Among your trailer-gear spares, you should carry an extra ball, in case wear or turning stresses force yours out of roundness. Like all trailer bolt fittings, the ball should be secured by a lock nut.

Safety Chains

The final legal requirement in most states is safety chains. These consist simply of a pair of chains ending in S-hooks and running from the tongue of the trailer to the towing hitch. The chains are crossed under the hitch in such a way that if the ball and socket fail, the trailer tongue won't hit the ground, dig in and cause a somersault. The chains should be just long enough to permit free turning and should be hooked with the S facing back toward the trailer, to prevent their jumping free. Although S hooks **are** acceptable, it is safer practice to use a shackle and safety wire in place of the S hook.

The chains themselves should be of welded steel, with a working test load equivalent to that of the trailer's recommended gross weight, which is marked on the trailer itself. Although a

single length of safety chain, looping through the eyes on the trailer tongue, may be used, individually-attached chains provide an extra safety factor. For obvious reasons, the chains should never be made fast to a fitting common with the ball.

The most important aspect of all is the trailer's support of your boat's hull. Even sturdy fiberglass boats can be badly wrenched out of shape if they're not braced at critical points. The problem is that no roller supporting system can act wholly correctly on a hull that was designed to be supported evenly at all points by water. You have to do the best you can with what's available, and there are a few things to watch out for.

10-10 Roller Supporting System

Support Points

For most hulls, vital support points are the forefoot, the keel, the turn of the bilge (especially where interior weights are concentrated) and the transom. Any other spot where a specially heavy downward force is exerted on the hull should also be braced from below when the hull is fully seated on the trailer. In the general category of concentrated weights you can include retractable keels or weighted centerboards, water and fuel tanks, batteries and engines. If your boat has an inboard engine, then this is an absolutely overriding weight concentration that must be carefully braced beneath the engine bed stringers.

On most commercial trailers, the rollers and bolsters are adjustable, both up and down and fore and aft, and the winch column and wheel assemblies can also be moved along the frame. Given a trailer of adequate length and width, therefore, it should be possible to adjust the various elements of the frame and the supports to match the boat with some precision. Remember to be careful when adjusting any element that has a matching component on the boat's other side: An inch or so of fore-and-aft difference between the wheels can make a serious riding problem for the whole rig.

Tires

A trailer's tires and wheels undergo far more strain than do the ones on your car. Not only are a trailer's wheels smaller to begin with, turning at far higher speeds, but they are also subject to immersion, often in corrosive salt water. Maximum tire load capacity and pressure are marked on the tire itself. These pressures are considerably higher than those of the tires on your family car. You should carrry a tire pressure gauge and check your trailer's tires frequently. If you err, it should be on the side of more air in the tires, not less: Low air pressure in small, high-speed tires causes them to heat up faster and fail sooner.

The Winch

Under way on the open road, a trailed boat is subject to a type of rapid motion that it will never encounter on the water. Not only should every unattached piece of gear in the trailed boat be firmly secured, but the boat itself should be firmly lashed in place. The primary point of attachment is forward, at the trailer winch. If you plan to launch and recover off the trailer with some frequency, this winch is an especially important piece of equipment. It's usually an extra-cost option, so you have some choice as to type.

Your winch should have an anti-reverse gear, so the boat can't escape, and unless the boat is very light, the standard rope on the winch drum should be replaced with stainless steel wire. For larger cruisers, geared winches and electrical winches running off the car's battery are available. The winch drum should be mounted, if possible, approximately on a line with the towing eye on your boat's bow when the boat is fully cradled. If there's no towing eye, the

10-11 Winch Cable Hooked to Eye of Stem

angle of pull from the bow chocks should be slightly downward.

Don't expect the winch alone to hold the bow in place. An additional wire cable, preferably with a turnbuckle, should connect the boat's stem to the winch pillar. There should also be a non-stretching strap across the after part of the boat — webbing like what's used for auto seat belts or hiking straps will do well enough, but pad the hull or wood trim directly under the strap with old carpeting to preserve gel coat and varnish. A pair of spring lines — these can be your boat's dock lines — should be run aft from the bow cleat to the trailer frame about even with the wheels.

Important extras, after a winch and brakes, include the following: spare trailer wheel, bearing grease and a complete set of wheel bearings, bulbs for the trailer's lights, a jack that suits the trailer's frame, a set of long-handled wrenches for tightening the various body bolts regularly, outside mirrors for the towing vehicle, flares, trouble flag and trouble light. If your rig is very heavy, you may also want to consider booster brakes and heavy-duty shock absorbers for the towing car.

10-12   Trailer Tongue Jack and Dolly Wheel

10-13   Mast Padded at the Rack and Transom

Proper Loading

Balancing the load on your trailer is really the key to successful towing. What it amounts to is adjusting the boat's gross weight — that is, the boat and her contents — so that the load on the trailer tongue is somewhere between five and seven percent of the **total** gross weight of the tow — boat + contents + trailer. For the average small passenger car, the weight at the tongue shouldn't be much more than 100 lb. Working backward, that indicates a gross weight of 2,000 lb. as the maximum an ordinary sedan should be asked to pull. If you're in doubt about the towing capabilities of your car, check with the dealer.

To measure tongue weight, load the boat (which is on the trailer) with the gear she would normally carry on the road. Then stack two or three cinder blocks under a set of bathroom scales and ease the trailer's tongue down on this makeshift platform. If the weight involved is over about 75 lb., consider fixing an accessory dolly wheel to the tongue.

If the weight at the trailer tongue is much more than the recommended maximum, the tow car will have too much load behind and be hard to handle at speed. If the tongue weight is too little, the trailer is likely to fishtail. What you want, then, is the happy medium. If you're pulling a load over about 4,000 lb., by the way,

you'll want a **tandem,** or four-wheel, trailer as well as a special towing vehicle.

Before setting out, you should check the items loaded in the boat to be sure they are properly secured in place. Make certain also that no one has tossed in last-minute items that can significantly alter the trailer's balance. Check also that the trailer's bolts are all tightened up: They can work loose slowly and insidiously. Check boat tie-downs, trailer lights and brakes: Spare a moment to make certain that the car-to-trailer umbilicals will stay put under way.

The mast and boom should be firmly lashed down, preferably in a padded rack. Some makers of trailerable boats supply just such a fitting, but you can usually rig one yourself. The standing and running rigging should be bundled together and tied to the spar at intervals so it can't work loose. If you travel rough roads or long distances, consider a covering for at least the winch cluster at the base of the spar and the sheave arrangement at the masthead, just to keep highway dirt out. If the mast protrudes aft, it should have a red flag lashed to its end.

Obviously the rudder will have been removed before trailering, if it's removable. A bracket-mounted outboard can stay on the boat and is probably safe enough, as long as the transom is supported directly beneath the motor. If your

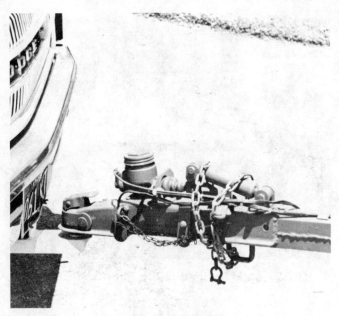

10-14 Front Hitch

boat has a swing keel or a weighted center-board, it should be lowered until it rests on a frame cross-member. This will save a lot of wear on the centerboard pennant and a certain amount of stress on the hull as well.

Under way, remember that you've got a long, heavy, awkward tail behind you. This sounds very obvious, until you see someone pulling a trailer cut in ahead of you, oblivious to the fact that his vehicle is 20 or 25 feet longer than normal.

Start your towing car slowly, in low gear, and take it up through the speeds gently and smoothly. Think twice about passing other cars, but if you decide to pass, pick a spot and go — don't hesitate. When rounding corners, swing wide, after having checked traffic just behind and alongside you.

Remain sensitive to any unusual sounds or handling factors, and if you notice anything at all out of the ordinary, pull over at once and check. If fact, you should get off the road and check out the entire rig every hour or so — look for high temperatures in the wheel bearings, loosening tie-downs, slacked-off bolts, brake and turn lights, tire pressure and car engine temperature.

Launching

Before you attempt a real launching, put in a couple of hours some Sunday in a supermarket parking lot, learning how to line up and back the trailer effectively. Have someone help you by acting as a guide, and develop a set of simple hand signals. Backing a trailer is a lot easier than docking, but it does take practice. If you have an exceptionally heavy or unwieldy rig, consider buying a front bumper hitch: With this accessory, you can make the launch while moving the towing vehicle forward, and close-quarters maneuvering will be a lot simpler.

When launching, try to avoid getting the trailer hubs in the water. If you can't avoid immersing them, at least let them cool off first, or the heat will simply suck the bearing full of water. One way to pass the time while waiting for the trailer wheels to come down from highway temperatures is by stepping the mast in the parking lot. Before you try this, check to be sure there are no low power lines or other overhead obstructions between you and the launching ramp: Many municipal ramps were laid out for outboard skiffs, not masted vessels.

Raising the Mast

Many sailboats usually have some form of **tabernacle** for raising the mast. This is essentially a mast stepped on a hinge, and most of them are so arranged that the mast swings up from astern. Smaller boats, of course, don't require this kind of fancy gear, and the mast goes into the normal step guided by a crewmember, as described earlier in this book.

Masts that pivot up and forward are simple to raise, but require a fair amount of muscle power from the crew. With the mast in its hinged tabernacle, attach the upper shrouds and the backstay and tie a pulling line — a good, thick one, comfortable to the hand — to the forestay just above the turnbuckle. As one person stands in the cockpit and raises the spar, the other crewmember at the bow, who should be the stronger of the two, if there's a difference in strength, pulls on the forestay extension.

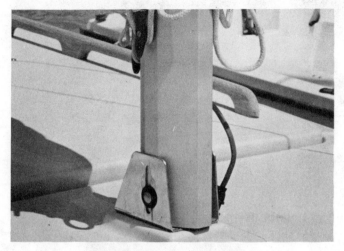

10-15 Mast Step on Hinge

10-16 Mast Tabernacle

If the boat is very small and light, the person raising the spar should stay out of the boat while doing it, which is not easy. As the mast approaches the point where the person aft can exert no more lift, it may be necessary to tie off the forestay extension until the cockpit hand can get around forward to help pull. Until you're used to the stresses involved, don't take anything for granted: Even a light mast can exert an enormous pull at certain acute angles.

The mast may, in some cases, swing up and aft from the bow. The spar thus lies flat over the foredeck after being made fast in its tabernacle. In this case, make fast the upper shrouds and the forestay first. Then attach the boom to its gooseneck at right angles to the mast, where it is held by the topping lift and temporary guys to the deck at either side. To raise the mast, you simply employ the four- or five-part mechanical advantage of the mainsheet tackle system, amplified if necessary by the genoa sheet winch.

Launching & Recovery

Before launching (or recovery, for that matter), make sure that there is nothing protruding down from the boat to snag on the trailer frame. The outboard should be raised and locked, and the centerboard or swing keel should be pulled all the way into its well and the pennant lashed. Although some professionals like to back the trailer fast down the ramp and shoot the boat off by braking suddenly, this is

not a good idea, as too many things can go wrong too fast.

Back slowly down until the boat's stern is afloat, then ease her off the trailer. A person ashore should hold a bow line while this is being done. When launching, never turn the car's engine off. If you have an automatic transmission, it should be in **park** with the brake set while you work the boat on or off. If the trailer's wheels do get wetted down, repack the bearings with grease. It doesn't take long and is a lot easier than changing a burnt-out bearing on the road home.

When the boat is on her trailer for any length of time, get the weight off the trailer suspension and wheels. Jack up the trailer frame and support it with cinder blocks, shimmed up if necessary with pieces of planking. Once the frame is fully jacked up, check underneath to be sure that the boat is still evenly supported — the frame can be easily and imperceptibly wrenched out of shape during the jacking process.

Although this seems complicated, in fact it is not, if you approach trailering in an orderly, plan-ahead fashion. The equipment has been developed to a high pitch of efficiency and the techniques tested over years and miles of use. The only thing to watch out for is taking too much for granted and failing to anticipate what might go wrong and then forestalling it.

10-17   **Backing Down the Launch Ramp**

10-18   **Releasing the Stem Hook**

10-19   **Launched**

10-20   **Beginning Recovery Process**

10-21   Boat Recovered and on Trailer

10-22   Preparing to Lower the Mast

10-23   Lowering the Mast

Chapter 11

Equipment for You and Your Boat

Although governmental authority dictates, to a certain degree, what equipment you must carry aboard your boat (see Chapter Six), the extent of those legal requirements is very narrow. Dealing only with safety-related equipment, the Coast Guard's regulations do not cover all safety gear — only certain vital items that apply to all people or all boats of a certain type. Even an obviously desirable item like an anchor is subject to so many variables in selection that it would be impossible to put together a workable regulation.

Beyond the regulations themselves, it's still possible to have a boat that's basically seaworthy, meets all the legal requirements plus the suggestions of the Courtesy Marine Examination (see page 6-10), and still operate a vessel that isn't safe. Safety on a boat is largely a state of mind, not a shopping list. Beyond having the proper gear, one must maintain it and know how and when to use it. And beyond that state is the knowledge of true seamanship — when the skipper may assume a risk, but does so in the knowledge of what's involved and the reasons for doing it.

The equipment dealt with in this chapter is mostly safety-related, but in the larger sense it's all conducive to a higher standard of seamanship, and thus a better-sailed, more effective boat, whether it's being raced or cruised.

Personal Gear

Having a well-equipped boat starts with a well-equipped crew. And the equipment includes virtually all the clothes on one's back (not to mention one's head and feet). Let's begin by considering what the well-dressed sailor wears — and more important, why.

Although it shouldn't detract from one's enjoyment of sailing, or any other watersport, it's important always to remember that water is an element that's basically hostile to humans. Nearly all the dangers associated with being on or in the water can be avoided by taking a few precautions. Most experienced sailors stay out of trouble without conscious thought, because of childhood training or experience; new sailors have to make an effort, until seamanlike behavior becomes second nature.

Unfortunately, talking about safety afloat has a negative effect on many people. It's understandable. You go out on the water to have fun, even to be adventurous, not to "be safe." As it happens, good seamanship (which is the same as skillful seamanship) is based on not taking needless personal chances. One of the oldest rules of seamanship is **one hand for the ship, one for yourself.**

Hand in this connection should be generalized to include all the gear that makes you a more alert, more effective sailor — clothing, personal rescue equipment, safety gear that's part of the boat itself.

11-1 Non-Skid Boat Boots

Shoes and Boots

Begin at the bottom, with deck shoes. On a small sailboat, you'll be standing seldom if at all, but many experienced sailors wear shoes anyway. Why? Every boat is literally studded with small, sharp fittings that seem to have been expressly designed as toe-stubbers, whatever their other functions. In addition, in small boats one frequently goes over the side while launching or recovering the boat from beach or trailer. Thanks largely to human carelessness, lake and bay bottoms today are coated with sharp-edged trash.

Sailors whose feet are frequently wet during the course of the sailing day usually opt for sneakers with non-skid soles and uppers of some artificial, rot-proof fabric such as Dacron or nylon. Crewmembers aboard larger boats have a wider choice, and many prefer moccasin-style

shoes that can be kicked off in an emergency. In cold weather, over-the-sock boots can be most welcome — but it's a good idea to get them large enough to fit properly over two pairs of socks.

Whatever style of shoe or boot appeals to you, make sure it has a non-skid boating sole — which may consist of any one of half a dozen different patterns of slits, treads, ridges or suction cups. Complement this by making sure your boat's deck is non-skid. Most stand-on surfaces aboard today's production fiberglass boats have molded-in non-skid patterns. Sometimes, however, the pattern doesn't cover a place that you frequently find yourself standing on. This is especially true aboard cruisers, where parts of the cabin roof may not be skid-proof.

11-2 Non-Skid Tape on Deck

It's easy to buy self-stick non-skid tape for these areas. Or if you paint your deck, most paint firms sell a non-abrasive non-skid compound that can be added to deck paint. Cheapest of all — but hard on clothing and skin — is a handful of sand in the deck paint.

Head and Hands

At the other end of the body, your head deserves the best protection you can give it. Boating caps and hats are available in virtually any shape, but a few things are worth bearing in mind. First, a hat or cap's primary function is usually to protect you from sun. On most boats,

11-3 Spinnaker Hat

11-4 Watch Cap

a flexible brim at least in front and preferably all the way around will be most comfortable. Many light-colored caps — which are much cooler — have dark-tinted under sides to their brims, to reduce glare off the water.

If your boat's rig is one that makes the boom a menace to your skull at every tack and jibe, a padded cap is a good idea, and centuries of design have failed to improve upon the old-fashioned sailor's watch cap, made of wool or synthetic. The double- or triple-rolled brim affords head protection and can, in cold weather, be pulled down to cover the ears and neck.

Hands are another vulnerable point, especially early in the season before callouses have time to form on tender palms. Ordinary cotton painters' gloves are most sailors' choice for hand protection — they're relatively warm, dry quickly, and when (as will sooner or later happen) they're lost overboard, the financial jolt isn't unbearable. Many skippers carry half a dozen pairs aboard, in several sizes. If you don't wear gloves — or even if you do — trim your fingernails off short: Long nails have a great

likelihood of being snapped when furling sails or handling lines.

Other Clothing

For the rest of your person, clothing will depend on weather. If your boat has any dry stowage lockers at all, it pays to carry aboard some old, warm clothing — a sweatshirt and warm trousers at least — for each crewmember, in addition to what he or she may be wearing. This is especially important aboard cruising craft, where one may be out in the weather for an extended period.

It also pays to learn the layer method of dressing in changeable spring and fall sailing. Start off with a warm, heavy layer under which is a lighter layer that's still reasonably presentable, so you can peel or put on clothes as the conditions demand. And, as every experienced sailor knows, it's far, far better practice to take a little trouble and stay warm and dry, rather than trying to regain that state. Once you've been wetted through in a boat, getting really dry again usually means going ashore, unless yours is an exceptionally large and well-equipped cruiser.

Foul Weather Gear

And staying dry means foul weather gear. Good waterproof clothing is extremely expensive, but it's worth the money. If you sail in anything but a board boat, where being wet is wholly unavoidable, you should have a first-rate set of foul weather gear. Most experienced sailors prefer a jacket-style top with a drawstring hood and cuffs that can be snapped tight to keep at least the major part of the spray from running up the sleeves. Pullover styles are dryer than the kind that open down the front, but are harder to get into. A jacket with a plastic zipper (far better than any metal closure) and a waterproof, snap-equipped flap to cover it is the most practical for most people. Good, big pockets with snap or zip closures are another must.

11-6 Wet Suit

11-5 Foul Weather Gear With Sailor's Vest Over

Where cold-weather sailing is a way of life, the so-called float-coats are very nice. These jackets are not wholly waterproof, but they have to be very thoroughly wetted down for soaking to occur. In addition, some contain enough foam flotation to serve as Coast Guard-approved personal flotation devices, thus serving two needs with a single garment.

Foul weather trousers are never fashionable-looking, but the kind that keep the wearer dry are loose-fitting and usually at least high enough to reach the bottom of the rib cage. Since few people have an indentation at this point, suspenders are required to hold the trousers up. As with jackets, foul weather trousers keep you dry, but they often cause perspiration. To keep from being soaked on the inside, wear at least one extra layer of moisture-absorbing clothing in addition to street (or deck) clothes.

All this gear can make one feel clumsy and awkward. Practice at moving about in foul weather clothing will dispel part of this feeling, but if you sail one of the small, high-performance boats where nimbleness is really vital, you may be better served by wearing an ordinary skindiver's wetsuit instead of foul weather clothing. Sailors' wetsuits are sometimes padded at wear points — seats, elbows, knees. In addition to the suit, you'll want a life vest specifically designed for activity.

Life Vests

The Coast Guard has approved many styles of these vests, but they are all basically much the same, consisting of slabs of high-flotation closed-cell foam encased in cloth or net covering. The vest is usually closed in front by a non-corrosive zipper and sometimes by a belt as well. Although there is a certain amount of adjustability for shape with straps at waist and shoulders, these life vests are much more closely related to the individual wearer's size than are

to wearing life vests, but if one considers them garments and if the skipper has his crew put them on as a matter of course when conditions warrant, it becomes less of a chore and more of an accepted thing.

As sailors and sailing authorities are only just realizing, cold is perhaps as big a danger as drowning to most people on the water — and a far less obvious menace. The effects of extreme or prolonged cold, technically known as **hypothermia,** are now undergoing serious study by the Coast Guard and many concerned sailing people. Although much remains to be learned, some facts are already glaringly obvious. Without going into detail, hypothermia causes a gradual, imperceptible slowing down of

11-7   Sailor's Life Vest

the bulkier life jackets.

Most experienced skippers buy this sort of closely-sized life vest for each member of the regular crew, and mark it with his or her name; standard, bulky-style vests are carried for guests, in **adult, large child** (45-90 lb) and **small child** sizes. It's hard for many people to get used

bodily and mental function ending in unconsciousness and, if not reversed, death. The great danger of hypothermia is that the victim is usually unaware that anything's happening to him or her. As one becomes more affected by cold, simple tasks take longer to accomplish or even understand.

11-8 "Awaiting Rescue" Position

The onset of hypothermia varies widely with individuals. Generally speaking, somewhat overweight people are less quickly affected than thin, wiry ones, but there are enough exceptions in either direction to make broad statements risky. Only by keeping warm and observing the actions of fellow crewmembers can one spot the first slowing down of reactions. If one's boat is spilled, unless it can be righted quickly, it's best to conserve one's body heat by not struggling without reason. Clothing that is not actually dragging one down will serve to retain some heat even when soaked — and it may well hold air and thus buoyancy as well.

The popular technique known as "drown-proofing" is especially unfortunate, for it leads to the loss of heat at an accelerated rate. The best defense, once in the water, is to cling to some floating object while assuming a crouched or huddled position to retain heat.

Other Boat Equipment

The Offshore Rating Council, a non-governmental body that supervises international distance sailboat racing, has issued its own list of equipment and construction standards for racers in four different categories of offshore races. One thing to bear in mind is that racers, unlike most other sailors, carry on as long as it's at all possible, so the equipment list is put together with that attitude considered. The resume that follows is a somewhat edited version of the ORC's 1973 regulation. After each item appears the number 1, 2, 3 and/or 4.

These stand for categories of race —
1 being long-distance contests where boats must be self-sufficient for days at a time;
2 longshore races where boats should be able to take care of themselves, but where help should be available within a few hours at the outside;
3 consists of races in protected water or along shore, including races for small cruising craft;
4 short races in warm or protected waters.

Skipper's Responsiblity

The safety of a yacht and her crew is the sole and inescapable responsiblity of the skipper, who must do his best to insure that the yacht is fully equipped, thoroughly seaworthy and manned by an experienced crew who are physically fit to face bad weather. He must be satisfied as to the soundness of hull, spars, rigging, sails and all gear. He must insure that all safety equipment is properly maintained and stowed and that the crew know where it is kept and how it is to be used.

Neither the establishment of these special regulations, their use by the sponsoring organizations, nor the inspection of a yacht under these regulations in any way limits or reduces the complete and unlimited responsiblity of the owner.

It is the sole and exclusive responsibility of each skipper to decide whether or not to start or continue to race.

Basic Standards

Hulls of offshore racing yachts shall be self-righting, strongly built, watertight and capable of withstanding solid water and knockdowns. They must be properly rigged and ballasted, be fully seaworthy and must meet the standards set forth herein.

"Self-righting" means that a yacht must have a positive righting arm when the masthead, with main and foresail set, touches the water.

"Properly rigged" means that the shrouds are never to be disconnected.

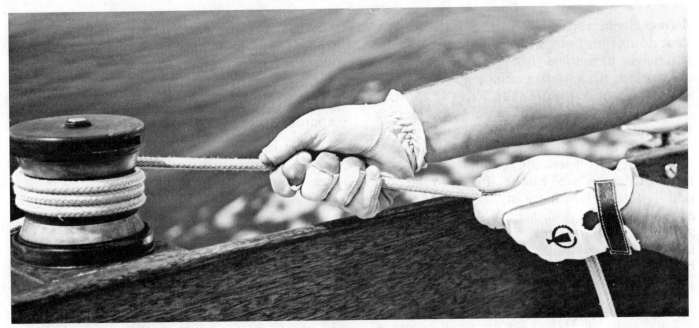

11-9 Sailor's Gloves

All equipment must function properly, be readily accessible and be of a type, size and capacity suitable and adequate for the intended use and the size of the yacht, and shall meet standards acceptable in the country of registry.

Structural Features

Hatches, companionways and ports must be essentially watertight, that is, capable of being strongly and rigidly secured. Cockpit companionways, if extended below main deck level, must be capable of being blocked off to main deck level. If cockpit opens aft to the sea, the lower edge of the companionway may not be below deck level. **1,2,3,4.**

Cockpits must be structurally strong, self-bailing and permanently incorporated as an integral part of the hull. They must be essentially watertight, that is, all openings to the hull below the main deck level must be capable of being strongly and rigidly secured. **1,2,3,4.**

Cockpit drains adequate to drain cockpit quickly but with a combined area (after allowance for screens, if attached) of not less than the equivalent of two 1" (2.5 cm) diameter drains. Yachts built after 1-1-72 must have drains with a combined area (after allowance for screens, if attached) of not less than the equivalent of four 3/4" (2.0 cm) drains. **1,2.**

Cockpit drains adequate to drain cockpit quickly but not less in combined area (after allowance for screens, if attached) than the equivalent of two 1" (2.5 cm) diameter drains. **3,4.**

Storm coverings for all windows more than two square feet in area. **1,2,3.**

Sea cocks or valves on all through-hull openings below LWL, except integral deck scuppers, shaft log, speed indicators, depth finders and the like; however, a means of closing such openings, when necessary to do so, shall be provided. **1,2,3.**

Soft wood plugs, tapered and of various sizes. **1,2,3,4.**

Lifelines and Pulpits

Fixed bow pulpit (forward of headstay) and stern pulpit (unless lifelines are arranged as to adequately substitute for a stern pulpit). Pulpits and stanchions must be through-bolted or welded, and the bases thereof must not be further inboard from the edge of the working deck than 5 percent of maximum beam or 6 inches (15 cm), whichever is greater. The head of a stanchion must not be angled from the point of its attachment to the hull at more than 10 degrees from vertical throughout the length. Taut double life lines, with upper life line of wire at a height of not less than 2 feet (60cm) above the working deck, to be permanently supported at intervals of not more than 7 feet (2.15m). A taut lanyard of synthetic rope may be used to secure lifelines, provided that when in position its length does not exceed 4 inches (10cm). Lower lifelines need not extend to the bow pulpit. Lifelines need not be affixed to the bow pulpit if they terminate at, or pass through, adequately braced stanchions 2 feet (60 cm) above the working deck, set inside of and over-lapping the bow pulpit, provided that the gap between the upper lifeline and the bow pulpit shall not exceed 6 inches (15 cm). **1,2,3.**

Yachts under 21 feet, as above, but with a single taut lifeline not less than 18 inches (45 cm) above the working deck, and a bow pulpit and a stern pulpit (unless lifelines are so arranged as to adequately substitute for a stern pulpit) to the same height. If the lifeline is at any point more than 22 inches (56 cm) above the rail cap, a second intermediate lifeline must be fitted. If the cockpit opens aft to the sea additional lifelines must be fitted so that no opening is greater in height than 22 inches (56 cm). The bow pulpit may be fitted abaft the forestay with its bases secured at any points on deck, but a point on its upper rail must be within 16 inches (40 cm) of the forestay on which the foremost headsail is hanked. **1,2,3.**

As above except that a stern pulpit is not required, provided the required height of life-line must be carried aft to at least the midpoint of the cockpit. **4.**

Ballast and Heavy Equipment. Inside ballast in a yacht shall be securely fastened in position. All other heavy internal fittings such as batteries, stoves, gas bottles, tanks, outboard motors, etc., shall be securely fastened. **1,2,3,4.**

Accommodations

Cooking stove, permanently installed with safe accessible fuel shutoff control. **1,2.**

Cooking stove, capable of being safely operated in a seaway. **3.**

Water tanks, permanently installed and capable of dividing the water supply into at least two separate containers. **1.**

At least one permanently installed water tank, plus at least one additional container capable of holding 2 gallons. **2.**

Water in suitable containers. **3,4.**

11-10 Fire Extinguishers Must Be Coast Guard Approved

General Equipment

Fire extinguishers, readily accessible and of the type and number required by the country of registry, provided there be at least one on yachts fitted with an engine or stove. **1,2,3,4.**

Bilge pumps, at least two, manually oper-ated, one of which must be operable with all cockpit seats and all hatches and companion-ways closed. **1,2.**

One manual bilge pump operable with all cockpit seats, hatches, and companionways closed. **3.**

One manual bilge pump. **4.**

Anchors, two with cables except yachts rating under 21 feet, which shall carry at least one such anchor and cable. **1,2,3.**

One anchor and cable. **4.**

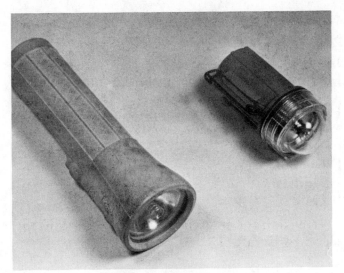

11-11   Flashlights

11-12   Compass - Direct Reading

Flashlights, one which is suitable for signaling, water resistant, with spare batteries and bulbs. **1,2,3.**

At least one flashlight, water resistant, with spare batteries and bulb. **4.**

First aid kit and manual. **1,2,3,4.**

Foghorn. 1,2,3,4.

Radar reflector. 1,2,3,4.

Set of international code flags and international code book. **1.**

Shutoff valves on all fuel tanks. **1,2,3,4.**

Navigation Equipment

Compass, marine type, properly installed and adjusted. **1,2,3,4.**

Spare compass. 1,2,3.

Charts, light list and piloting equipment. 1,2,3.

Sextant, tables and accurate time piece. 1.

Radio direction finder. 1,2.

Lead line or echo sounder. 1,2,3,4.

Speedometer or distance measuring instrument. 1,2,3.

Navigation lights, to be shown as required by the International Regulations for Preventing Collision at Sea, mounted so that they will not be masked by sails or the heeling of the yacht. **1,2,3,4.**

Emergency Equipment

Emergency navigation lights and power source. **1,2.**

Special storm sail(s) capable of taking the yacht to windward in heavy weather. **1,2.**

Heavy weather jib and reefing equipment for mainsail. **3,4.**

Emergency steering equipment. 1,2,3.

Tools and spare parts, including a hacksaw. **1,2,3,4.**

Yacht's name on miscellaneous buoyant equipment, such as life jackets, oars, cushions, etc. Portable sail number. **1,2,3.**

Marine radio transmitter and receiver, with minimum transmitter power of 25 watts. If the regular antenna depends upon the mast, an emergency antenna must be provided. **1.**

Radio receiver capable of receiving weather bulletins. **2,3,4.**

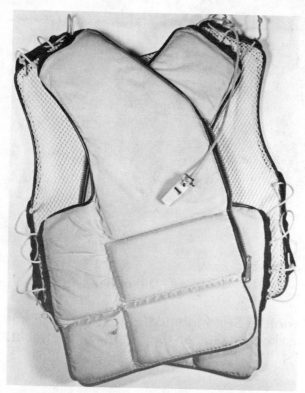

11-13 Life Vest With Whistle Attached

Safety Equipment

Life jackets, one for each crew member. **1,2,3,4.**

Whistles attached to the life jackets. **1,2,3.**

Safety belt (harness type) one for each crew member. **1,2,3.**

Life raft(s) capable of carrying the entire crew and meeting the following requirements: **1,2,3.**

Must be carried on deck (not under a dinghy) or in a special stowage opening immediately to the deck and containing life raft(s) only.

Must be designed and used solely for saving life at sea.

Must have at least two separate buoyancy compartments, each of which must be automatically inflatable, each raft must be capable of carrying its rated capacity with one compartment deflated.

Must have a canopy to cover the occupants.

Must have been inspected, tested and approved within two years by the manufacturer or other competent authority; and

Must have the following equipment appropriately secured to each raft.

1 Sea anchor or drogue
1 Bellows, pump or other means for maintaining inflation of air chambers
1 Signaling light
3 Hand flares
1 Bailer
1 Repair kit
2 Paddles
1 Knife

Provision for emergency water and rations to accompany raft. **1.**

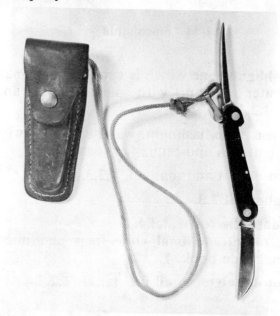

11-14 Rigging Knife With Marlinspike

Life ring(s), at least one horseshoe type life ring equipped with a waterproof light and drogue within reach of the helmsman and ready for instant use. **4.**

At least one horseshoe type life ring equipped with a self-igniting high-intensity water light and a drogue within reach of the helmsman and ready for instant use. **1,2,3.**

At least one more horseshoe type life ring equipped with a whistle, dye marker, drogue, a self-igniting high intensity water light, and a pole and flag. The pole is to be attached to the ring with 25 feet (8 m) of floating line and is to be of a length and so ballasted that the flag will fly at least 8 feet (2.45 m) off the water. **1,2.**

Distress signals to be stowed in a waterproof container and meeting the following requirements for each category, as indicated: **1,2,3,4.**

Twelve red parachute flares. **1.**

Four red parachute flares. **2,3.**

Four red hand flares. **1,2,3,4.**

Four white hand flares. **1,2,3,4.**

Heaving line (50 foot (16 m) minimum length, floating type line) readily accessible to cockpit. **1,2,3,4.**

Chapter 12

Sailboat Piloting

Introduction

All navigation, from the most elementary to the most complex, involves two things — determining the present position of one's ship or plane, and directing that vehicle from one known position to another. Navigation is frequently described as both an art and a science; it's an **art** because of the skills and techniques required, and a **science** because it's based on the systematic application of physical laws.

In a basic text like this, we only have space to deal with the essentials of one branch of the larger subject — **coastal navigation,** often referred to as **piloting.** As the name suggests, this subject involves directing the movements of a ship or boat along the coast, by using visible landmarks ashore, navigational aids, and soundings (measurements of the sea bottom's depth and composition). Although piloting isn't generally considered as complex or demanding as the two other kinds of navigation, **electronic and celestial,** it isn't necessarily easier, if only because there is less elbow room for mistakes in shallow, rock-strewn coastal waters.

Sailboat navigation is of course based on the same principles that hold true for other vessels, but because sailboats are relatively so slow, they are more affected by **current** (the horizontal movement of water caused by tide or wind). In addition, sailboats have greater draft than powerboats of equivalent length, and as a result, sailboat navigators are especially sensitive to **tide,** the vertical rise and fall of the water level, which obviously has an effect on depth.

Navigation as practiced aboard modern ocean-racing sailboats is a truly scientific art (or artistic science) functioning at a high level, aided by instruments of great accuracy. For most occasional sailors, however, navigation is a much rougher and simpler operation, carried out in an open cockpit or on a slanting dinette table, with rather variable results.

This chapter is addressed to that sometime navigator, to the skipper or crewmember who merely wants to be able to find his or her way from place to place with tolerable accuracy, if not with pinpoint precision. Having mastered the material in this section, one must then go out on the water and use it. If there is any key to offhand navigation, it's practice.

The tools required are minimal, and one should avoid heavy investments in equipment until the basic techniques are well in hand. What you will need aboard your boat will vary according to your stowage space and the conditions under which you'll be working, but here is a list of the initial gear, most of which is described in fuller detail later in the chapter:

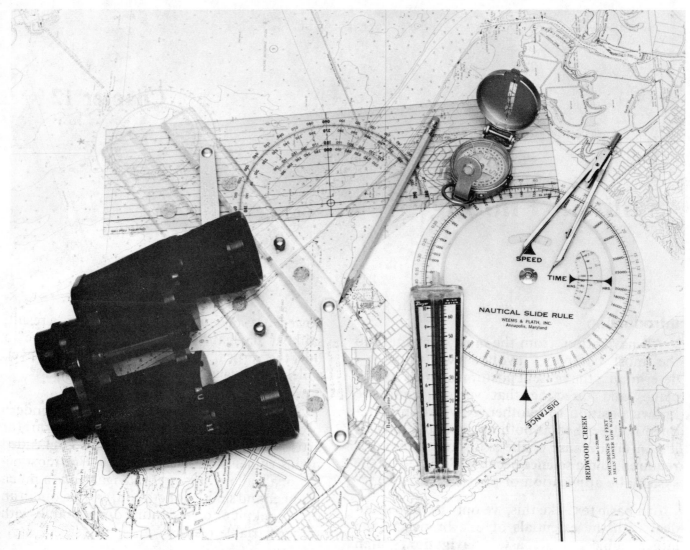

12-1 The Pilot's Basic Instruments

Charts of the area in which you sail;
A good-quality magnetic compass;
Binoculars, 7x35 or, if you have room, 7x50;
Parallel rules or course protractor;
Dividers, for measuring off distance;
Pencils, preferably medium-soft #2.

The Nautical Chart

Maps are what make serious navigation possible, and a map has been defined as "a symbolic picture of a portion of the earth drawn to scale." A nautical chart is only a map that emphasizes features useful to the mariner — the shape of the coastline, landmarks visible from the sea, manmade aids to navigation, and depths.

Today's chart is a technological marvel, containing as much information as several large books. This compression is possible in part because of the use of symbols that stand for various objects that can't be represented on a

29th Ed., Sept. 4/**76**

12273

(formerly C&GS 1226)

LORAN-C OVERPRINTED

12-2 Chart Number, Edition and Date

(MLLW)	
Lower Water at	Extreme Low Water feet
0	−2.5
.0	−2.5
.0	−2.5

UNITED STATES – WEST COAST

CALIFORNIA

GULF OF THE FARALLONES

CAUTION

marine radiobeacons have been calibrated for
use.. Limitations on the use of certain other
gnals as aids to marine navigation can be
n the U.S. Coast Guard Light Lists and
e Mapping Agency Hydrographic Center
ion H.O. 117 (A&B).
o direction-finder bearings to commercial
sting stations are subject to error and should
with caution.
n positions are shown thus:

:urate location)   o(Approximate location)

Mercator Projection
1:100,000 at Lat. 37°46′

SOUNDINGS IN FATHOMS
(FATHOMS AND FEET TO ELEVEN FATHOMS) _____
AT MEAN LOWER LOW WATER

For Symbols and Abbreviations see Chart No. 1

NOTE F
NITIONS DUMPING AREA –
RESTRICTION

ised or designated for U.S. chemical
Such use has been discontinued.
rea in no way constitutes authority

AUTHORITIES

Hydrography and topography by the National Ocean Survey (formerly the Coast and
Geodetic Survey) with additional data from the Corps of Engineers, Geological Survey
and U.S. Coast Guard.

HEIGHTS

12-3 Chart Title, Type of Projection, Scale of the Chart and Datum of Soundings

chart in a scaled-down version of their true shapes. We'll come back to the symbols used on a chart in a while, but first let's consider the kinds of charts available to the American coastal sailor.

Charts of U.S. waters are prepared and published by the National Ocean Survey (NOS), and free catalogs are available directly from that organization (Distribution Division, C44, National Ocean Survey, Riverdale, MD 20737); these catalogs are also provided by authorized chart sales outlets, which include map stores, major boatyards and marine dealers. Charts are only as good as the information on them, and because that information changes, you should be sure to buy and use up-to-date charts. It pays to get new charts every couple of years, and when an area is subject to frequent change because of soft bottom, strong tides and the like, to check at the local chart outlet every year to see if a new edition of your local chart has been issued.

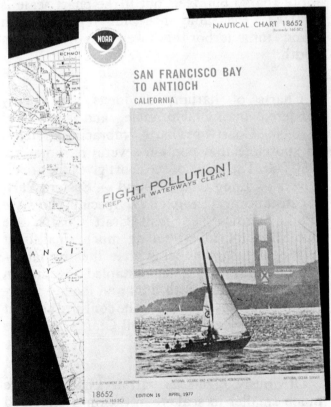

12-4 A Typical Small Craft or Folio Style Chart

A valuable and reliable source of information concerning changes to charts, navigational aids, channel conditions, and hazards to navigation is the Local Notice To Mariners. These notices are disseminated by either Broadcast Notices, Local Notices, and/or Weekly Notices. Urgent notices concerning changes or deficiencies in aids to navigation are issued by means of radio broadcast. The Local Notice, aimed primarily at the boater in local waters, is mailed and can be obtained free of charge by application to the Commander of the Coast Guard District in which the boat is principally operated. The Weekly Notice to Mariners is intended for those mariners who will be sailing over a much wider geographical area and is also free of charge. It is published by the Defence Mapping Agency.

Generally speaking, charts are classified according to **scale.** This term simply refers to the size of an object on the chart relative to its size in reality: A harbor may be one inch wide on your chart. If the chart's scale is 1:20,000, the harbor's actual width is 20,000 times charted size, or more than 1,650 feet; but if the chart scale is 1:40,000, the same inch-wide representation stands for a harbor that's well over 3,000 feet in width.

Charts of harbors or inlets are usually rendered in 1:20,000 scale, and sometimes 1:10,000. Coastwise charts, embracing stretches of shoreline that contain several harbors, are 1:80,000. The name of the chart gives the area it covers — **Long Island Sound — Eastern Part,** for instance, or **Tampa Bay.** Special folio-style charts, known as Small Craft Charts, are published for areas having much small-boat traffic, the theory being that the format — several fold-out segments stapled together in protective covers, with tidal and facility information — is easier to use in the confined cockpit of a skiff or daysailer. Small Craft Charts are 1:40,000 in scale.

Obviously, high-seas craft use charts that are much smaller in scale than the ones described here, over 1:1,000,000 in some cases. (A small-scale chart is one in which features are presented in smaller size and less detail than on a **large**-scale chart.) As a rule of thumb, the casual navigator should carry a chart on which the entire projected voyage can be encompassed, as well as larger-scale charts for any bays or harbors he might have to enter. In practical terms, a day-sailor's afternoon cruise will seldom require more than one large-scale chart, and even a harbor chart will usually be quite comprehensive enough for serious piloting.

If yours is a largely open boat, you will want to protect your chart by encasing it in a transparent plastic cover that will allow you to lay the chart out flat in the open, without fear of its being damaged by spray or rain. Although charts are printed on specially-treated paper, they are not improved by being wetted.

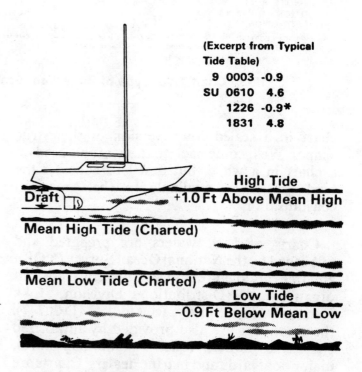

(Excerpt from Typical
Tide Table)
```
 9  0003  -0.9
SU  0610   4.6
    1226  -0.9*
    1831   4.8
```

High Tide
+1.0 Ft Above Mean High

Mean High Tide (Charted)

Mean Low Tide (Charted)

Low Tide
-0.9 Ft Below Mean Low

12-5 Tide — the Vertical Movement of Water

Datum and Sea Level

One technical term requires definition for you to get the most from your chart: **Datum** refers to the base line from which a map's vertical measurements are made — heights of land or landmarks or, in the case of a chart, depths of water. Most landsman's maps use sea level as a

1		*Ground*
2	*S*	*Sand*
3	*M*	*Mud; Muddy*
4	*Oz*	*Ooze*
5	*Ml*	*Marl*
6	*Cl*	*Clay*
7	*G*	*Gravel*
8	*Sn*	*Shingle*

12-6 Symbols for Quality of the Bottom from CHART NUMBER 1

I. Buildings and Struct

1		*City or Town (large scale)*
(1a)		*City or Town (small scale)*
2		*Suburb*
3	*Vil*	*Village*
3a		*Buildings in general*
4	*Cas*	*Castle*
5		*House*

12-7 Symbols for Buildings and Structures from CHART NUMBER 1

datum, and that's quite good enough for them. But to a sailor, the depth of the water is vitally important, and that depth is constantly changing.

On a nautical chart, water depth is measured downward from sea level, while the heights of landmarks are given in feet above sea level. But because of **tide,** which changes sea level in saltwater areas on a regular basis, some allowance must be made on the chart for the fact that the depth isn't always the same.

Tidal rise and fall is reasonably predictable, so chartmakers have selected a given point in the tidal cycle as the one at which heights and depths are measured. For safety's sake, depth measurements (called **soundings**) are noted on the chart as of **low water** (or low tide) — the point in the tide's cycle when there will be the **least** depth at a given point. On the East Coast of the United States, the tidal datum is **Mean** (or normal) **Low Water;** on the Gulf Coast the datum is **GULF COAST WATER DATUM;** the actual low water depth on any given day in a month will vary somewhat from this figure according to a number of factors.

On the Pacific Coast, there are two high tides and two low tides each day, as on the Atlantic and Gulf of Mexico, but on the West Coast one set of daily tides is markedly higher than the other. Thus, the datum on Pacific Coast charts is **Mean Lower Low Water,** or the lower of two average low tides.

Depths of water are usually given in feet on U.S. charts, but some older, small-scale charts show soundings in **fathoms** (1 fathom=6 feet). The kind of measurement, the scale and the datum are prominently noted on each chart. Besides depths, charts also note the type of bottom, using any of a number of abbreviations, the more common of which are shown here. This information is especially useful when trying to select a place to anchor, as good holding ground — sand or hard mud — is an essential aspect of a safe anchorage.

Obstructions and dangers in the water are also charted, and symbols tell the mariner what to be ready for. It is worth bearing in mind that a wreck, even one that's largely exposed, soon ceases to look much like the ship it once was, and may be difficult to recognize.

As a rule, shallow water is tinted light blue on a chart, while deeper water is white. This allows the navigator a ready, visual reference without having to look at each charted sounding. You should learn to relate the shallow-water blue tint to your own boat's draft.

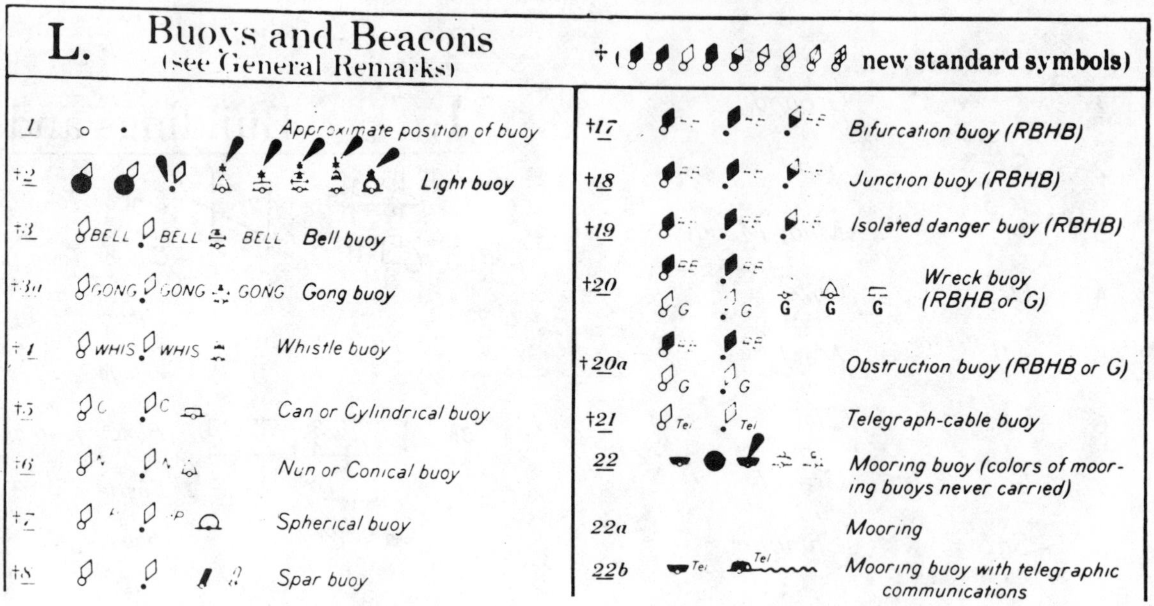

12-8 Symbols for Buoys and Beacons from CHART NUMBER 1

Charted Details

Charted features ashore include prominent structures, especially ones that stand out because of their recognizable shape (such as churches and water towers); land contours are frequently charted; bridges of all types are listed in detail, The vertical clearance of a bridge, however, is based on Mean High Water, so that some factor of safety is included in the printed chart. The navigator should remember that buildings only appear on the chart when someone tells the chartmaker to put them there; conversely, a structure that was once prominent enough to chart may have been destroyed or screened by a larger building while it still appears on a chart. That's why aids to navigation are far more reliable to use as landmarks.

The actual shoreline contour itself is one of the chart's most important features. Once tinted pale yellow, now **gold,** land sometimes appears as light **green,** if it's swampy or if it covers and uncovers with changes in water level.

Aids to Navigation

Manmade structures, both fixed and floating, serve as signposts, beacons, direction signals and warnings of dangers to the mariner. Aids to navigation, placed and serviced by the U.S. Coast Guard, occur either in patterned groups that indicate a channel, or path of deep water, or as individual aids that serve as warnings of isolated dangers or points of special significance.

The small-boat sailor will normally find himself using aids to navigation as individual recognition or reference points, but owners of larger, fixed-keel vessels will often need to keep within a channel's boundaries in order to stay afloat. Even if you don't regularly use the channels for their intended purpose, you ought to know what the various floating aids (collectively called **buoys**) and fixed markers mean.

The accompanying diagrams illustrate a simplified channel system. Some points about it should be emphasized.

1. There is no functional difference between lighted and unlighted buoys or between buoys and fixed aids, although simpler and less costly aids are used where they are adequate for the purpose.

2. The only significant buoy shapes are the cylindrical **cans** and the cone-topped **nuns:** The former mark the left-hand side of a channel going from open water toward an anchorage or smaller body of water; nuns mark the right-hand side.

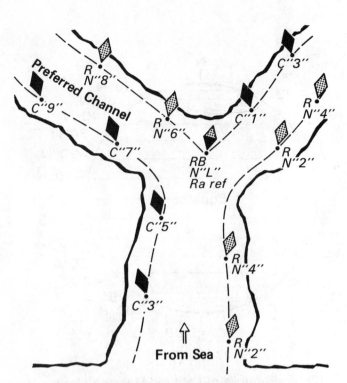

12-9 Simplified Channel System

3. Significant buoy colors are **red** and **black**. Although cans are generally black and nuns red, buoys of varied shape may be either color. The thing to remember is that red aids mark the right side of inbound channels, black the left. Red-and-black horizontally striped buoys mark obstructions in the channel or channel junctions. Black-and-white vertically striped buoys mark inlet entrances or mid-channel.

4. Red lights go with red aids; green lights appear on black aids. White lights may be placed on aids of any color.

5. Light patterns tell you, in some cases, not only which buoy you're looking at, but what it does. Most aids use very simple flashing patterns. The more complex multi-colored patterns identify major lighthouses.

6. Aids are numbered from open water toward sheltered water, with "1" or "2" being the first buoy in a channel series. A new channel branching off a main channel will begin a new series of buoy numbers. Red-and-black and black-and-white buoys are not numbered at all.

7. Sound-producing aids — all lighthouses and many buoys are equipped with sound-producing instruments to aid in identification in low visibility. Diaphones, diaphragm horns, sirens, whistles, and bells are used to give each aid a distinctive sound to facilitate identification. Bells, gongs and whistles are activated by wave action and will not work in flat water. Atmospheric conditions at times alter some sounds on the water and may cause certain tones to be inaudible or varied.

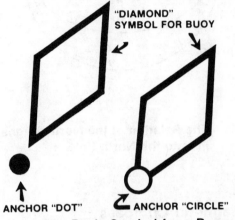

12-10 Basic Symbol for a Buoy

Obviously, aids to navigation — except for major lighthouses — are far too small to appear on the chart in their true shape. Instead, symbols are used to indicate the position, type, number and color of aids. A chart on these pages shows how the more common symbols relate to the buoys for which they stand.

The actual location of an aid to navigation is the small dot or circle (dot on older charts, small circle on newer ones) at the bottom of the diamond (when it's a buoy), or the isolated circle that indicates a fixed aid. Lighted buoys are distinguished by light-purple circles over-printed around the position circle. Lighted fixed aids have a light-purple exclamation mark with its sharp end pointing toward the position circle.

In practical piloting, you should remember that buoys are anchored in place, and at low tide they may move off their charted position — may even wind up outside the channel they mark. They may also be sunk or displaced by ice, collision or vandalism. Fixed aids, on the other hand, stay put. Even if their lights are extinguished, they are usually recognizable.

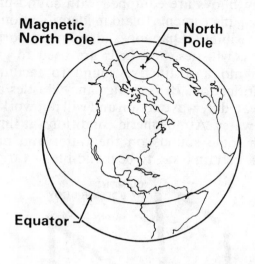

12-11   The Relation of the North Magnetic Pole to the North Pole

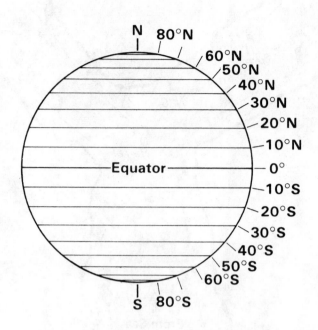

12-12   Parallels of Latitude Measure North and South from the Equator - 0° to 90° at Either Pole

The Magnetic Compass

Many centuries ago, mariners oriented themselves by the sun's place of rising and setting or by the direction of prevailing winds. This was less than precise (especially on windless, cloudy days), and the magnetic compass, slowly perfected over the ages, became the sailor's most common and reliable direction-indicating instrument.

In principle, the magnetic compass remains as simple as when it was invented by some unknown traveler in early medieval times. It is a linear magnet balanced so it can pivot freely in a horizontal plane and line up — as any magnet so suspended will — with the earth's magnetic field. The linear magnet, properly suspended and unaffected by nearby ferrous metal or electrical influence, will point toward the North Magnetic Pole, an area on earth whose location changes slightly and very slowly, but which lies in far northern Canada, at some distance from the "true" North Pole — a fictional location that serves as a base point for the familiar grid of latitude and longitude lines seen on all maps and charts.

Latitude and Longitude

Parallels of latitude are numbered north and south from 0° at the Equator to 90° North and 90° South at the true North and South Poles respectively. Each degree is subdivided into 60 equal segments called **minutes,** and each minute into either 60 seconds or 10 tenths of minutes, according to the notational system one prefers. On charts, true North is usually located at the top, and the parallels are indicated along the side margins by divisions in the black-and-white border, as well as by actual lines running across the chart surface at stated intervals that depend on the chart scale. It's handy to remember that one minute of latitude (but not longitude) equals one nautical mile (6076.1 feet or 1852 meters). Each chart also contains at least one printed scale, in nautical miles, kilometers, statute miles and/or yards. (Small Craft Charts are sometimes printed to show a maximum stretch of shoreline per sheet, and when this is the case, the top edge of the chart may not be North.)

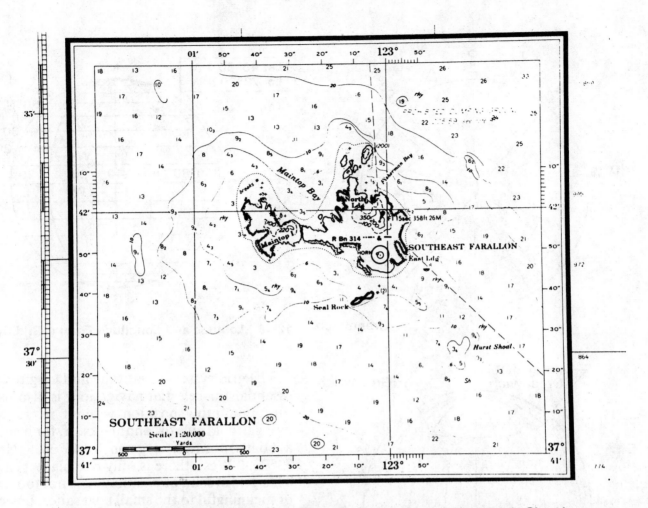

12-13 Latitude is Measured along the Vertical Margins. Note that the Basic Chart is in Minutes and Tenths of Minutes. The Inset has both Latitude and Longitude Divided into Minutes and Seconds

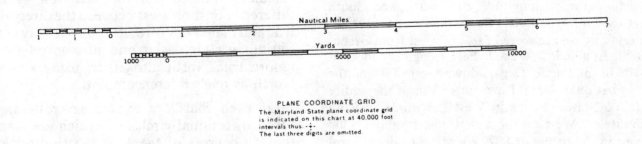

12-14 Scales may be Printed in Nautical Miles, Kilometers, Statute Miles and/or Yards.

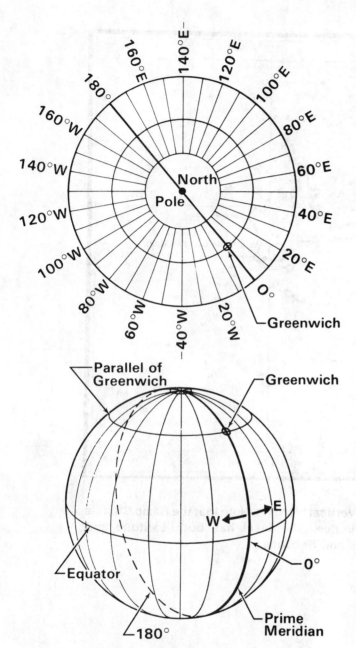

12-15 **Meridians of Longitude Measure East or West from the Prime Meridian to 180°**

Meridians of longitude run north and south between the true poles. By an ancient convention, meridians are numbered east and west from Greenwich, England. West and East Longitude meet at 180° in the Pacific Ocean, down most of which the International Date Line runs. Almost the entire United States is thus in West Longitude — from about 60° West on the East Coast to about 130° West in California or 150° West in Hawaii. Several islands of the Aleutian Chain in Alaska are over the 180th meridian and in East Longitude.

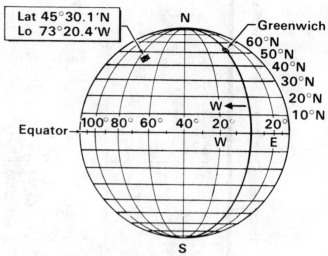

12-16 **Latitude and Longitude Form a Grid System**

The grid system of latitude and longitude, so essential for celestial navigation, is also useful for pinpointing position without reference to navigational aids or landmarks. If, for instance, a boat's position is given as 45° 30.1′ North, 73° 20.4′ West, there is only one place it can be. This grid system of positioning is not too useful or meaningful to the small boat sailor, however, and a grid based on true North does make it difficult for the mariner whose compass points to magnetic North. For obvious reasons, charts can only accommodate one reference grid. The navigator with a magnetic compass is left with two choices — "correct" his compass reading to the true North equivalent of its magnetic direction, or use an angular measuring device or system that reads out in magnetic degrees.

Traditional navigators make an arithmetic calculation to correct for **variation** — local difference East or West between the direction of true and magnetic North. For day-to-day course setting, it's far easier and just as reliable to ignore true North altogether, using magnetic North as one's reference point.

On each chart are printed several **compass roses**, directional circles on which are marked the 360 degrees of the True North directional circle in an outer ring, with the 360° Magnetic circle in an inner ring, and a written notation of

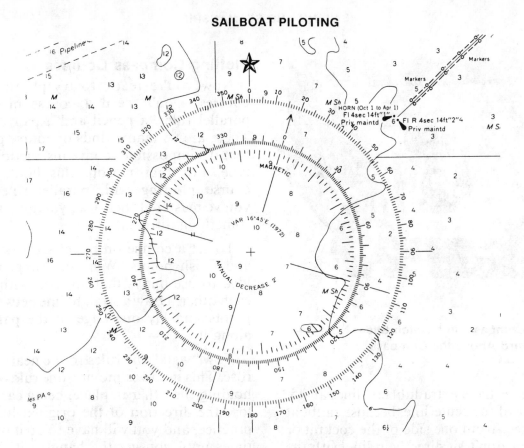

12-17 Usually Several Compass Roses are Placed Conveniently on the Chart. Some Charts May Only Require One

the local amount of variation. Later in this chapter we'll show how to plot and set courses by the inner, or magnetic, rose using either parallel rules or a course protractor; for the moment, merely bear in mind that any **course** — the direction from one point to another — can be expressed equally well in degrees true, related to True North, or degrees magnetic, based on the direction of magnetic north.

Selecting a Compass

When choosing a magnetic compass, you should first consider where on the boat it will be sited. Aboard cruising sailboats, the preferred location is usually the aft bulkhead of the deckhouse, where it can easily be seen from the helm. Boats with wheel steering usually have a **binnacle** for the wheel mounting, and the compass is fixed there. But for small daysailers, compass location can be a real problem. Mounting it in a removable bracket on the centerboard trunk is a common compromise, adequate **unless** your boat has a steel or iron centerboard.

12-18 The Magnetic Compass - the Sailor's Most Common and Reliable Direction-Indicating Instrument

Try to locate the instrument so you can sight over it in all directions, and be sure the fore-and-aft marks — the center pivot and the **lubber's line** — are in line with the keel. Many good sail-

12-19 A Compass on a Hatch Slide. Note the Guard Above the Compass

boat compasses have extra lubber's lines at 45° on either side of the centerline, because sailboat helmsmen steer from one side of the cockpit or the other, but don't sit directly in line with the compass.

A good compass nearly always has **internal compensators,** small magnets that allow the instrument to be adjusted for local metal or electrical influence (known as **deviation).** If you plan to sail at night, and if your boat has an electrical system, it's handy also to have a compass with a built-in red light.

The compass should be located at least three feet from radios, other electronic instruments or masses of ferrous metal. This may be hard to achieve in a small boat. When you've done your best, sail out and anchor at a place in the harbor where you can see several charted landmarks or fixed aids to navigation.

When the boat is riding steadily, face north according to the compass and orient yourself on the chart. Pick out as many natural and man-made features as you can and find their corresponding symbols on the chart. Do this from several points in your home waters and then try it underway. You'll soon find that it's not hard to relate reality to the chart, as long as you don't commit the navigator's cardinal sin — losing track of where you are.

Plotting Compass Courses

Now you're ready to try plotting compass courses. You'll need a course protractor or parallel rules, a pencil and a pair of dividers. There are so many kinds of course protractors that it's impossible to give instructions for each type. For that reason, this book will show course plotting with parallel rules — after you've mastered their use, you may want to try something different.

To set a course on the chart, first pick start and finish points. While learning, it's a good idea to use buoys that are well within sight of each other. Draw a straight line between the two points and lay one edge of the parallel rules along it.

Now "walk" the rules to the nearest compass rose. This involves moving one rule while firmly holding the other in place, being careful not to lose the direction of the original line. It takes practice, and you will have to do it over several times until you get the hang of it. You'll also need a flat, smooth surface under your chart, the larger the better, but no smaller than about two by two feet. When one edge of the rule has been walked to the compass rose, move it slowly and carefully until it intersects the small + that marks the rose's center.

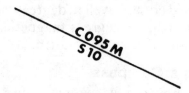

12-20 Labeling a Magnetic Course Line With Direction and Speed

From the **inner** degree circle, read out the course where the rule's edge intersects the circle, on the side in which you are heading. This is your **magnetic** course. Write it along the top edge of the penciled course line as three digits followed by the letter "M" (for magnetic): a course of 90° would thus be **090 M.**

Checking the Compass

Having plotted a buoy-to-buoy course, take your boat out and carefully put her on that course. It's a good idea to plot several possible courses in directions that are at least 45° different one from the other, and sail a beam reach, broad reach or run to minimize leeway. Using the course noted above, your compass should read 90°, or East, the same thing. When you arrive at the mark for the other end of the charted course, reverse your heading and reach back, if possible. Your compass should now read 180° different from the first heading, or 270°. (This 180° reverse is called the **reciprocal**).

If your original compass course and its reciprocal are the same as what you've plotted on the chart, or within 2-3 degrees either way, your compass is adequately free from deviation, the error caused by magnetic influences within the boat. If, on the other hand, you have an error of 5° or more on any heading, first check the accuracy of your plotting, then try running the courses again. If the error persists, check for a mass of ferrous metal, an electronic device or wiring near the compass. Presuming you find no removable source of interference, you must either move the compass, compensate the instrument according to the manufacturer's instructions, or make a **deviation table,** a record that indicates the amount of compass error on various evenly-spaced headings. Both compensation and making a deviation table are beyond the scope of this book, but are seldom necessary on small sailing craft.

Positioning

Assuming, however, that your compass is reasonably accurate, you can now employ it for positioning your boat. To do this, pick out two identifiable landmarks or (preferably) navigational aids that form a 90° angle more or less with your boat as the apex. Now locate the two markers on your chart. Remember buoys are floating and therefore cannot be used for absolutely precise positions.

Head the boat directly at one mark and note the compass course. As soon as you've written it down, head for the other mark and make a note of the compass heading to it.

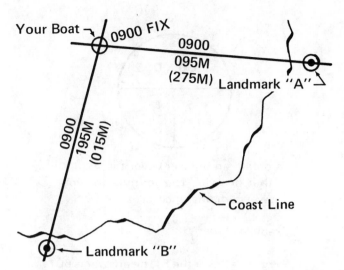

12-21 Plotting Two Lines of Position or Two LOPs

For the sake of argument, let's assume your first direction (called a **bearing**) was 095 M and the second was 195 M. Calculate the reciprocals of each bearing: 095 + 180 = 275; and 195 + 180 = 375, or 015 (when you pass 360°, of course, you have to begin over with 001).

Next, plot these reciprocals — 275° and 015° — **from** the charted positions of the respective marks. Each of these plotted lines is called a **Line of Position**, and your boat must be somewhere along it. Where two lines of position cross is obviously where you are.

To double-check your work, try three lines of position. In theory, they should intersect at one point, but they most probably won't. Practice doing the same thing over and over until they do, or at least form a reasonably small triangle.

Speed-Time-Distance

In setting courses, it's important to know how long it'll take you to get from place to place. Unfortunately, it's hard to figure such times with much precision in the average small sailboat, for several reasons.

To begin with, a sailboat's speed is constantly changing, and it's hard for a beginner to arrive at an average estimate over an extended distance. Second, even if your boat has a speedometer, these instruments are not terribly

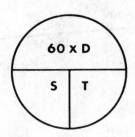

To obtain an answer cover the symbol of that answer. The formula for your answer remains uncovered.

Example:

SPEED — Cover the S. The answer is 60 multiplied by Distance divided by Time.

DISTANCE — Cover the D. The answer is Speed multiplied by Time divided by 60.

TIME — Cover the T. The answer is 60 multiplied by Distance divided by Speed.

12-22 Time, Speed and Distance Formula

accurate or reliable at the slow speeds typical of sailboats. Finally, your boat's speed over the bottom — her real speed — will be invisibly affected by the current, the movement of the water in which you're floating.

If you're attempting to pilot accurately, you just have to do the best you can. One helpful fact to bear in mind is that the average non-planing sailboat's cruising speed is something like the equal in knots of the square root of her waterline length. This apparently formidable thought is really quite simple: If your boat is 16 feet at the waterline, she will probably be able to average about four knots over an extended period.

If you have a stopwatch, try timing yourself between buoys on various points of sailing and at various wind strengths. Write down the two buoy numbers and the times, and plot your speed at home. In a surprisingly short time you'll be able to estimate your boat's speed with considerable accuracy, just from the feel of the

boat moving through the water, the size of the quarter wave and the force of the apparent wind.

Auxiliary inboard engines usually have tachometers, and a boat's speed through the water at a given tachometer setting is often quite predictable. Again, time yourself between buoys with a stopwatch and work out a speed-tachometer table.

The basic formula for determining speed when distance and time are known is:

$$S = \frac{60D}{T}$$

The result is in units of speed (MPH or NMPH). From that formula, it follows that:

$$D = \frac{S \times T}{60} \quad \text{and} \quad T = \frac{60D}{S}$$

Tides and Currents

We've mentioned the forces called tide and current several times in this chapter, but now we must come to grips with them. If you sail in tidal waters, you should be aware of the amount of rise from low to high water — it's marked on some charts — and the force and direction of the normal tidal current.

This information is available from many sources. Tide tables in one form or another give the time of high and low tide at several selected points for a full year at a time. Probably your local newspaper lists the time of high or low water at a prominent location. Although the state of the tide can be surprisingly different at two points not far from each other, most of the time the tide in a given harbor or bay is at much the same point in its cycle at any given time.

Bear in mind, too, that tide predictions are just that — with a strong wind or a serious change in barometric pressure, the time of high

DAY	TIME h.m.	HT. ft.	DAY	TIME h.m.	HT. ft.
1 W	0249	-1.5	16 TH	0316	-0.5
	0911	4.2		0945	3.7
	1413	1.3		1421	2.1
	2030	6.9		2034	5.8
2 TH	0337	-1.7	17 F	0348	-0.5
	1003	4.2		1017	3.7
	1502	1.5		1453	2.2
	2115	6.7		2106	5.7
3 F	0425	-1.6	18 SA	0421	-0.5
	1057	4.2		1056	3.7
	1553	1.7		1529	2.3
	2203	6.4		2137	5.5

12-23 Typical Excerpt from the Tide Tables

12-25 Can Buoy with Radar Reflector and Green Reflective Paint Band. Note Current Flowing Past the Buoy

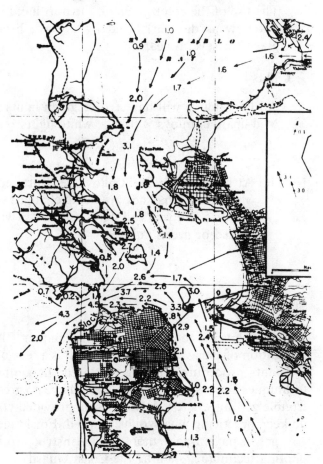

12-24 This Current Chart Shows Maximum Ebb Velocities in San Francisco Bay and at the Golden Gate

or low tide, and the amount of tidal rise or fall, may be considerably different from the forecast.

To figure tide, use a reference point near your boat's location. If you have a time for predicted high or low, you can work out a rough-and-ready but generally reliable prediction of the state of the tide at a time between high and low using the **rule of 12**: Take the total amount of tidal fluctuation in feet and divide it into twelfths (say the charted high water is 6.0 feet and the low water datum of soundings is 0.0; each twelfth is 0.5, or half a foot).

Then: Low water = 0	0 feet (datum)
1 hour after Low, add 1/12	½ foot above datum
2 hours after Low, add 3/12	1½ feet above datum
3 hours after Low, add 6/12	3 feet above datum
4 hours after Low, add 9/12	4½ feet above datum
5 hours after Low, add 11/12	5½ feet above datum
6 hours after Low, add 12/12	High water.

This simple system is based on a six-hour cycle from high to low or the other way, approximately the standard interval in most areas.

The forces and directions of tidal currents are listed in a government publication called **Tidal Current Tables** for each day of the year at selected reference stations. Currents are related to tides, but the two forces do not operate on the same schedule. The current of a rising tide is

12-26 Nun Buoy with Radar Reflector and Red Reflective Paint Band

called the **flood,** the current of falling tide is the **ebb.** Normally, the current turns in the other direction some time **after** the tide has ceased to rise or fall, but this is not always the case. With practice, you can learn to estimate the force of the existing current by looking at the shape of water piled up against fixed objects, and then make a freehand adjustment for its effect. You will need to have the **Tidal Current Tables,** published by National Ocean Survey, for your region.

If you live and sail in one of the major tidal boating areas covered by a set of **Tidal Current Charts,** this NOS publication will make current prediction easy. Each set consists of 12 simplified charts of a given area bound in booklet form. Instead of soundings and aids to navigation, the current chart is marked for the direction and force of current in various points in each of the 12 hours of a complete high-low-high cycle. All you need to know is approximately where you are, the present time, and have Tidal Current Tables for the region. Follow the instructions given in the Tidal Current Chart.

IALA-Maritime Buoyage System

The lateral buoyage stystem of the International Association of Lighthouse Authorities (IALA) has been adopted by the United States for waters navigated by international commercial shipping. Buoys of this system are being put in place. See Note.

Buoys:

Starboard hand buoys - red

Port hand buoys - green

Junction/Bifurcation buoys - green and red, or red and green horizontal bands

Mid-channel buoys - red and white vertical stripes

Special buoys - yellow

The use of the color green on the port hand is not new as daymarks and lights have been green for several years.

Lights:

All lateral aids will have red or green lights
Mid-channel buoys will have white lights

NOTE: At present significant buoy colors are red, black or green. They are being changed so that in 5 to 6 years all significant buoys will be red or green only.

Summary

As noted at the beginning of this chapter, the navigation of the average small sailboat is a seat-of-the-pants procedure. Having mastered the simple techniques discussed here, you should have no great trouble getting where you want to go, provided you do keep practicing what you've learned. For longer voyages, it pays to take more serious instruction in piloting technique, such as the Coast Guard Auxiliary Coastal Piloting Course.

Chapter 13

Radiotelephone

General

This chapter is addressed to owners and operators of vessels voluntarily equipped for radiotelephone communication. For practical purposes, recreational boats are not required by Federal law to carry radiotelephone equipment. If you do decide to equip your boat, there are certain regulations of the Federal Communications Commission that you must observe. These regulations are reflected in the text of this chapter, and are set forth in Volume IV, Part 83, of the FCC Rules and Regulations available from the Superintendent of Documents, U. S. Government Printing Office, Washington, D. C. 20402.

Boats carrying more than six passengers for hire, as well as many other commercial craft, are required to carry radio equipment. If you operate any type of commercial vessel, consult your nearest FCC office to determine the requirements which may apply to you and your boat.

Communications Purposes

With the distress, safety and calling frequencies — Channel 16 (156.8 MHz) VHF-FM and the 2182 kHz MF-SSB — as the keystones, the marine radiotelephone system is designed to accomplish all the following communications functions:

1. Provide monitored distress and safety frequencies. By designating the distress frequencies as calling frequencies, the radio regulations ensure that a maximum number of stations will be listening at any given time. *The success of this arrangement depends on cooperation,* both in maintaining a listening watch on 2182 kHz or Channel 16 (156.8 MHz) and in keeping those frequencies clear of all unnecessary communication.

2. Allow for communication between your vessel and local and Federal agencies.

3. Provide frequencies for the exchange of information pertaining to navigation, movement or management of vessels.

4. Provide special frequencies for stations and vessels engaged in commerce.

5. Provide noncommercial frequencies for the special needs of recreational boating people.

6. Provide separate frequencies for vessels to communicate with shore telephones.

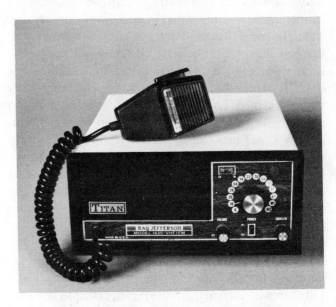

13-1 Radiotelephone Set

How To Get Ship Station and Operator Licenses

Ship Station Licenses

All radio stations aboard vessels must be licensed by the Federal Communications Commission. Ship stations are licensed primarily for the safety of life and property; therefore, distress and safety communications must have absolute priority. The licensee is responsible at all times for the lawful and proper operation of his station.

Each licensee must have a copy of Part 83 of the FCC Rules or a copy of the Simplified Rules, "How to Use Your VHF Marine Radio." This copy may be aboard your vessel or at a readily accessible place at your home or business.

Application for a ship station license including radionavigation (radar) and EPIRB (see a later section for special information concerning EPIRBs) is made on FCC Form 506. This form may be obtained from any FCC Field Office. The completed application is sent to the Federal Communications Commission, P.O. Box 1040, Gettysburg, PA 17325. Application processing time is approximately 6 to 8 weeks. The regular term of a ship station license is 5 years.

Temporary Station License

The Commission realizes that some individuals may want to start operating their radiotelephones immediately and not wait the 6 to 8 week processing time. To meet this need, the applicant may obtain an interim ship station license. This may be done by the applicant filing a properly completed application (FCC Form 506) and posting 506A, the temporary station license. This license, valid for sixty days from the date Form 506 is mailed to Gettysburg, Pennsylvania, permits the applicant to operate his ship radiotelephone station while awaiting receipt of the regular term license. The regular term license will be mailed to the licensee prior to the expiration of the temporary permit.

Renewal of Ship Station License

An application for renewal of a ship radiotelephone station license is made on FCC Form 405-B. This form is ordinarily mailed to the station licensee 60 days prior to the expiration date of his license. If the form has not been received 30 days prior to the expiration of current license, FCC Form 405-B may be obtained upon request from any FCC office. Application for renewal must be received by the Commission prior to the expiration date of the station license.

Discontinuing Ship Station Operation

If you permanently discontinue the operation of the ship radio station, as for example, if you sell your boat, you are required to promptly return the station license to the Secretary, Federal Communications Commission, Washington, D. C. 20554. In the event that the license is not available for this purpose, a letter or telegram must be sent to the Secretary stating the reason why the license is not available and requesting that the license be cancelled. Otherwise, any violations committed in the operation of the station may be your responsibility.

Modification of Ship Station License

An application for modification of the station license must be filed when any transmitting equipment is added that does not operate in a frequency band or bands authorized in the ship station license. This application should be filed on FCC Form 506.

No application for modification is required for additions and/or replacement of FCC type accepted radiotelephone transmitters that operate in the same frequency band(s) as specified in the station license.

The licensee must promptly notify the Commission when the name of the licensee is changed, when the mailing address of the licensee is changed, or in the event that the vessel's name is changed. This notice, which may be in letter form, should be sent to the Federal Communications Commission, P. O. Box 1040, Gettysburg, PA 17325, or to the Secretary, Federal Communications Commission, Washington, D. C. 20554. A copy of the letter should be posted with the station license until a new license is issued. No formal application or fee is required in these cases.

VHF Equipment

All ship stations employing frequencies in the 2 MHz band must also be equipped to operate in the 156-162 MHz band. Licensees authorized by their existing licenses to operate in the 2 MHz band may install and operate VHF equipment under authority of their existing licenses.

Operator Permit or License

The radiotelephone transmitter in a ship station may be operated only by a person holding a permit or operator license. The authorized operator may permit others to speak over the microphone if he starts, supervises, and ends the operation, makes the necessary log entries, and gives the necessary identification. The authorization usually held by radio operators aboard small vessels is the Restricted Radiotelephone Operator Permit.

The Restricted Radiotelephone Operator Permit is the minimum authorization required for the operation of a ship station. Neither the Restricted Radiotelephone Operator Permit nor the Third Class Radiotelephone Operator Permit allow the operator to make any transmitter adjustment that may affect the proper operation of the station. Any such adjustments may only be made by the holder of a First- or Second-Class Radiotelegraph or Radiotelephone License. The Restricted Radiotelephone Operator Permit or verification card of a higher class license must be posted or kept on the operator's person.

An application for a Restricted Radiotelephone Operator Permit is made on FCC Form 753. The completed form is sent to the Federal Communications Commission, P. O. Box 1050, Gettysbrug, PA 17325. No oral or written examination is required. Applicants must be at least 14 years of age. Part III of Form 753 is filled out and detatched to serve as a temporary Restricted Operator's Permit until the licensee's lifetime permit is issued.

Special Provisions for Aliens

Except for foreign governments and representatives of foreign governments, aliens may be granted ship station licenses and Restricted Radiotelephone Operator Permits. The operator permit granted to an alien is valid only for operating the ship station licensed in his name. Special forms and provisions are applicable to aliens and, therefore, an alien should contact an FCC Field Office for information before applying for his license and permit.

Radiotelephone Equipment

FCC Type Acceptance

All radiotelephone transmitters used in a ship station must be type accepted under Part 83 of the FCC Regulations. A list of all equipment acceptable for licensing in the marine service is included in the Commission's Radio Equipment List. Any FCC Field Office can advise you whether the radiotelephone you propose to use is type accepted under Part 83, if you furnish them with the manufacturer's name and the model or type number of the transmitter.

Adjustments of Transmitting Equipment

The station licensee is responsible for the proper technical operation of his equipment. All transmitter measurements, adjustments, or repairs that may affect the proper operation of the transmitter must be made by or under the immediate supervision and responsibility of a person holding a valid First- or Second-Class Radiotelegraph or Radiotelephone Operator License. A special license endorsement is required to service a ship radar set.

Selecting a VHF Radiotelephone

Before purchasing a VHF-FM radiotelephone, you should carefully consider your requirements and select a unit that will meet these needs. You should remember that VHF communications are essentially "line of sight." The average ship-to-ship

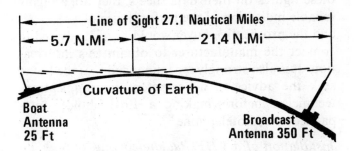

13-2 Line of Sight Distances for Radio

range is about 10 to 15 miles, while the normally expected ship-to-shore range is 20 to 30 miles. These figures vary depending upon transmitter power, antenna height, and terrain.

The FCC limits the transmitter power for VHF-FM to 25 watts for vessels and also requires the capability to reduce transmitter power to not more than one watt for short range communication. No matter how powerful your transmitter is, if you can't hear the other station — you can't communicate. The receiver performance of your radiotelephone is therefore an important aspect of your communication capability.

Two of the most important receiver specifications are sensitivity and adjacent channel rejection. These two factors are usually a good indication of how a particular receiver will perform.

In a VHF-FM receiver, the sensitivity is usually given as the number of microvolts required to produce 20 decibels (dB) of quieting. The lower or smaller the number of microvolts for the same amount of quieting, the better the sensitivity of the receiver; for example, 0.5 microvolt is better than 2.0 microvolts. (Note: Some manufacturers specify the sensitivity at other than 20 dB, so you should be sure you are comparing receivers based on the same criteria.)

The adjacent channel rejection is one of several different specifications that indicate the receiver's ability to reject unwanted signals and accept only the desired signal. It is usually given as a negative number of dB. The larger the absolute number of dB, the better the adjacent channel rejection of the receiver. For example, a receiver with an adjacent channel rejection of –70 dB would normally perform much better than one with an adjacent channel rejection of –50 dB.

Although many manufacturers do not include these figures on their data sheets, they are a highly reliable indication of the performance of a receiver; and the prospective buyer would be well advised to contact the manufacturer to obtain this information. It is also strongly recommended that the buyer seek the advice of a competent communications technician before making a final choice on a particular radiotelephone.

Installation of a VHF Radiotelephone

The licensee of a ship station may install a *pretested* VHF marine radiotelephone transmitter in his ship station. No operator license is required to perform this kind of installation. This permission does NOT authorize the ship station licensee to add or substitute channels or to make any modifications to the transmitter, with the exception that where the FCC has type accepted a transmitter in which factory sealed pretested "plug-in" modules are used for the addition or substitution of channels in the transmitter, the licensee may add or substitute channels using these "plug-in" modules. Unless the individual is familiar with working with coaxial cable, he should have a technician attach the coaxial cable plug to the antenna cable.

Required Frequencies and Equipment Channelization

All ship radiotelephone stations in the 156 to 162 MHz band must be equipped to operate on:
1. Ch. 16 (156.8 MHz)   International Distress, Safety and Calling frequency for VHF.
2. Ch. 6 (156.3 MHz) Intership Safety Channel.
3. At least one working frequency.

The number of channels installed in your set will depend largely on how the set will be used, where the vessel will be operated, and what coast stations are operating in your area. While fewer than twelve channels may be satisfactory for some vessels, installation of a radiotelephone with less than twelve channel capability is not recommended.

The marine VHF band in the United States consists of 47 channels including three weather channels.

13-3 Thunderstorm

The following tables include a listing of the noncommercial frequencies available, an explanation of the use of the various channels and some suggestions on the selection of channels for recreational (noncommercial) vessels.

The more channels you have in your set, the better your communication capability will be. Caution must be exercised, however, in selecting and using channels in accordance with their authorized purposes as set out in Table II.

The following table can be used as an aid in selecting the proper channels to install in your VHF radio. The suggested number of channels to be selected from each group is given for recreational vessels equipped with radiotelephones having six and twelve channel capability. An explanation of the use of each channel is given in Table II.

TABLE I

Channel Numbers	Type of Communication	Suggested Channel Selection for Recreational Vessels	
		6 Ch.	12 Ch.
16	DISTRESS, SAFETY & CALLING Intership & ship to coast	*	*
6	INTERSHIP SAFETY Intership. NOT to be used for non-safety intership communications	*	*
22	Communications with U. S. Coast Guard ship, coast, or aircraft stations.	1	1
65, 66, 12, 73, 14, 74, 20	PORT OPERATIONS Intership & ship to coast		1
13	NAVIGATIONAL		1
68, 9	NON-COMMERCIAL Intership & ship to coast	1	2
69, 71, 78	NON-COMMERCIAL Ship to coast		1
70, 72	NON-COMMERCIAL Intership		2
24, 84, 25, 85, 26, 86, 27, 87, 28	PUBLIC CORRESPONDENCE Ship to public coast	2	2
162.40 & 162.475 MHz 162.55 MHz	NOAA WEATHER SERVICE Ship receive only Ship receive only	** **	** **

* These stations are required to be installed in every ship station equipped with a VHF radio.

**The weather receive channels are half-channels (receive only) one or both of which are recommended to be installed in each ship station. Many manufacturers include one or both of these channels in their sets in addition to the normal six or twelve channel capacity.

TABLE II

CHANNEL USAGE

Channel Number	Ship Transmit	Ship Receive	Intended Use
6	156.300	156.300	INTERSHIP SAFETY. Required for all VHF-FM equipped vessels for intership safety purposes and search and rescue (SAR) communications with ships and aircraft of the U. S. Coast Guard. Must not be used for non-safety communications.
9	156.450	156.450	COMMERCIAL AND NON-COMMERCIAL (INTERSHIP AND SHIP-TO-COAST). Some examples of use are communications with commercial marinas and public docks to obtain supplies to schedule repairs and contacting commercial vessels about matters of common concern.
12	156.600	156.600	PORT OPERATIONS (INTERSHIP AND SHIP-TO-COAST). Available to all vessels. This is a traffic advisory channel for use by agencies directing the movement of vessels in or near ports, locks, or waterways. Messages are restricted to the operational handling, movement and safety to ships and, in emergency, to the safety of persons. It should be noted, however, in the Ports of New York and New Orleans channels 11, 12 and 14 are to be used exclusively for the Vessel Traffic System being developed by the United States Coast Guard.
13	156.650	156.650	NAVIGATIONAL — (SHIP'S) BRIDGE TO (SHIP'S) BRIDGE. This channel is available to all vessels and is required on large passenger and commercial vessels (including many tugs). Use is limited to navigational communications such as in meeting and passing situations. Abbreviated short

operating procedures and 1 watt maximum power (except in certain special instances) are used on this channel for both calling and working. For recreational vessels, this channel should be used for *listening* to determine the intentions of large vessels. This is also the primary channel used at locks and bridges operated by the U. S. Army Corps of Engineers.

14	156.700	156.700	PORT OPERATIONS (INTERSHIP AND SHIP-TO-COAST). Same as channel 12.
15	156.750	156.750	ENVIRONMENTAL (RECEIVE ONLY). A receive only channel used to broadcast environmental information to ships such as weather, sea conditions, time signals for navigation, notices to mariners, etc. Most of this information is also broadcast on the weather (WX) channels.
16	156.800	156.800	DISTRESS, SAFETY AND CALLING (INTERSHIP AND SHIP-TO-COAST). Required channel for all VHF-FM equipped vessels. Must be monitored at all times station is in operation (except when actually communicating on another channel). This channel is monitored also by the Coast Guard, public coast stations and many limited coast stations. Calls to other vessels are normally initiated on this channel. Then, except in an emergency, you must switch to a working channel. For additional information see the sections on operating procedures.
17	156.850	156.850	STATE CONTROL. Available to all vessels to communicate with ships and coast stations operated by state or local governments. Messages are restricted to regulation and control, or rendering assistance. Use of low power (1 watt) setting is required by international treaty.
20	157.000	161.600	PORT OPERATIONS (SHIP-TO-COAST). Available to all vessels. This is a traffic advisory channel for use by agencies directing the movement of vessels in or near ports, locks, or waterways. Messages are restricted to the operational handling, movement and safety of ships and, in emergency, to the safety of persons.
21A	157.050	157.050	U. S. GOVERNMENT ONLY.
22A	157.100	157.100	COAST GUARD LIAISON. This channel is used for communications with U. S. Coast Guard ship, coast and aircraft stations after first establishing communications on channel 16. *It is strongly recommended that every VHF radiotelephone include this channel.*
23A	157.150	157.150	U. S. GOVERNMENT ONLY
24	157.200	161.800	PUBLIC CORRESPONDENCE (SHIP-TO-COAST). Available to all vessels to communicate with public coast stations operated by telephone companies. Channels 26 and 28 are the primary public correspondence channels and therefore become the first choice for the cruising vessel having limited channel capacity.
25	157.250	161.850	PUBLIC CORRESPONDENCE (SHIP-TO-COAST). Same as channel 24.
26	157.300	161.900	PUBLIC CORRESPONDENCE (SHIP-TO-COAST). Same as channel 24.
27	157.350	161.950	PUBLIC CORRESPONDENCE (SHIP-TO-COAST). Same as channel 24.

28	157.400	162.000	PUBLIC CORRESPONDENCE (SHIP-TO-COAST). Same as channel 24.
65A	156.275	156.275	PORT OPERATIONS (INTERSHIP AND SHIP-TO-COAST). Same as channel 12.
66A	156.325	156.325	PORT OPERATIONS (INTERSHIP AND SHIP-TO-COAST). Same as channel 12.
68	156.425	156.425	NON-COMMERCIAL (INTERSHIP AND SHIP-TO-COAST). A working channel for non-commercial vessels. May be used for obtaining supplies, scheduling repairs, berthing and accommodations, etc. from yacht clubs or marinas, and intership operational communications such as piloting or arranging for rendezvous with other vessels. It should be noted that channel 68 (and channel 70 for intership only) is the most popular non-commercial channel and therefore is the first choice for vessels having limited channel capacity.
69	156.475	156.475	NON-COMMERCIAL WORKING. For pleasure boats ship-to-ship and ship-to-shore communications only.
70	156.525	156.525	NON-COMMERCIAL WORKING. For pleasure boats ship-to-ship communications only.
71	156.575	156.575	NON-COMMERCIAL WORKING. For pleasure boats ship-to-ship and ship-to-shore communications only.
72	156.625	156.625	NON-COMMERCIAL (INTERSHIP). Same as channel 68 except limited to intership communications.
73	156.675	156.675	PORT OPERATIONS (INTERSHIP AND SHIP-TO-COAST). Same as channel 20.
74	156.725	156.725	PORT OPERATIONS (INTERSHIP AND SHIP-TO-COAST). Same as channel 20.
78A	156.925	156.925	NON-COMMERCIAL WORKING. For pleasure boats ship-to-ship and ship-to-shore communications only. (Not available for pleasure boat use in Canada.)
81A	157.075	157.075	U. S. GOVERNMENT ONLY.
82A	157.125	157.125	U. S. GOVERNMENT ONLY.
83A	157.175	157.175	U. S. GOVERNMENT ONLY.
84	157.225	161.825	PUBLIC CORRESPONDENCE (SHIP-TO-COAST). Same as channel 24.
85	157.275	161.875	PUBLIC CORRESPONDENCE (SHIP-TO-COAST). Same as channel 24.
86	157.325	161.925	PUBLIC CORRESPONDENCE (SHIP-TO-COAST). Same as channel 24.
87	157.375	161.975	PUBLIC CORRESPONDENCE (SHIP-TO-COAST). Same as channel 24.
WX1	—	162.550	WEATHER (RECEIVE ONLY). To receive weather broadcasts of the Department of Commerce, National Oceanic and Atmospheric Administration (NOAA).
WX2	—	162.400	WEATHER (RECEIVE ONLY). Same as WX1.
WX3	—	162.479	WEATHER (RECEIVE ONLY). Same as WX1.

NOTE: The addition of the letter "A" to the channel number indicates that the ship receive channel used in the United States is different from the one used by vessels and coast stations of other countries. Vessels equipped for U. S. operations only, will experience difficulty communicating with foreign ships and coast stations on these channels.

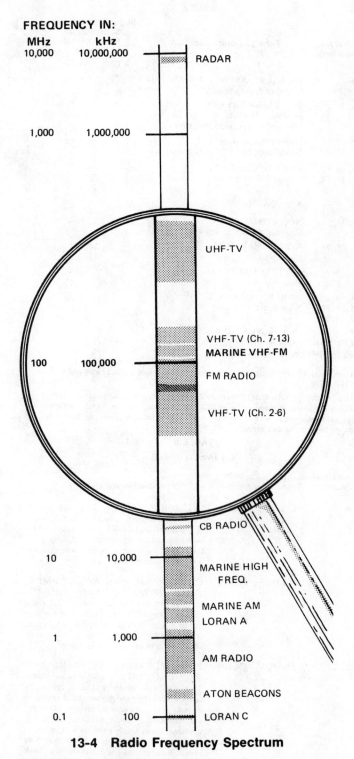

13-4 Radio Frequency Spectrum

Medium and High Frequency Radiotelephone Equipment

Previously, most marine radiotelephones operated in the 2-3 MHz medium frequency (MF) band. This equipment, which is now obsolete, employed double sideband (DSB) full carrier type of amplitude modulation (AM). These DSB radiotelephones have been superseded by single sideband (SSB) equipment. The FCC requires that all installations in the medium frequency (MF) band employ the SSB mode.

Single sideband provides a number of advantages over DSB equipment. Most important, the occupied bandwidth is narrower. Therefore, more stations can be accommodated in the marine bands. The SSB mode is more efficient than DSB. This permits longer range communications with less battery consumption than for DSB radiotelephones.

SSB medium and high frequency radiotelephones are primarily for offshore and high-seas service. For that reason, information on SSB technique is beyond the scope of this chapter.

Emergency Position Radio Beacon

The EPIRB is basically a small VHF transmitter available in three classes, A, B, and C. The A and B classes send out a distinctive signal on two frequencies. These are the aeronautical emergency frequencies of 121.5 MHz monitored by commercial and private aircraft and 243 MHz monitored by military aircraft.

The Class A EPIRB is capable of floating free of a sinking vessel and activating automatically while the Class B EPIRB must be activated manually.

The Class C EPIRB has been authorized by the FCC specifically for vessels within range of a VHF installation (Inland waters and within 20 miles of shore). It operates alternately on VHF marine channels 16 and 15, transmitting a short, distinctive warbling signal on Channel 16 to alert the monitoring station to the distress call and shifts automatically to Channel 15 with a longer transmission time to allow rescuers to home in on the signal with direction finding equipment.

All three must be FCC licensed.

In making application for FCC license, use FCC Form 506, whether the EPIRB is to be a part of the complement of transmitting equipment aboard or even if an EPIRB only is to be authorized.

27 MHz Citizens Radio Band (CB)

Operation in the Citizens Radio Service is intended primarily to provide an individual means of conducting personal or business communications over a typical range of 5 to 15 miles. You may operate CB equipment aboard your boat on any of the 40 channels that have been made available in the 27 MHz Class D service on a shared basis.

FCC regulations limit the maximum power output from the transmitter to 4 watts carrier power (PEP) for Double Sideband (DSB) amplitude modulation (AM) equipment, and 12 watts PEP for single sideband (SSB) transmitters, with a maximum antenna height of 20 feet above the highest point of the vessel.

Channel 9 in the Citizens Band has been designated as an emergency channel for emergency communications involving the safety of life of individuals, protection of private property, or for rendering assistance to a motorist.

No operator permit or operator license is required; however, a station license is required prior to operation of a CB radio. The application should be filed with the FCC using Form 505. Mail the application to the Federal Communications Commission, P.O. Box 1010, Gettysburg, PA 17325.

A Temporary Permit is Available Using Form 555-B

Commencing 1 April 1978, the Coast Guard will monitor Channel 9, Citizens Band Radio Service (CB), not to interfere with existing communications system (i.e. Channel 16 VHF-FM or 2182.). The Coast Guard recommends that the boaters use VHF-FM for distress communications.

Operating Procedures (Other than Distress, Urgency and Safety)

Maintain a Watch

Whenever your radio is turned on, keep the receiver tuned to the appropriate distress and calling frequency, 156.8 MHz or 2182 kHz. This listening watch must be maintained at all times the station is in operation and you are not actually communicating.

Since this watch is required for safety and to facilitate communications by providing a common calling channel, it is not permissible for one vessel in a fleet of vessels traveling together to maintain this watch while the other vessels guard another channel, such as common intership channel. You may maintain a watch on a working channel, however, and may establish communications directly on that channel provided you simultaneously maintain your watch on the distress and calling channel.

Don't forget to record the times you maintain this watch in your Radio Log.

Choose the Correct Channel or Frequency

Each of the marine frequencies and channels is authorized for a specific type of communication. It is therefore required that you choose the correct channel for the type of communications you wish to engage in. For example, certain channels are set aside exclusively for intership use and may not be used for ship to coast communications. Channels are further classified according to the subject matter or content of the communications. For example, Commercial communications are limited to commercial operations and may be used only to discuss matters pertaining to the commercial enterprise the vessel is engaged in.

The authorized use of each of the VHF channels is given in Table II. For recreational boats, most of the communications will be limited to what is known as Non-commercial (Operational in the MF band) communications and Public Correspondence.

Public Correspondence

By using the channels set aside for Public Correspondence and establishing communications through the facilities of the public coast stations, you are able to make and receive calls from any telephone on shore. There is no restriction on the content of your communication and you do not have to limit your messages strictly to ship's business. Except for distress calls, public coast stations will charge for this service.

Non-Commercial or Operational

These channels have been set aside to fulfill the wide scope of needs of the recreational (non-commercial) vessel. Frequencies are available for both intership and ship to shore (with limited coast stations) communications. Permissible communications on these channels are those concerning the movement of vessels, obtaining supplies and service and, in general, anything else that pertains to the needs and normal operation of the vessel. "Chitchat" is not permitted.

Coast Guard

The government frequencies 157.1 MHz (Channel 22) and 2670 kHz are widely used by recreational boating operators for communicating with U. S. Coast Guard shore stations and ship stations, and with USCG Auxiliary vessels when these vessels are operating under orders. When using these channels, you must first establish communications on the appropriate calling frequency (Channel 16 or 2182 kHz).

13-5 Coast Guard Communication Station

Calling Intership

Turn your radiotelephone on and listen on the appropriate distress and calling frequency, Channel 16 or 2182 kHz, to make sure it is not being used. If it is clear, put your transmitter on the air. This is usually done by depressing the "push to talk" button on the microphone. (To hear a reply, you must release this button.)

Speak directly into the microphone in a normal tone of voice. Speak clearly and distinctly. Call the vessel with which you wish to communicate by using its name; then identify your vessel with its name and FCC assigned call sign. Do not add unnecessary words and phrases such as "come in, Bob" or "Do you read me?" Limit the use of phonetics to poor transmission conditions.

This preliminary call must not exceed 30 seconds. If contact is not made, wait at least 2 minutes before repeating the call. After this time interval, make the call in the same manner. This procedure may be repeated no more than three times. If contact is not made during this period, you must wait at least 15 minutes before making your next attempt.

Once contact is established on Channel 16 or 2182 kHz, you must switch to an appropriate frequency for further communication. You may only use Channel 16 and 2182 kHz for calling and in emergency situations.

Since switching to a "working" frequency is required to carry out the actual communications, it is often helpful to monitor the "working" frequency you wish to use, briefly, before initiating the call on Channel 16 or 2182 kHz. This will help prevent you from interrupting other users of the channel.

All communications should be kept as brief as possible and at the end of the communication each vessel is required to give its call sign, after which, both vessels switch back to the distress and calling channel in order to reestablish the watch.

Two examples of acceptable forms for establishing communication with another vessel follow:

EXAMPLE I

Vessel	Voice Transmission
BLUE DUCK (on Channel 16)	"MARY JANE — THIS IS — BLUE DUCK — WHISKEY ALFA 1234" (The name of the vessel being called may be said two or three times if conditions demand).
MARY JANE (on Channel 16)	"BLUE DUCK — THIS IS — MARY JANE WHISKEY ALFA 5678 — REPLY 68" (Or some other proper working channel.)
BLUE DUCK (on Channel 16)	"68 or "ROGER" (If unable to reply on the channel selected, an appropriate alternate should be selected.)
BLUE DUCK (on working channel)	"BLUE DUCK"
MARY JANE (on working channel)	"MARY JANE"
BLUE DUCK (on working channel)	(Continues with message and terminates communication within 3 minutes. At the end of the communication, each vessel gives its call sign.)

EXAMPLE II — A short form most useful when both parties are familiar with it.

BLUE DUCK (on Channel 16)	"MARY JANE — BLUE DUCK — WHISKEY ALFA 1234 — REPLY 68"
MARY JANE (on Channel 68)	"MARY JANE — WHISKEY ALFA 5678"
BLUE DUCK (on Channel 68)	"BLUE DUCK" (Continues message and terminates communications as indicated in EXAMPLE I.)

Calling Ship to Coast (Other than U. S. Coast Guard)

The procedures for calling coast stations are similar to those used in making intership calls with the exception that you normally initiate the call on the assigned frequency of the coast station.

Routine Radio Check

Radio checks may be made on 156.8 MHz (Channel 16) but should be completed by immediately shifting to a working channel.

Listen to make sure that the Distress and Calling frequency is not busy. If it is free, put your transmitter on the air and call a specific station or vessel and include the phrase "request a radio check" in your initial call. For example, "MARY JANE - THIS IS BLUE DUCK - WHISKEY ALFA 1234 - REQUEST RADIO CHECK CHANNEL _____ (names working channel) - OVER." After the reply by Mary Jane, Blue Duck would then say "HOW DO YOU HEAR ME? - OVER." The proper response by Mary Jane, depending on the respective conditions, would be:

"I HEAR YOU LOUD AND CLEAR," or

"I HEAR YOU WEAK BUT CLEAR," or

"YOU ARE LOUD BUT DISTORTED," etc.

Do not respond to a request for a radio check with such phrases as:

"I HEAR YOU FIVE BY FIVE," or

"I *READ* YOU LOUD AND CLEAR."

Figures are not a clear response as to the character of the transmission and the word *"read"* implies a radio check by a meter.

It is illegal to call a Coast Guard Station on 2182 kHz for a radio check. This prohibition does not apply to tests conducted during investigations by FCC representatives or when qualified radio technicians are installing equipment or correcting deficiencies in the station radiotelephone equipment.

Radiotelephone Station Log

A radio log is required; each page must (1) be numbered; (2) bear the name of the vessel and call sign; and (3) be signed by the operator. Entries must show the time each watch begins and ends. All distress and alarm signals must be recorded as completely as possible. This requirement applies to all related communications transmitted or intercepted, and to all urgency and safety signals and communications transmitted. A record of all installations, services, or maintenance work performed that may affect the proper operation of the station must also be entered by the licensed operator doing the work, including his address and the class, serial number, and expiration date of his license.

The 24-hour system is used in a radio log for recording time; that is, 8:45 a.m. is written as 0845 and 1:00 p.m. as 1300. Local time is normally used, but Eastern Standard Time (EST) or Universal Coordinated Time (UTC) - must be used throughout the Great Lakes. Vessels on international voyages use UTC exclusively. Whichever time is used, the appropriate abbreviation for the time zone must be entered at the head of the time column.

Radio logs must be retained for at least a year, and for 3 years if they contain entries concerning distress, and for longer periods if they concern communications being investigated by the FCC or against which claims or complaints have been filed.

Station logs must be made available for inspection at the request of an FCC representative, who may remove them from the licensee's possession. On request, the licensee shall mail them to the FCC by either registered or certified mail, return receipt requested.

A sample "Ship Radio Station Log Sheet" and a "Ship Radio Station Maintenance Log Sheet" are shown.

SAMPLE

SHIP RADIO STATION LOG SHEET
(Recreational Vessels)

Page No. _____ Name of Vessel _____ Radio Call _____

DATE /1	DISTRESS LISTENING WATCH TIME /2 /3 (EST, GMT, ETC.)		Channel or Freq. /4	Priority MESSAGE TIME /2	MESSAGE /5	OPERATOR'S SIGNATURE
	Start	Stop				

1 Log: Day, Month, Year

2 Use UTC or Local Time. Show which used. Use 24-hour system; that is, 8:45 a.m. is entered as 0845, and 2:15 p.m. as 1415.

3 Log time when radiotelephone is turned on and when turned off.

4 Log VHF Channel 16 (156.800 MHz) or 2182 kHz, as appropriate.

5 Record as completely as possible all distress communications transmitted or intercepted and all urgency and safety communications transmitted. Retain logs for at least one year; for 3 years if they include entries related to distress; longer if they concern communications being investigated by the FCC or against which claims or complaints have been filed.

SAMPLE

SHIP RADIO STATION MAINTENANCE LOG
(Recreational Vessels)

Page No. _____ Name of Vessel _____ Radio Call _____

DATE	SERVICE RECORD	TECHNICIAN'S LICENSE DATA
		Class _____ Number _____ Expiration Date _____ Signature _____ Address _____
		Class _____ Number _____ Expiration Date _____ Signature _____ Address _____

Include record of installations, repairs, adjustments and service performed by FCC licensed Radiotelegraph or Radiotelephone 1st or 2nd Class Radio Operator. Special endorsement required for Radar installation and repair.

Secrecy of Communications

The Communications Act prohibits divulging interstate or foreign communications transmitted, received, or intercepted by wire or radio to anyone other than the addressee or his agent or attorney, or to persons necessarily involved in the handling of the communications, unless the sender authorizes the divulgence of the contents of the communication. Persons intercepting such communications or becoming acquainted with them are also prohibited from divulging the contents or using the contents for the benefit of themselves or others.

Obviously, this requirement of secrecy does not apply to radio communications relating to ships in distress, nor to radio communications transmitted by amateurs or broadcasts by others for use of the general public. It does apply, however, to all other communications. These statutory secrecy provisions cover messages addressed to a specific ship station or coast station or to a person via such station.

Obscenity, Indecency and Profanity

When two or more ship stations are communicating with each other, they are talking over an extensive party line. Users should always bear this fact in mind and assume that many persons are listening. All users therefore have a compelling moral obligation to avoid offensive remarks. They also have a strict legal obligation inasmuch as it is a criminal offense for any person to transmit communications containing obscene, indecent, or profane words, language, or meaning. Whoever utters any obscene, indecent or profane language by means of radio communication may be fined not more than $10,000 or imprisoned not more than 2 years, or both.

Procedure Words

One way of cutting down the length of radio transmissions without loss of meaning is by the use of Procedure Words. These are individual words and short phrases which express complex thoughts in abbreviated form. They are employed in transmitting situations which frequently recur — the most obvious example, perhaps, is the word "OUT," which (when spoken at the end of a message) signifies: "THIS IS THE END OF MY TRANSMISSION TO YOU AND NO ANSWER IS REQUIRED OR EXPECTED."

Procedure words can only be successful in shortening message sending when (1) their meaning is fully understood by sender and listener and (2) they are properly used. The phrase over and out, for instance, is improper, since the two terms are contradictory.

Following is a list of procedure words and their meanings. It will take time for the novice operator to become used to this form of verbal shorthand, but effort spent in learning these few phrases will be repaid in clearer, shorter messages.

PROCEDURE WORD	MEANING
OUT	This is the end of my transmission to you and no answer is required or expected.
OVER	This is the end of my transmission to you and a response is necessary. Go ahead and transmit.
	(Note: Observe the considerable difference between "Over," used during a message exchange, and "Out," employed at the end of an exchange. "Over" should be omitted when the context of a transmission makes it clear that it is unnecessary.)
ROGER	I have received your last transmission satisfactorily.
WILCO	Your last message has been received, understood, and will be complied with.
THIS IS	This transmission is from the station whose name or call sign immediately follows.
	(Note: Normally used at the beginning of a transmission: "BLUE DUCK — THIS IS — GIMLET — WHISKEY ZULU ECHO 3488." Sometimes omitted in transmissions between experienced operators familiar with each other's boat names.)
FIGURES	Figures or numbers follow.
	(Used when numbers occur in the middle of a message: "Vessel length is figures two three feet.")
SPEAK SLOWER	Your transmission is at too fast a speed, speak more slowly.
SAY AGAIN	Repeat.
WORDS TWICE	Communication is difficult — give every phrase twice.

PHONETIC ALPHABET

Letter	Phonetic Equivalent	Pronunciation

I SPELL

I shall spell the next word phonetically.

(Note: Often used where a proper name or unusual word is important to a message; "Boat name is *Martha*. I spell — Mike; Alfa; Romeo; Tango; Hotel; Alfa." See phonetic alphabet.)

MESSAGE FOLLOWS

A message that requires recording is about to follow.

BREAK

I separate the text from other portions of the message; or one message from one immediately following.

WAIT

I must pause for a few seconds; stand by for further transmission.

(Note: This is normally used when a message must be interrupted by the *sender*. If, for instance, one station is asked for information not instantly available, its operator might send "WAIT" while looking up the required data. In addition, WAIT may also be used to suspend the transmission of an on-the-air test. If a station announces its intention of making such a test, another station using the channel may transmit the word "WAIT;" the test shall then be suspended.

AFFIRMATIVE

You are correct, or what you have transmitted is correct.

NEGATIVE

No.

SILENCE (said three times)

Cease all transmissions immediately. Silence will be maintained until lifted.

(Note: Used to clear routine business from a channel when an emergency is in progress. In this meaning *Silence* is correctly pronounced SEE LONSS.)

SILENCE FINI

Silence is lifted.

(Note: Signifies the end of the emergency and the resumption of normal traffic. Correctly pronounced SEE LONSS FEE NEE.)

Letter	Phonetic Equivalent	Pronunciation
A	ALFA	*AL* FAH
B	BRAVO	*BRAH* VOH
C	CHARLIE	*CHAR* LEE
D	DELTA	*DELL* TAH
E	ECHO	*ECK* OH
F	FOXTROT	*FOKS* TROT
G	GOLF	GOLF
H	HOTEL	HO *TELL*
I	INDIA	*IN* DEE AH
J	JULIETT	JEW LEE *ETT*
K	KILO	*KEY* LOH
L	LIMA	*LEE* MAH
M	MIKE	MIKE
N	NOVEMBER	NO *VEM* BER
O	OSCAR	*OSS* CAH
P	PAPA	PAH *PAH*
Q	QUEBEC	KEH *BECK*
R	ROMEO	*ROW* ME OH
S	SIERRA	SEE *AIR* RAH
T	TANGO	*TANG* GO
U	UNIFORM	*YOU* NEE FORM
V	VICTOR	*VIK* TAH
W	WHISKEY	*WISS* KEY
X	XRAY	*ECKS* RAY
Y	YANKEE	*YANG* KEY
Z	ZULU	*ZOO* LOO
0	ZERO	ZERO
1	ONE	WUN
2	TWO	TOO
3	THREE	THUH REE
4	FOUR	FO WER
5	FIVE	FI YIV
6	SIX	SIX
7	SEVEN	SEVEN
8	EIGHT	ATE
9	NINE	NINER

Operating Procedures (Distress, Urgency and Safety)

General

If you are in distress, you may use any means at your disposal to attract attention and obtain assistance. You are by no means limited to the use of your marine radiotelephone. Often, visual signals, including flags, flares, lights, smoke, etc., or audible signals such as your boat's horn or siren, or a whistle, or megaphone will get the attention and help you need.

For boats equipped with a marine radiotelephone, help is just a radio signal away. Two marine radiotelephone channels have been set aside for use in emergencies. Channel 16 (156.8 MHz), the VHF-FM Distress, Safety and Calling frequency is the primary emergency channel in the VHF marine band. For those who have medium frequency (MF) radiotelephone also, 2182 kHz is the emergency frequency for use in that band. You are not limited to the use of these channels; you may use any other frequency channel available to you. The working frequency of the local marine operator (public telephone coast station) is a good example of a channel that is monitored.

There are other types of marine stations located ashore that are listening to Channel 16 and 2182 kHz along with the marine radio equipped vessels operating in the area. Because of this coverage, almost any kind of a call for assistance on Channel 16 (or 2182 kHz) will probably get a response. There are times, however, when the situation demands immediate attention; when you just can't tolerate delay. These are the times when you need to know how to use (or respond to) the Distress and Urgency signals and how to respond to the Safety signal.

Spoken Emergency Signals

There are three spoken emergency signals:

1. *Distress Signal: MAYDAY*
   The distress signal MAYDAY is used to indicate that a mobile station is threatened by grave and imminent danger and requests immediate assistance. MAYDAY has priority over all other communications.

2. *Urgency Signal: PAN (Properly pronounced PAHN)*
   Used when the safety of the vessel or person is in jeopardy. "Man overboard" messages are sent with the Urgency signal. PAN has priority over all other communications with the exception of distress traffic.

3. *Safety Signal: SECURITY (Pronounced SAY-CURITAY)*
   Used for messages concerning the safety of navigation or giving important meteorological warnings.

Any message headed by one of the emergency signals (MAYDAY, PAN, or SECURITY), must be given precedence over routine communications. This means listen. Don't transmit. Be prepared to help if you can. The decision of which of these emergency signals to use is the responsibility of the person in charge of the vessel.

Radiotelephone Alarm Signal

This signal consists of two audio frequency tones transmitted alternately. This signal is similar in sound to a two-tone siren used by some ambulances. When generated by automatic means, it shall be sent as continuously as practicable over a period of not less than 30 seconds nor more than 1 minute. The purpose of the signal is to attract attention of the person on watch or to actuate automatic devices giving the alarm. The radiotelephone alarm signal shall be used only with the distress signal except in two situations dealing with the Urgency Signal.

Sending Distress Call and Message

First send the Radiotelephone Alarm Signal, if available.

1. Distress signal MAYDAY (spoken three times)
2. The words THIS IS (spoken once)
3. Name of vessel in distress (spoken three times) and call sign (spoken once)

The Distress Message immediately follows the Distress Call and consists of:

4. Distress signal MAYDAY (spoken once)
5. Name of vessel (spoken once)

6. Position of vessel in distress by latitude and longitude or by bearing (true or magnetic, state which) and distance to a well-known landmark such as a navigational aid or small island, or in any terms which will assist a responding station in locating the vessel in distress

7. Nature of distress (sinking, fire, etc.)

8. Kind of assistance desired

9. Any other information which might facilitate rescue, such as:
   length or tonnage of vessel
   number of persons on board and number needing medical attention
   color of hull, decks, cabin, masts, etc.

10. The word OVER

EXAMPLE: Distress Call and Message

(Send Radiotelephone Alarm Signal, if available, for at least 30 seconds but not more than 1 minute.)

"MAYDAY - MAYDAY - MAYDAY
THIS IS — BLUE DUCK — BLUE DUCK — BLUE DUCK — WHISKEY ALFA 1234
MAYDAY — BLUE DUCK
DUNGENESS LIGHT BEARS 185 DEGREES MAGNETIC — DISTANCE 2 MILES
STRUCK SUBMERGED OBJECT
NEED PUMPS — MEDICAL ASSISTANCE AND TOW
THREE ADULTS — TWO CHILDREN ABOARD
ONE PERSON COMPOUND FRACTURE OF ARM
ESTIMATE CAN REMAIN AFLOAT TWO HOURS
BLUE DUCK IS THIRTY-TWO FOOT CABIN CRUISER — BLUE HULL — WHITE DECK HOUSE
OVER"

NOTE: Repeat at intervals until answer is received. If no answer is received on the Distress frequency, repeat using any other available channel on which attention might be attracted.

Acknowledgement of Distress Message

If you hear a Distress Message from a vessel and it is not answered, then YOU must answer. If you are reasonably sure that the distressed vessel is not in your vicinity, you should wait a short time for others to acknowledge. In any event, you must log all pertinent details of the Distress Call and Message.

Offer of Assistance

After you acknowledge receipt of the distress message, allow a short interval of time for other stations to acknowledge receipt, if there are any in a position to assist. When you are sure of not interfering with other distress-related communications, contact the vessel in distress and advise them what assistance you can render. Make every effort to notify the Coast Guard. The offer-of assistance message shall be sent only with permission of the person in charge of your vessel.

Urgency Call and Message Procedures

The emergency signal PAN (pronounced PAHN), spoken three times, begins the Urgency Call. The Urgency Call and Message is transmitted on Channel 16 (or on 2182 kHz) in the same way as the Distress Call and Distress Message. The Urgency signal PAN indicates that the calling person has a message concerning the safety of the vessel, or a person in jeopardy. The Urgency signal is authorized for situations like the following:

—Transmission of an urgent storm warning by an authorized shore station.

—Loss of person overboard but only when the assistance of other vessels is required.

—No steering or power in shipping lane.

Sending Urgency Call and Message

The Urgency Call and Message usually includes the following:

1. The Urgency signal PAN (spoken three times)

2. Addressee ALL STATIONS (or a particular station)

3. The words THIS IS

4. Name of calling vessel (spoken three times) and call sign (spoken once)

5. The Urgency Message (state the urgent problem)

6. Position of vessel and any other information that will assist responding vessels. Include description of your vessel, etc.

7. The words THIS IS

MARINE DISTRESS COMMUNICATIONS FORM

Instructions: Complete this form now (except for items 6 through 9) and post near your radiotelephone for use if you are in DISTRESS.

****

SPEAK: SLOWLY — CLEARLY — CALMLY

1. Make sure your radiotelephone is on.
2. Select either <u>VHF Channel 16</u> (156.8 MHz) or <u>2182 kHz.</u>
3. Press microphone button and say: "MAYDAY—MAYDAY—MAYDAY."
4. Say: "THIS IS _____
   Your Call Sign/Boat Name repeated three times
5. Say: "MAYDAY_____."
   Your Boat Name
6. TELL WHERE YOU ARE (What navigational aids or landmarks are near?).
7. STATE THE NATURE OF YOUR DISTRESS.
8. GIVE NUMBER OF PERSONS ABOARD AND CONDITIONS OF ANY INJURED.
9. ESTIMATE PRESENT SEAWORTHINESS OF YOUR BOAT.
10. BRIEFLY DESCRIBE YOUR BOAT: _____FEET; _____ ; _____HULL;
    Length   *Type*   *Color*
    _____ TRIM; _____ MASTS; _____
    Color   *Number*   * *Anything else you think will help rescuers find you.*
11. Say: "I WILL BE LISTENING ON <u>CHANNEL 16/2182</u>."
    Cross out one which does not apply

12. End Message by saying: "THIS IS _____. OVER"
    Your Boat Name and Call Sign
13. Release microphone button and listen: Someone should answer.
    IF THEY DO NOT, REPEAT CALL, BEGINNING AT ITEM NO. 3 ABOVE.
    If there is still no answer, switch to another channel and begin again.

Radiotelephone Reminders

- Post station license and have operator license available.

- Whenever the radio is turned on, keep the receiver tuned to the distress frequency (2182 kHz or 156.8 MHz).

- Use 2182 kHz and 156.8 MHz for calling, distress, urgency or safety only.

- Listen before transmitting on any frequency to avoid interfering with other communications.

- If you hear a MAYDAY, talk only if you can help. Be prepared to render assistance or relay the distress message if necessary.

- Identify by call sign at the beginning and end of each communication.

- Keep all communications as brief as possible.

- Keep your radio equipment shipshape. Have it checked periodically by a qualified, licensed technician.

- Notify FCC of changes to mailing address, licensees name and vessel name.

- False distress signals are prohibited.

- Radiocommunications are private and divulgence of content without permission is prohibited.

- Don't use profane or indecent language.

VESSEL INFORMATION DATA SHEET

When requesting assistance from the Coast Guard, you may be asked to furnish the following details. This list should, therefore, be filled out as completely as possible and posted alongside your transmitter with the *Distress Communications Form.*

1. *Description of Vessel Requiring Assistance.*

Hull markings _____

Home port _____

Draft _____

Sails: Color _____

        Markings _____

Bowsprit ? _____

Outriggers ? _____

Flying Bridge ? _____

Other prominent features _____

2. *Survival Gear Aboard (Circle Yes or No)*

Personal Flotation Devices	Yes	No
Flares	Yes	No
Flashlight	Yes	No
Raft	Yes	No
Dinghy or Tender	Yes	No
Anchor	Yes	No
Spotlight	Yes	No
Auxiliary power	Yes	No
Horn	Yes	No

3. *Electronic Equipment*

	VHF	MF	HF
Radiotelephone(s)			
Channels/Frequencies	*22*	Yes	No;
available	*2670* kHz	Yes	No
Radar		Yes	No
Depth Finder		Yes	No
Loran		Yes	No
Direction Finder		Yes	No
EPIRB		Yes	No

4. *Vessel Owner/Operator*

Owner name _____

    Address _____

    _____

    Telephone number _____

Operator's name _____

    Address _____

    _____

    Telephone number _____

Is owner/operator an experienced sailor?   Yes   No

5. *Miscellaneous*

Be prepared to describe local weather conditions.

8. Name of calling vessel and radio call sign (spoken once)

9. The word OVER

EXAMPLE: Urgency Call and Message

(Not involving possible use of radiotelephone alarm)

> "PAN — PAN — PAN — ALL STATIONS (or a particular station)
> THIS IS — BLUE DUCK — BLUE DUCK — BLUE DUCK — WHISKEY ALFA 1234
> THREE MILES EAST OFF BARNEGAT LIGHT
> HAVE LOST MY RUDDER
> AM DRIFTING TOWARD SHORE AND REQUIRE TOW
> SEVEN PERSONS ON BOARD
> BLUE DUCK IS THIRTY-TWO FOOT CABIN CRUISER — BLUE HULL — WHITE DECK HOUSE
> THIS IS — BLUE DUCK — WHISKEY ALFA 1234
> OVER"

Safety Call and Message Procedures

The Safety Call, headed with the word SECURITY (Say-curitay, spoken three times), is transmitted on the Distress and Calling frequency (Channel 16 or 2182 kHz), together with a request to shift to a working frequency where the Safety Message will be given. The Safety Message may be given on any available working frequency.

United States Coast Guard stations routinely use the Safety Call SECURITY to alert boating operators that they are preparing to broadcast a message concerning safety of navigation. The call also precedes an important meteorological warning. The Safety Message itself usually is broadcast on Coast Guard Channel 22 (157.1 MHz) and 2670 kHz. Although recreational boating operators may use the Safety Signal and Message, in many cases they would get better results and perhaps suffer less criticism by giving the information to the Coast Guard without making a formal Safety Call. The Coast Guard usually has better broadcast coverage from its shore stations and will rebroadcast the information if it is appropriate.

Sending the Safety Call and Message

The Safety Call usually includes the following: (On Channel 16 or 2182 kHz.)

1. The Safety Signal SECURITY (spoken three times)

2. Addressee - ALL STATIONS (or a particular station)

3. The words THIS IS (spoken once)

4. Name of vessel calling and radio call sign

5. Announcement of the working channel (frequency) where the Safety Message will be given

6. Radio Call Sign

7. The word OUT

The Safety Message usually includes the following:

1. Select working channel (frequency) announced in step 5 above

2. The Safety Signal SECURITY (spoken three times)

3. The words ALL STATIONS (spoken once)

4. The words THIS IS (spoken once)

5. Name of vessel calling and radio call sign

6. Give the Safety Message

7. Repeat the Radio Call Sign

8. The word OUT

EXAMPLES: Safety Call and Message

on Channel 16

> "SECURITY — SECURITY — SECURITY — ALL STATIONS
> THIS IS — BLUE DUCK — WHISKEY ALFA 1234
> LISTEN CHANNEL 68
> WHISKEY ALFA 1234 — OUT

on Channel 68

> "SECURITY — SECURITY — SECURITY — ALL STATIONS
> THIS IS — BLUE DUCK — WHISKEY ALFA 1234
> A LOG APPROXIMATELY TWENTY FEET LONG TWO FEET IN DIAMETER ADRIFT OFF HAINS POINT POTOMAC RIVER
> WHISKEY ALFA 1234 — OUT"

Public Coast Stations

General

By utilizing the services of Public Coast Stations, ships may make and receive telephone calls to and from any telephone with access to the nationwide telephone network, including telephones overseas and on other ships and aircraft. In effect, these coast stations extend the talking range of ship telephones almost without limit.

Description of Public Coast Stations

Three categories of Public Coast Stations operate in different frequency bands to provide for telephone service over a wide range of situations. The following brief descriptions of these services are of interest in selecting a service appropriate for your requirements. This information is followed by some suggestions for operating ship stations on public correspondence channels.

VHF-FM Service

VHF-FM service offers reliable operation with good transmission quality over relatively short distances up to 20-50 miles, using channels in the 157-162 MHz range. Channels 24, 25, 26, 27, 28, 84, 85, 86 and 87 are available for assignment to public coast stations in the United States. Channels 26 and 28 are used in more areas than any others. To obtain information on VHF-FM ship-to-shore telephone coverage in your area, call your local Marine Operator, according to instructions in your telephone directory.

In addition, in some localities not yet served by VHF-FM coast stations, ships are permitted to make telephone calls through local VHF-FM base stations operating in the land mobile radio telephone service. In these instances, a different license authorization as well as different transmitting equipment is required.

Medium Frequency Service

The Medium Frequency Service operates over considerably greater distance ranges than VHF-FM, but ranges vary widely with time of day and a variety of other circumstances. Distances in excess of 1,000 miles are possible at certain times, but may be limited to less than 100 miles at other times.

Medium Frequency Coast Stations operate on frequencies in the 2 MHz band along the sea coasts and Gulf of Mexico. Stations serving the Great Lakes and the Mississippi River valley also operate on frequencies in the high-frequency bands.

High Frequency

A High Seas Service using high frequencies provides long-range radiotelephone communications with suitably equipped vessels throughout the world. Service is provided via four coast stations within the United States coastal areas plus one station in the state of Hawaii. These stations operate on various radio channels in the 4 through 23 MHz bands and are equipped for single sideband operation.

Registration With Your Public Coast Station

It is important for the vessel owner who plans on using the public radiotelephone service to register with the telephone company in the location where you wish to be billed.

This registration provides all coast stations with the name and address to be used in billing for ship-originated calls. Public coast stations are supported by charges made in accordance with tariffs filed with regulatory authorities. If a ship is not registered, billing information must be passed to the coast station operator each time a call is made, with consequent expenditure of time and effort. Registration may also serve to establish the procedures under which a coast station will call the ship in completing land-originated calls. Should you encounter any problems, contact your local telephone company business office and request assistance in registering your vessel.

Making Ship-To-Shore Calls

Use the VHF-FM Service (up to 20 to 40 miles) in preference to the Medium Frequency or High Frequency Services, if within range.

1. Select the public correspondence channel assigned to the desired shore station. Do not call on Channel 16 or on 2182 kHz except in an emergency.

2. Listen to determine if the working channel of the desired coast station is busy. A busy condition is evidenced by hearing speech, signalling tones, or a busy signal.

3. If the channel is busy, wait until it clears or switch to an alternate channel if available.

4. If the channel is not busy, press the push-to-talk button and say: (Name of the coast station) — THIS IS — (your call sign once). Do not call for more than a few seconds.

5. Listen for a reply. If none is received, repeat call after an interval of two minutes.

When the coast station operator answers, say:

THIS IS — Name of vessel, call sign, and ship's telephone or billing number (if assigned), CALL-ING (city, telephone number desired).

If your vessel is not registered or if the coast station operator does not have the listing, the operator will ask for additional information for billing purposes. At completion of call say:

Name of vessel — Call sign — OUT.

Receiving Shore-to-Ship Calls

Obviously, to receive public coast station calls, a receiver must be in operation on the proper channel. When calling on VHF-FM frequencies, coast stations will call on Channel 16 unless you have selective signalling, in which case the shore station will dial your number on a working channel. When calling on SSB medium frequencies, the preferred channel is the working channel of the coast station. Bell System coast stations operating on channels in the 2 MHz band routinely call on a working channel, but will call on 2182 kHz when requested to do so by the calling party. If you are expecting calls on medium frequencies and are not planning to monitor the working channel, you should tell prospective calling parties to so advise the Marine Operator. Note: A guard must be maintained on the distress, safety and calling channel; therefore a second channel receiver capability is essential if a guard is to be maintained on a coast station working channel.

Selective signalling, of course, requires a second receiver, since monitoring of the working channel would be essential. It is illegal to send dial pulses over Channel 16 or 2182 kHz.

Making Ship-to-Ship Calls Through a Coast Station

Although contacts between ships are normally made directly, ship-to-ship calls can be made by going through your coast station, using the same procedure as you do for the ship-to-shore calls.

How to Place a Shore-to-Ship Call

The basic procedure that the telephone subscriber should follow in placing a telephone call to a ship station from his home or office is found in the first few pages of most Telephone Directories. These instructions generally consist of dialing "0" (Zero) for the Operator, and asking for the "Marine Operator."

It is further necessary to know the name of the vessel being called (not the owner's name) and the approximate location so that the Marine Operator may judge which coast station to place the call through.

More specific information about the vessel is often useful. For instance, the channel generally monitored for receiving calls, a selective signalling number (if applicable), and the coast station through which calls can generally be received.

Remember that the ship station generally operates using push-to-talk techniques, so that it is impossible for you to break in while the ship station is being received.

Limited Coast Stations

The term *limited coast stations* includes coast stations which are there to serve the operational and business needs of vessels, but are not open to public correspondence. Many, such as those operated by a harbor master coordinating the movement of vessels within a confined area, or a station at a highway bridge, serve a safety function as well. Shore stations operated by the United States Coast Guard provide a safety communications service rather than business or operational. They are classified as Government stations rather than as limited coast stations although they also are not open to public correspondence.

While limited coast stations are not new to the Marine Service, most small vessel operators are finding this service available for the first time on VHF-FM. Thus, tug companies may have a limited coast station for the purpose of dispatching their own tugs. A fleet of fishing vessels may be directed from a limited coast station operated by a fish cannery.

Yacht clubs having docking facilities, marina operators, ship chandlers, boatels, harbor masters, dock-side restaurants, marine police, and marine radio service shops are among those who maintain and operate limited coast stations as a part of their regular operations. No charge is made for the communications service, which is incidental to their business.

How to Use the Services of Limited Coast Stations

Vessels should call limited coast stations on the limited coast station's working channel. All limited coast stations have Channel 16 plus one or more working channels. Limited coast stations, on the other hand, will call boats on Channel 16; therefore you do not need to monitor his working channel even if you are expecting a call.

As a general rule, limited coast stations operate only during their normal working hours. The calling procedure to use is the same as you would use to call another vessel except that you should initiate the call on the coast station's working channel. Be sure to give them plenty of time to answer your call as operating the radio is secondary to the operator's normal tasks. Many of these stations monitor Channel 16 as well as their working channels. If you don't know their assigned working channel, or if they don't appear to be watching their working channel, call on Channel 16.

Bibliography

Blanchard, Fessenden S., *The Sailboat Classes of North America*. Garden City, N.Y.: Doubleday & Co., 1968 (revised).

Bowker, R.M. and Budd, S.A., *Make Your Own Sails*. New York: St. Martin's Press, 1959.

Coles, Adlard, *Heavy Weather Sailing*. Tuckahoe, N.Y.: John de Graff, Inc., 1972 (revised).

Cotter, Edward F., *Multihull Sailboats*. New York: Crown Publishers, 1966.

Duffett, John, *Modern Marine Maintenance*. New York: Motor Boating & Sailing Books, 1973.

Falk, Stephen, *The Fundamentals of Sailboat Racing*. New York: St. Martin's Press, 1973.

Giannoni, Frances and John, *Useful Knots and Line Handling*. New York: Golden Press, 1968.

Gibbs, Tony, *Advanced Sailing*. New York: St. Martin's Press, 1975.

Hankinson, Ken, *Rigging Small Sailboats*. Bellflower, Calif.: Glen-L, 1973.

Henderson, Richard, *Better Sailing*. Chicago,: Henry Regnery Co., 1977.

Henderson, Richard, *Sea Sense*. Camden, Me.: International Marine Publishing Co., 1972.

Howard-Williams, Jeremy, *Sails*. Tuckahoe, N.Y.: John de Graff, Inc., 1971.

Imhoff, Fred, and Pranger, Lex, *Boat Tuning for Speed*. Boston: Sail Books, Inc., 1975.

Kotsch, William J., *Weather for the Mariner*. Annapolis, Md.: Naval Institute Press, 1977 (revised).

McCollam, Jim, *The Yachtsman's Weather Manual*. New York: Dodd, Mead & Co., 1973.

Phillips-Birt, Douglas, *Sailing Yacht Design*. London: Adlard Coles, Ltd., 1966.

Robinson, Bill (ed.), *The Science of Sailing*. New York: Charles Scribner's Sons, 1961.

Ross, Wallace, *Sail Power*. New York: Alfred A. Knopf, 1974.

Sail, *The Best of Sail Trim*. Boston: Sail Books, Inc., 1975.

Ship's Medicine Chest and Medical Aid at Sea. U. S. Dept. of Health, Education and Welfare. 1978.

Shufeldt, H.H. and Dunlap, G.D., *Piloting and Dead Reckoning*. Annapolis, Md.: Naval Institute Press, 1970.

Smith, Hervey Garrett, *The Arts of the Sailor*. New York: Funk & Wagnalls, 1968.

Watts, Alan, *Wind and Sailing Boats*. Chicago: Quadrangle Books, 1970.

Glossary

A

ABAFT - Toward the rear (stern) of the boat. Behind.

ABEAM - A direction at right angles to the keel of the boat.

ABOARD - On or within the boat.

ABOVE DECK - On the deck (not over it — see ALOFT).

ABREAST - Side by side; by the side of.

ADRIFT - Loose, not on moorings or towline.

AFT - Toward the stern of the boat.

AGROUND - Touching or fast to the bottom.

AHEAD - Toward the bow or forward.

AIDS TO NAVIGATION - Artificial objects to supplement natural landmarks in indicating safe and unsafe waters.

ALEE - Away from the direction of the wind. Opposite of windward.

ALOFT - High above the deck of the boat.

AMIDSHIPS - In or toward the center of the boat.

ANCHORAGE - A place suitable for anchoring in relation to the wind, seas and bottom.

ANEMOMETER - A device which measures the velocity of the wind.

APPARENT WIND - The wind perceived in a moving boat which is the combination of the true wind and the wind of motion.

ASTERN - In back of the boat, opposite of ahead.

ATHWARTSHIPS - At right angles to the centerline of the boat; rowboat seats are generally athwartships.

AWEIGH - The position of anchor as it is raised clear of the bottom.

B

BACKSTAY - Standing rigging that supports the mast from aft to keep it in an upright position. *Running backstays* (always in pairs) perform the same function, but may be quickly slackened to avoid interfering with the boom.

BACKWIND - When wind is deflected from one sail to the lee side of another sail, as when the jib is backwinding the main.

BALLAST - Heavy material placed in the bottom of a boat to provide stability.

BARE POLES - When a sailboat is under way with no sails set.

BAROMETER - An instrument for measuring the atmospheric pressure.

BATTEN - A thin semi-rigid strip inserted in the leach of the sail to provide support for the sail material.

BATTEN DOWN - Secure hatches and loose objects both within the hull and on deck.

BEAM - The greatest width of the boat.

BEAM REACH - Sailing with the apparent wind coming at right angles to the boat.

BEAR - To "bear down" is to approach from windward, to "bear off" is to sail away to leeward.

BEARING - The direction of an object expressed either as a true bearing as shown on the chart, or as a bearing relative to the heading of the boat.

BEAT - To sail to windward, generally in a series of tacks. Beating is one of the three points of sailing, also referred to as sailing *close hauled* or *by the wind.*

BECALMED - Having no wind to provide movement of the boat through the water.

BECKET - A looped rope, hook and eye, strap, or grommet used for holding ropes, spars, or oars in position.

BEFORE THE WIND - Traveling in the same direction the wind is blowing toward; sailing before the wind is a point of sailing, also called running.

BELAY - To make a line fast. A command to stop.

BELOW - Beneath the deck.

BEND - To attach a sail to a spar. Also used as a term to describe a knot which fastens one line to another.

BIGHT - A loop in a line of rope; a bend in a river; a bend in the shoreline making a cove or a bay.

BILGE - The interior of the hull below the floor boards.

BINNACLE - A stand holding the steering compass.

BITT - A heavy and firmly mounted piece of wood or metal used for securing lines.

BITTER END - The last part of a rope or chain. The inboard end of the anchor rode.

BLANKET - To deprive a sail of the wind by interposing another object.

BLOCK - A wooden or metal case enclosing one or more pulleys and having a hook, eye, or strap by which it may be attached (see SHEAVE).

BOAT - A fairly indefinite term. A waterborne vehicle smaller than a ship. One definition is a small craft carried aboard a ship.

BOAT HOOK - A staff with a fitting at one end shaped to facilitate use in putting a line over a piling, recovering an object dropped overboard, or in pushing or fending off.

BOLLARD - A heavy post set into the edge of a wharf or pier to which the lines of a ship may be made fast.

BOLT ROPE - Line attached to the foot and luff of a sail to give it strength or to substitute for sail slides.

BOOM - A spar attached to the mast for extending the foot of the sail.

BOOM CROTCH or CRUTCH - A notched board or X-shaped frame that supports the main boom and keeps it from swinging when the sail is not raised.

BOOMKIN - A short spar or structure projecting from the stern to which a sheet block is attached for an overhanging boom, and to which, on boats without running backstays, is attached the fixed backstay.

BOOM VANG - A tackle running from the boom to the deck which will flatten the curve of the sail by pulling downward on the boom.

BOOT TOP - A line (of several inches' width) painted above and along the waterline.

BOW - The forward part of a boat.

BOW LINE - A docking line leading from the bow.

BOWLINE - A knot used to form a temporary loop in the end of a line.

BOWSPRIT - A spar extending forward from the bow.

BRIDGE - The location from which certain vessels are conned and controlled. (for sailboats, see COCKPIT).

BRIDLE - A line or wire secured at both ends in order to distribute a strain between two points.

BRIGHTWORK - Varnished woodwork and or polished metal.

BROACH - The turning of a boat broadside to the waves, subjecting it to possible capsizing.

BROAD ON THE BEAM - Bearing at right angles to the direction. To the boat's heading.

BROAD ON THE BOW - A direction midway between abeam and dead ahead.

BROAD ON THE QUARTER - A direction midway between abeam and dead astern.

BROAD REACH - Sailing with the apparent wind coming over either quarter.

BULKHEAD - A vertical partition separating compartments.

BULWARK - The side of a vessel when carried above the level of the deck.

BUOY - An anchored float used for marking a position on the water or a hazard or a shoal and for mooring.

BURDENED VESSEL - That vessel which, according to the applicable Rules of the Road, must give way to the privileged vessel. The term has been superceded by the term "give-way".

BURGEE - A small yachting flag which is either swallow tailed or pointed.

BY THE LEE - Sailing with the wind on the same side as the boom; not a recommended point of sailing as it could cause an accidental jibe.

BY THE WIND - Sailing close hauled, beating.

C

CABIN - A compartment for passengers or crew.

CAPSIZE - To turn over.

CARVEL - Smooth planked hull construction (see LAPSTRAKE).

CAST OFF - To let go mooring lines.

CATAMARAN - A twin-hulled boat, with hulls side by side.

CATBOAT - A sailboat with a single sail attached to a mast stepped well forward.

CAULK - To stop up and make watertight by filling with a waterproof compound or material.

CENTERBOARD - A plate, in a vertical fore-and-aft plane, that is pivoted at the lower forward end, and can be lowered or raised through a slot in the bottom of the boat to reduce leeway.

CENTER OF EFFORT - The center of wind pressure on a sail.

CENTER OF LATERAL RESISTANCE - The center of underwater resistance which is approximately the center of underwater profile.

CHAFING GEAR - Tubing or cloth wrapping used to protect a line from chafing on a rough surface.

CHAIN PLATE - Metal strap fastened to the side of a boat, to which a stay or shroud is attached.

CHART - A map for use by navigators.

CHART NO. 1 - A booklet prepared by the National Ocean Survey which contains symbols and abbreviations that have been approved for use on nautical charts published by the U.S. Government. Past editions of this chart were in actual chart form.

CHINE - The intersection of the bottom and sides of a boat (see HARD CHINE).

CHOCK - A fitting through which anchor or mooring lines are led. Usually U-shaped to reduce chafe.

CLEAT - A fitting to which lines are made fast. The classic cleat to which lines are belayed is approximately anvil-shaped.

CLEW - The after, lower corner of a sail to which is attached the sheets.

CLOSE ABOARD - Not on but near to a vessel.

CLOSE HAULED - Sailing as close to the wind as is possible, beating, or by the wind, one of the three points of sailing.

CLOSE REACH - Sailing with the sheets slightly eased and the apparent wind forward of the beam.

CLOVE HITCH - A knot for temporarily fastening a line to a spar or piling.

COAMING - A vertical piece around the edge of a cockpit, hatch, etc. to prevent water on deck from running below.

COCKPIT - An opening in the deck from which the boat is handled.

COIL - A series of loops or rings of line or rope. An electrical component of a boat's engine which transforms direct current from the battery into alternating current.

COIL DOWN - To flemish down.

COLLAR - The reinforced opening in the deck or cabin roof through which the mast passes. This opening is constructed to take the strain of the mast.

COMING ABOUT - The changing of course when close hauled by swinging the bow through the eye of the wind and changing from one tack to another.

COURSE - The direction in which a boat is steered.

CRADLE - A framework, generally of wood, to support a boat when it is out of the water.

CRINGLE - A ring sewn into a sail through which a line may be passed.

CUDDY - A small shelter cabin in a boat.

CUNNINGHAM - A grommeted hole in the mainsail luff slightly above the foot through which a line or hook is pulled downward to exert stress on the luff, thereby flattening the sail.

CURRENT - The horizontal movement of water.

CUTTER - A single masted sailboat with the mast stepped further aft than that of a sloop.

D

DAGGERBOARD - A plate, in a vertical fore-and-aft plane which can be lowered and raised vertically through a slot in the bottom of a boat to reduce leeway.

DAVITS - Mechanical arms extending over the side or stern of a vessel, or over a sea wall, to lift a smaller boat (Pronounced "DAY-VITS").

DEAD AHEAD - Directly ahead.

DEAD ASTERN - Opposite of dead ahead.

DEAD RECKONING - A plot of courses steered and distances traveled through the water.

DECK - A permanent covering over a compartment, hull or any part thereof.

DINGHY - A small open boat. A dinghy is often used as a tender for a larger craft.

DISPLACEMENT - The weight of water displaced by a floating vessel, thus, a boat's weight.

DISPLACEMENT HULL - A type of hull that plows through the water, displacing a weight of water equal to its own weight, even when more power is added.

DOCK - A protected water area in which vessels are moored. The term is often used to denote a pier or a wharf.

DOLPHIN - A group of piles driven close together and bound with wire cables into a single structure.

DOUSE - To lower sails quickly.

DOWNHAUL - A line attached to the boom at the tack area of the sail in order to pull the luff of the sail downward.

DRAFT - The depth of water a boat draws.

DROGUE - Any device streamed astern to check a vessel's speed, or to keep its stern up to the waves in a following sea.

E

EASE OFF - To slacken or relieve tension on a line.

EBB TIDE - A receding tide.

ENSIGN - A national or organizational flag flown aboard a vessel.

EVEN KEEL - When a boat is floating on its designed waterline it is said to be floating on an even keel.

EYE BOLT - A bolt having a looped head designed to receive a hook or towing line. This bolt is usually bolted through the deck or stem.

EYE OF THE WIND - The direction from which the wind is blowing.

EYE SPLICE - A permanent loop spliced in the end of a line.

F

FAIRLEAD - A fitting used to change the direction of a line.

FALL OFF - To turn the bow of the boat away from the eye of the wind.

FAST - Said of an object that is secured to another.

FATHOM - Six feet.

FENDER - A cushion or pad used between boats, or between a boat and a pier to prevent chafing.

FIGURE EIGHT KNOT - A knot in the form of a figure eight, placed in the end of a line to prevent the line from passing through a grommet or block.

FIN KEEL - A thin narrow keel bolted to the bottom of the hull.

FISHERMAN'S BEND - A knot for making fast to a buoy or spar or to the ring of an anchor.

FLARE - The outward curve of a vessel's sides near the bow. A distress signal.

FLEMISH DOWN - A decorative but useless method of coiling a line flat on the deck or dock.

FLOOD TIDE - A rising tide.

FLOORBOARDS - The surface of the cockpit on which the crew stand.

FLUKE - The palm of an anchor.

FLY - A pennant at the masthead.

FOLLOWING SEA - Waves moving as the same direction as the boat.

FOOT - The lower edge of a sail.

FORE-AND-AFT - In a line parallel to the keel.

FOREPEAK - A compartment in the bow of a small boat.

FORESAIL - The sail set abaft the foremast of a schooner.

FORWARD - Toward the bow of the boat.

FOULED - Any piece of equipment that is jammed, entangled, or dirtied.

FOUNDER - When a vessel fills with water and sinks.

FREEBOARD - The minimum vertical distance from the surface of the water to the gunwale.

FULL AND BY - Close hauled.

FURL - To roll up a sail on top of a boom or spar and secure it with small lines.

G

GAFF - A spar to support the head of a gaff sail.

GALLEY - The kitchen area of a boat.

GANGWAY - The area of a ship's side where people board and disembark.

GANGPLANK - The temporary ramp or platform between the vessel and the wharf or pier.

GASKET - A sail stop.

GEAR - A general term for ropes, blocks, tackle and other equipment.

GIVE-WAY VESSEL - A term used to describe the vessel which must yield in meeting, crossing, or overtaking situations.

GOOSENECK - A universal joint connecting the mast and the boom, allowing movement of the boom in any direction.

GRAB RAILS - Hand-hold fittings mounted on cabin tops and sides for personal safety when moving around the boat.

GROUND TACKLE - A collective term for the anchor and its associated gear.

GUDGEON - The eye supports for the rudder mounted on the transom which receive the pintles of the rudder.

GUNWALE - The upper edge of a boat's sides (Pronounced "GUN'L").

H

HALYARD - A line or wire used to hoist the sails or flags.

HANKS - Snap hooks which attach the luff of a headsail to the forestay.

HARD ALEE - The operation of putting the helm (tiller) to the lee side of the boat when coming about.

HARD CHINE - An abrupt intersection between the hull side and the hull bottom of a boat so constructed.

HATCH - An opening in a boat's deck fitted with a watertight cover.

HAWSER - A heavy rope or cable used for mooring or towing.

HEAD - A marine toilet. Also the upper corner of a triangular sail.

HEADER - A change in wind direction which will head or impede progress in an intended direction.

HEADSAILS - Sails forward of the foremost mast.

HEAD UP - Swing the bow closer to the eye of the wind.

HEADING - The direction in which a vessel's bow points at any given time.

HEADWAY - The forward motion of a boat. Opposite of sternway.

HEAVE TO - To bring a vessel up in a position where it will maintain little or no headway, usually with the bow into the wind or nearly so.

HEEL - To tip to one side temporarily because of an external force such as the wind's pressure on the sails. Also, the base or bottom of the mast.

HELM - The wheel or tiller controlling the rudder. (Also see LEE HELM, WEATHER HELM).

HELMSPERSON - The person who steers the boat.

HIKING OUT - The position one assumes when positioned on the weather rail in an effort to balance the heeling forces of the wind upon the sails and or rigging.

HIKING STICK - A short stick attached to the tiller which allows the helmsperson to hike out while steering the boat.

HITCH - A knot used to secure a rope to another object or to another rope, or to form a loop or a noose in a rope.

HOLD - A compartment below deck in a large vessel, used solely for carrying cargo.

HORSE - The wire or rope bridle to which is attached the block through which the sheet(s) run through.

HULL - The main body of a vessel.

HULL SPEED - The maximum displacement speed.

I

IN IRONS - Stalled. Said of a sailboat headed into the eye of the wind, with no wind pressure on either side of the sails.

INITIAL STABILITY - A boat's tendency to resist initial heel from the upright position.

J

JIB - A triangular sail set forward of the mainmast (sloop, cutter, ketch, yawl) or the foremast (schooner).

JIBE - The maneuver of changing the sail (and boom) from one side of the boat to the other. Usually used as a method of changing course while keeping the wind astern.

JIB SHEET - The line, usually paired, controlling the lateral movement of the jib.

JIB STAY - A stay running from the bow to the upper part of the mast on which the jib is attached.

JUMPER - A stay on the upper forward part of the mast.

JUMPER STAYS - The wire which runs over the ends of the jumper strut to provide support for the mast against the pull of the backstay.

JUMPER STRUTS - Short horizontal spars placed above the union of the forestay and the mast designed to balance the pull of the backstay upon the mast.

K

KEDGE - A light anchor used for moving a boat. Also the traditional yachtsman's anchor.

KEEL - The centerline of a boat running fore and aft; the backbone of a vessel.

KEEL BOAT - A boat with a fixed keel as opposed to a boat with a centerboard or daggerboard.

KETCH - A two-masted sailboat with the smaller after mast stepped ahead of the rudder post.

KNOCKDOWN - When a boat is laid over on its beam ends by wind or sea, allowing water to come in over the gunwales.

KNOT - A measure of speed equal to one nautical mile (6076.1 feet) per hour.

KNOT - A fastening made by interweaving rope to form a stopper, to enclose or bind an object, to form a loop or a noose, to tie a small rope to an object, or to tie the ends of two small ropes together.

L

LAPSTRAKE - Hull construction of overlapping planks; also known as clinker-built construction (see CARVEL).

LATEEN RIG - A fore and aft sailing rig originating in the near east and still found there, consisting of a triangular (lateen) sail, one side of which is very short, slung from a lateen yard, a long, moveable spar which crosses the relatively short mast at an angle.

LATERAL RESISTANCE - That resistance to the leeway or sideways movement of a boat caused by wind or wave forces determined by the amount of heel, keel or centerboard below the water line.

LATITUDE - The distance north or south of the equator measured and expressed in degrees.

LAY - To *lay a mark* is to be able to reach it without tacking, close hauled. The lay of a line is the direction in which its strands are twisted.

LAZARETTE - A storage space in a boat's stern area.

LEE - The side sheltered from the wind.

LEEBOARD - Pivoted board attached to the side of a sailboat to reduce leeway; usually one on either side, that to leeward being lowered when in use.

LEECH - The after edge of a fore-and-aft sail.

LEE HELM - The condition, in a sailing vessel, when the helm must be kept to leeward to hold a boat on her course.

LEEWARD - The direction away from the wind. Opposite of windward.

LEEWAY - The sideways movement of the boat caused by either wind or current.

LIFT - An increase in the wind's force, causing an increase of heel of a boat close-hauled, shifting the center of effort forward, allowing the boat to sail, often advantageously, closer to the wind and faster; sometimes said of a similarly advantageous shift in wind direction; being lifted is the opposite of being headed (see HEADER; also see TOPPING LIFT).

LINE - Rope and cordage used aboard a vessel.

LOG - A record of courses or operation. Also, a device to measure speed.

LONGITUDE - The distance in degrees east or west of the meridian at Greenwich, England.

LONG SPLICE - A method of joining two ropes by splicing without increasing the diameter of the rope.

LOOSE-FOOTED - A sail secured to the boom at the tack and the clew only as opposed to a sail secured with slides.

LOWER SHROUDS - The shrouds which run from the chain plates at the sides of the boat to the mast just beneath the intersection of the spreaders.

LUBBER'S LINE - A mark or permanent line on a compass indicating the direction forward parallel to the keel when properly installed.

LUFF - The forward edge of a sail; also the action of heading up into the wind causing the sail to flutter.

M

MAINMAST - The principal mast of a sailboat.

MAINSAIL - The principal sail that sets on the mainmast.

MAINSHEET - The sheet controlling the athwartships movement of a mainsail.

MARLINSPIKE - A tool for opening the strands of a rope while splicing.

MAST - A spar set upright to support rigging and sails.

MAST STEP - The shaped brace on which, or into which, the butt of the mast rests.

MIDSHIP - Approximately in the location equally distant from the bow and stern.

MIZZEN - The after and smaller mast of a ketch or yawl; also a sail set on that mast.

MIZZENMAST - (see MIZZEN).

MOORING - An arrangement for securing a boat to a mooring buoy or a pier.

MOORING PENNANT - A line used to secure a boat to a mooring buoy, which is permanently attached to the buoy's ring.

N

NAUTICAL MILE - The length of 1 minute of latitude of any great circle of the earth (such as the Equator), considered to be exactly 1852 meters, approximately 6076.1 feet; about 1.15 statute miles.

NAVIGATION - The art and science of conducting a boat safely from one point to another.

O

OFF THE WIND - Sailing downwind (away from the eye of the wind).

OUTBOARD - Toward or beyond the boat's sides. A detachable engine mounted on a boat's stern.

OUTHAUL - A line, or block and tackle, for stretching the foot of a sail out along the boom.

OVERBOARD - Over the side or out of the boat.

P

PAINTER - A line attached to the bow of a boat for use in towing or making fast.

PALM - A leather fitting placed over the hand to assist in sewing heavy material with a needle and thread.

PAY OUT - To ease out a line, or let it run in a controlled manner.

PEAK - The upper outer corner of a gaff sail.

PENNANT (sometimes PENDANT) - The line by which a boat is made fast to a mooring buoy.

PIER - A loading platform extending at an angle from the shore.

PILE - A wood, metal or concrete pole driven into the bottom. Craft may be made fast to a pile; it may be used to support a pier (see PILING) or a float.

PILING - Support, protection for wharves, piers, etc. constructed of piles (see PILE).

PILOTING - Navigation by use of visible references, the depth of the water, etc.

PINCH - To sail a boat too close to the wind causing the sails to stall.

PINTLE - The pin-like fittings of the rudder which are inserted into the gudgeons mounted on the transom.

PITCHPOLING - A boat is being thrown end-over-end in very rough seas.

PLANING - A boat is said to be planing when it is essentially moving over the top of the water rather than through the water.

PLANING HULL - A type of hull shaped to glide easily across the water at high speed.

POINT - One of 32 points of the compass. Equals 11 1/4 degrees.

PORT - The left side of a boat looking forward. A harbor.

PORT TACK - Sailing with the wind coming over the port side of the boat causing the main boom to be on the starboard side of the boat.

PRIVILEGED VESSEL - A vessel which, according to the applicable Rules of the Road, has right-of-way (this term has been superceded by the term "stand-on").

PUFF - A term used to describe a gust of wind.

Q

QUARTER - The corners of the transom; the sides of a boat aft of amidships.

QUARTERING SEA - Sea coming on a boat's quarter.

R

RAKE - The angle of a mast from the perpendicular, usually aft.

REACH - The point of sailing between close hauled and running, one of the points of sailing. Subdivided into *close, beam* and *broad* reach.

READY ABOUT - The preparatory command given before "hard alee" when tacking (passing the bow through the eye of the wind).

REEF - To reduce the sail area.

REEF POINTS - Short lines set into the lower portion of the sail to secure its foot when reefed.

REEVE - To pass a line through a block or other opening.

RIG - The arrangement of a boat's sails, masts and rigging.

RIGGING - The general term for all the lines and fittings of a vessel.

ROACH - The outward curve at the leech of a sail.

RODE - The anchor line and/or chain.

ROLLER FURLING - Type of jib rigged to furl by rolling up around its own luff.

ROLLER REEFING - Reefing by rolling a mainsail around a boom.

ROPE - In general, cordage as it is purchased at the store. When it comes aboard a vessel and is put to use it becomes line.

RUDDER - A vertical plate or board for steering a boat.

RULES OF THE ROAD - The regulations governing the movement of vessels in relation to each other, generally called steering and sailing rules.

RUN - To allow a line to feed freely.

RUNNING - Sailing before the wind; sailing with the wind astern.

RUNNING LIGHTS - Lights required to be shown on boats underway between sundown and sunup.

RUNNING RIGGING - Sheets, halyards, topping lifts, downhauls, vangs, etc., used for raising and adjusting sails (see STANDING RIGGING).

S

SAILING FREE - Sailing with the wind aft (running).

SAILS - Flexible vertical airfoils, generally made of cloth, that use wind pressure to propel a boat.

SAIL STOPS - Short length of line used to wrap around the sail when it is bundled up or furled.

SAMSON POST - A single bitt in the bow or stern of a boat, fastened to structural members.

SCOPE - The ratio of the length of an anchor line, from a vessel's bow to the anchor, to the depth of the water.

SCREW - A boat's propeller.

SCULLING - Moving the tiller or an oar back and forth to propel a boat ahead.

SEA ANCHOR - Any device used to reduce a boat's drift before the wind. Compare with DROGUE.

SEA ROOM - A safe distance from the shore or other hazards.

SEA WORTHY - A boat or a boat's gear able to meet the usual sea conditions.

SECURE - To make fast.

SEIZE - To bind two lines together with light line.

SET - Direction toward which the current is flowing.

SET FLYING - Said of a sail made fast only at its corners, such as a spinnaker.

SHACKLE - A "U" shaped connector with a pin or bolt across the open end.

SHEAVE - The grooved wheel or roller in a block (pulley). Sheave is pronounced "shiv".

SHEER - The fore-and-aft curvature of the deck as shown in side elevation.

SHEET - The line used to control the forward or athwartships movement of a sail.

SHEET BEND - A knot used to join two ropes. Functionally different from a square knot in that it can be used between lines of different diameters.

SHIP - A larger vessel usually thought of as being used for ocean travel. A vessel able to carry a "boat" on board.

SHORT SPLICE - A method of permanently joining the ends of two ropes.

SHROUD - The standing rigging that supports the mast at the sides of the boat.

SLACK - Not fastened; loose. Also, to loosen.

SLACK WATER - The period of tide change when there is no movement of water.

SLIDES - The hardware which attaches either the foot or the luff of the sail to a track on the respective spar.

SLOOP - A single masted sailing vessel with working sails (jib and main) set fore and aft.

SLUG - A fitting which is inserted into a groove on either the mast or the boom providing attachment for either the luff or the foot of the sail respectively.

SNATCH BLOCK - A block that opens at the side to allow a line to be inserted or removed without reeving the entire length of line.

SOLE - Cabin or saloon floor. Timber extensions on the bottom of the rudder. Also the molded fiberglass deck of a cockpit.

SOUNDING - A measurement of the depth of water.

SPAR - A general term for masts, yards, booms, etc.

SPINNAKER - A large, light-weather headsail used for running or reaching.

SPLICE - To permanently join two ropes by tucking their strands alternately over and under each other.

SPREADER - A horizontal strut used to increase the angle at which the shrouds approach the mast.

SPRING LINE - A pivot line used in docking, undocking, or to prevent the boat from moving forward or astern while made fast to a dock.

SQUALL - A sudden, violent wind often accompanied by rain.

SQUARE KNOT - A knot used to join two lines of similar size. Also called a reef knot.

STANDING PART - That part of a line which is made fast. The main part of a line as distinguished from the bight and the end.

STANDING RIGGING - The permanent shrouds and stays that support the mast.

STAND-ON VESSEL - That vessel which has right-of-way during a meeting, crossing, or overtaking situation.

STARBOARD - The right side of a boat when looking forward.

STARBOARD TACK - Sailing with the wind coming over the starboard side of the boat and with the boom out over the port side of the boat.

STAY - That part of the standing rigging supporting the mast from forward and aft.

STAYSAIL - A sail (usually triangular) set on one of the stays.

STEM - The foremost upright timber of a vessel to which the keel and ends of the planks are attached.

STEM - The forwardmost part of the bow.

STEP - A socket in the bottom of the boat which receives the heel of the mast.

STERN - The after part of the boat.

STERN LINE - A docking line leading from the stern.

STOCK - The cross bar of an anchor.

STORM SAILS - Small sails for heavy weather sailing.

STOW - To put an item in its proper place.

SWAMP - To fill with water, but not settle to the bottom.

SWING KEEL - A weighted extension of the keel which can be partially retracted into the hull or locked in the fully-lowered position.

T

TABERNACLE - A hinged fitting at the base of the mast to enable the mast to be easily raised or lowered.

TABLING - An extra thickness of cloth sewn around the sail's edges and at the corners.

TACK - To come about; the lower forward corner of a sail; sailing with the wind on a given side of the boat, as starboard or port tack.

TACKING - Moving the boat's bow through the wind's eye from close hauled on one tack to close hauled on the other tack. Same as coming about.

TACKLE - A combination of blocks and line to increase mechanical advantage. Pronounced "taakle".

TANG - A fitting on a spar to which standing rigging is secured.

THWART - A seat or brace running laterally across a boat.

THWARTSHIPS - At right angles to the centerline of the boat.

TIDE - The periodic rise and fall of water level in the oceans.

TILLER - A bar or handle for turning a boat's rudder or an outboard motor.

TOGGLE - Small fittings which allow the turnbuckle to lie in the same straight line as the stay or shroud to which it is fitted. Also, a pin thru eye or bight of rope used as a quick release.

TOPPING LIFT - A line used to support the weight of or to adjust the horizontal set of a spar such as a boom or a spinnaker pole.

TOPSIDES - The sides of a vessel between the waterline and the deck.

TRANSOM - The stern cross-section of a square sterned boat.

TRAVELER - A device that allows sheets to slide athwartships.

TRIM - Fore and aft balance of a boat.

TRUE WIND - The actual direction from which the wind is blowing.

TRUNK - The structure which houses the centerboard.

TURNBUCKLE - A threaded fitting to pull two eyes together for adjustment of standing rigging.

U

UNDERWAY - Vessel in motion; i.e., when not moored, at anchor, or aground.

UNREEVE - To run a line completely through and out of a block.

UPPER SHROUDS - The shrouds which run from the chain plates at the sides of the boat over the spreaders to the masthead.

V

VANG - See *boom vang*.

V BOTTOM - A hull with the bottom section in the shape of a "V".

W

WAKE - Moving waves, track or path that a boat leaves behind it, when moving across the waters.

WATERLINE - A line painted on a hull which shows the point to which a boat sinks when it is properly trimmed (see BOOT TOP).

WAY - Movement of a vessel through the water such as headway, sternway or leeway.

WEATHER - Windward side of a boat.

WEATHER HELM - The tendency of a boat to turn into the wind when its rudder is set amidships.

WHARF - A man-made structure bounding the edge of a dock and built along or at an angle to the shoreline, used for loading, unloading, or tying up vessels.

WHIPPING - The act of wrapping the end of a piece of rope with small line, tape or plastic to prevent it from fraying.

WHISKER POLE - A spar used to extend the jib when running.

WINCH - A device to increase hauling power when raising or trimming sails.

WIND OF MOTION - That wind which is perceived on a boat as the result of the movement of the boat itself.

WINDWARD - Toward the direction from which the wind is coming.

WING AND WING - Running with the mainsail set on one side of the boat and the jib set on the other side.

WORKING SAILS - Sails for use under normal conditions; on a sloop, the mainsail and jib.

Y

YAW - To swing off course, as when due to the impact of a following or quartering sea.

YAWL - A two-masted sailboat with the small mizzen mast stepped abaft the rudder post.

Index

INDEX

AIDS TO NAVIGATION ON WESTERN RIVERS
(MISSISSIPPI RIVER SYSTEM)

AS SEEN ENTERING FROM SEAWARD

PORT SIDE

■ GREEN OR □ WHITE LIGHTS
FLASHING

LIGHTED BUOY

CAN

SG

PASSING DAYMARK

CG

CROSSING DAYMARK

176.9

MILE BOARD

JUNCTION

MARK JUNCTIONS AND OBSTRUCTIONS
INTERRUPTED QUICK FLASHING

**PREFERRED CHANNEL
TO STARBOARD**
TOPMOST BAND BLACK

**PREFERRED CHANNEL
TO PORT**
TOPMOST BAND RED

□ WHITE OR
■ GREEN LIGHTS

□ WHITE OR
■ RED LIGHTS

LIGHTED

CAN

NUN

JG

JR

STARBOARD SIDE

■ RED OR □ WHITE LIGHTS
GROUP FLASHING (2)

LIGHTED BUOY

NUN

TR

PASSING DAYMARK

CR

CROSSING DAYMARK

123.5

MILE BOARD

RANGE DAYMARKS AS FOUND ON

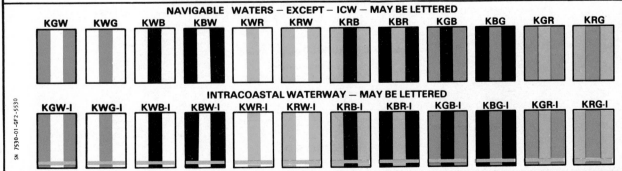

NAVIGABLE WATERS – EXCEPT – ICW – MAY BE LETTERED

| KGW | KWG | KWB | KBW | KWR | KRW | KRB | KBR | KGB | KBG | KGR | KRG |

INTRACOASTAL WATERWAY – MAY BE LETTERED

| KGW-I | KWG-I | KWB-I | KBW-I | KWR-I | KRW-I | KRB-I | KBR-I | KGB-I | KBG-I | KGR-I | KRG-I |

SN 7530-01-GF2-5530

STATE WATERS AND DESIGNATED STATE WATERS FOR PRIVATE AIDS TO NAVIGATION

REGULATORY MARKERS

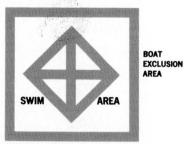

BOAT EXCLUSION AREA

EXPLANATION MAY BE PLACED OUTSIDE THE CROSSED DIAMOND SHAPE, SUCH AS DAM, RAPIDS, SWIM AREA, ETC.

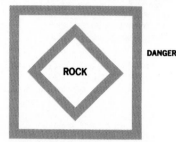

DANGER

THE NATURE OF DANGER MAY BE INDICATED INSIDE THE DIAMOND SHAPE, SUCH AS ROCK, WRECK, SHOAL, DAM, ETC.

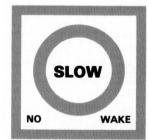

CONTROLLED AREA

TYPE OF CONTROL IS INDICATED IN THE CIRCLE, SUCH AS SLOW, NO WAKE, ANCHORING, ETC.

INFORMATION

FOR DISPLAYING INFORMATION SUCH AS DIRECTIONS, DISTANCES, LOCATIONS, ETC.

BUOY USED TO DISPLAY REGULATORY MARKERS

MAY SHOW WHITE LIGHT
MAY BE LETTERED

AIDS TO NAVIGATION

MAY SHOW WHITE REFLECTOR OR LIGHT

MOORING BUOY

WHITE WITH BLUE BAND

MAY SHOW WHITE REFLECTOR OR LIGHT

RED-STRIPED WHITE BUOY

MAY BE LETTERED
DO NOT PASS BETWEEN BUOY AND NEAREST SHORE

BLACK-TOPPED WHITE BUOY

MAY BE NUMBERED

PASS TO NORTH OR EAST OF BUOY

RED-TOPPED WHITE BUOY

PASS TO SOUTH OR WEST OF BUOY

CARDINAL SYSTEM

MAY SHOW GREEN REFLECTOR OR LIGHT

MAY SHOW RED REFLECTOR OR LIGHT

SOLID RED AND SOLID BLACK BUOYS

USUALLY FOUND IN PAIRS
PASS BETWEEN THESE BUOYS

PORT SIDE ——— LOOKING UPSTREAM ——— STARBOARD SIDE

LATERAL SYSTEM

SN 7530-01-GF2-5540

AIDS TO NAVIGATION ON NAVIGABLE WATERS
except Western Rivers and Intracoastal Waterway

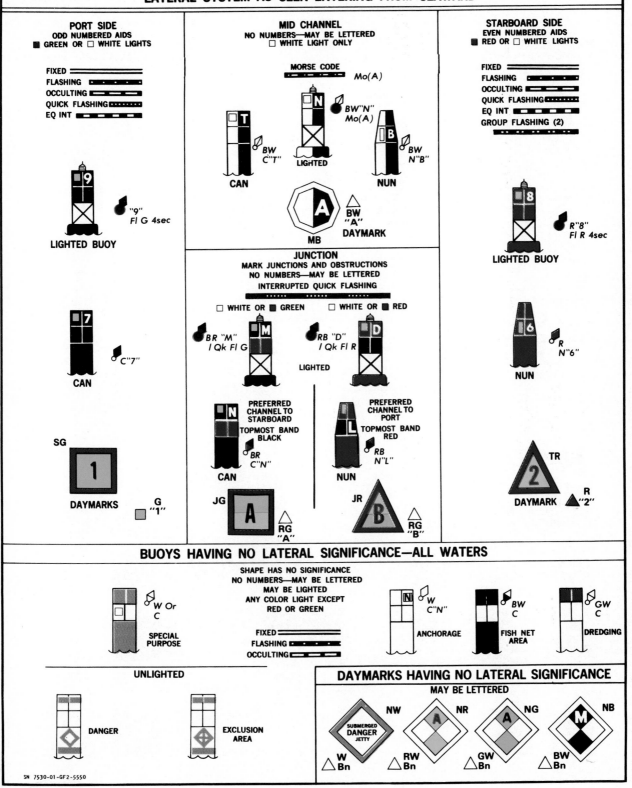

LATERAL SYSTEM AS SEEN ENTERING FROM SEAWARD

PORT SIDE
ODD NUMBERED AIDS
■ GREEN OR □ WHITE LIGHTS

FIXED
FLASHING
OCCULTING
QUICK FLASHING
EQ INT

LIGHTED BUOY — "9" Fl G 4sec

CAN — C"7"

SG — DAYMARKS — G "1"

MID CHANNEL
NO NUMBERS—MAY BE LETTERED
□ WHITE LIGHT ONLY

MORSE CODE — Mo(A)

CAN — BW C"T"

LIGHTED — BW"N" Mo(A)

NUN — BW N"B"

MB — BW "A" DAYMARK

JUNCTION
MARK JUNCTIONS AND OBSTRUCTIONS
NO NUMBERS—MAY BE LETTERED
INTERRUPTED QUICK FLASHING

□ WHITE OR ■ GREEN   □ WHITE OR ■ RED

BR "M" I Qk Fl G   RB "D" I Qk Fl R — LIGHTED

PREFERRED CHANNEL TO STARBOARD — TOPMOST BAND BLACK — CAN — BR C"N"

PREFERRED CHANNEL TO PORT — TOPMOST BAND RED — NUN — RB N"L"

JG — A — RG "A"   JR — B — RG "B"

STARBOARD SIDE
EVEN NUMBERED AIDS
■ RED OR □ WHITE LIGHTS

FIXED
FLASHING
OCCULTING
QUICK FLASHING
EQ INT
GROUP FLASHING (2)

LIGHTED BUOY — R"8" Fl R 4sec

NUN — R N"6"

TR — DAYMARK — R "2"

BUOYS HAVING NO LATERAL SIGNIFICANCE—ALL WATERS

SHAPE HAS NO SIGNIFICANCE
NO NUMBERS—MAY BE LETTERED
MAY BE LIGHTED
ANY COLOR LIGHT EXCEPT
RED OR GREEN

FIXED
FLASHING
OCCULTING

SPECIAL PURPOSE — W Or C

ANCHORAGE — W C"N"

FISH NET AREA — BW C

DREDGING — GW C

UNLIGHTED

DANGER

EXCLUSION AREA

DAYMARKS HAVING NO LATERAL SIGNIFICANCE
MAY BE LETTERED

SUBMERGED DANGER JETTY — NW — W Bn

NR — RW Bn

NG — GW Bn

NB — BW Bn

AIDS TO NAVIGATION ON THE INTRACOASTAL WATERWAY

AS SEEN ENTERING FROM NORTH AND EAST—PROCEEDING TO SOUTH AND WEST

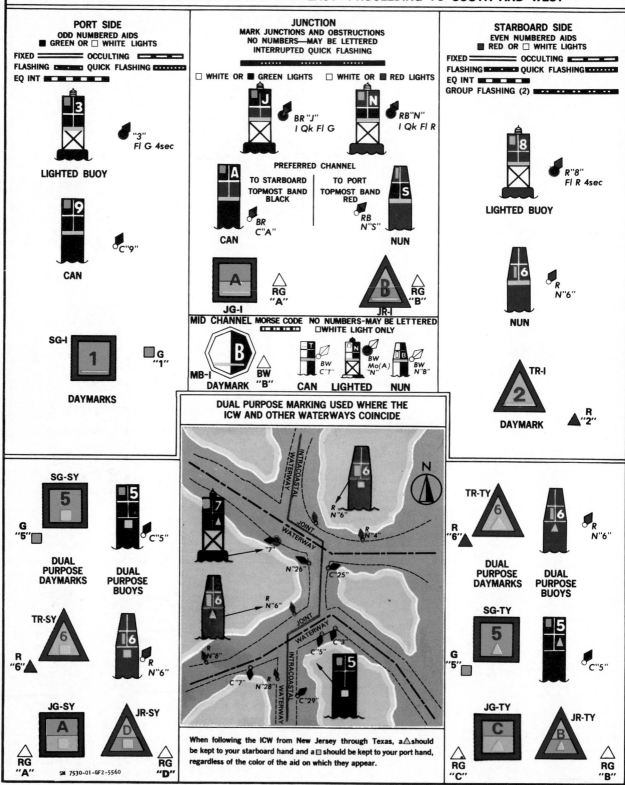